FINANCIAL TIMES

PERSONAL FINANCE LIBRARY

RRSPs 1992

Everything You Need to Know to
Make the Right Choices

By Steven G. Kelman

Penguin Books

PENGUIN BOOKS
Published by the Penguin Group
Penguin Books Canada Ltd., 10 Alcorn Avenue, Suite 300, Toronto, Canada, M4V 3B2
Penguin Books Ltd., 27 Wrights Lane, London W8 5TZ, England
Viking Penguin Inc., 40 West 23rd Street, New York, New York 10010, USA
Penguin Books Australia Ltd., Ringwood, Victoria, Australia
Penguin Books (NZ) Ltd., 182-190 Wairau Road, Auckland 10, New Zealand
Penguin Books Ltd., Registered Offices: Harmondsworth, Middlesex, England
Published in Penguin Books, 1991

10 9 8 7 6 5 4 3 2 1

Copyright © Financial Times of Canada, 1991
All rights reserved. Except in the United States of America, this book is sold subject to the condition that it shall not, by way of trade or otherwise, be lent, re-sold, hired out, or otherwise circulated without the publisher's prior consent in any form of binding or cover other than that in which it is published and without a similar condition, including this condition, being imposed on the subsequent purchaser. The information in appendices four and five was compiled by Southam Business Communications Inc. from data contained in its *Mutual Fund Sourcebook*, Sourcedisk and mutual fund data bank.

Canadian Cataloguing in Publication Data
Kelman, Steven G. (Steven Gershon), 1945 –
RRSPs
1986 –
Annual.
Vols. for in series: Financial times personal finance library.
Continues: Kelman, Steven G. (Steven Gershon), 1945 –   .No nonsense guide to RRSPs/RHOSPs and other tax shelters.
ISSN 0832-0659
ISBN 0-14-016859-1 (1992)

1. Registered Retirement Savings Plans – Periodicals.*
2. Retirement income – Canada – Periodicals.
I. Title. II. Series: Financial times personal finance library.

HD7106.C2K45   332.6'042   C86-031550-9 rev

Cover design: Creative Network
Cover illustration: Thomas Dannenberg

The information contained in this book is intended only as a general guide and may not be suitable for certain individuals. If expert advice is warranted, readers are urged to consult a competent professional. While the investment, legal, tax and accounting information contained in this book has been obtained from sources believed to be accurate, constant changes in the legal and financial environment make it imperative that readers confirm this information before making financial decisions.

CONTENTS

		Introduction	i
		PART I	
		THE ADVANTAGES AND THE RULES	
CHAPTER 1		More Than Just a Tax Break	1
CHAPTER 2		The Rules of the Game	7
		PART II	
		INVESTMENT STRATEGIES	
CHAPTER 3		Risk, Reward and Essential Strategies	21
CHAPTER 4		Guaranteed Plans: Playing It Safe	33
CHAPTER 5		Using Mutual Funds in Your RRSP	41
CHAPTER 6		Income Funds: Better Returns, Little Risk	45
CHAPTER 7		Equity Funds: For Long-Term Growth	55
CHAPTER 8		Balanced, Real Estate and Specialty Funds	63
CHAPTER 9		Self-Directed Plans: Are They Right for You?	67
CHAPTER 10		Putting Your Mortgage in Your RRSP	77
CHAPTER 11		Making Your RRSP Work Harder for You	79
		PART III	
		SPECIAL RRSP CONSIDERATIONS	
CHAPTER 12		Group RRSPs: Understand Your Choices	83
CHAPTER 13		DPSPS and Individual Pension Plans	87
CHAPTER 14		Spousal Plans: A Second Stream of Income	93

CHAPTER 15	How Much Will You Have?	97
CHAPTER 16	Unwinding Your Plan: RRIFs and Annuities	101
CHAPTER 17	Gimmicks to Avoid	111
CHAPTER 18	A Capsule Review	115
CHAPTER 19	The Most Often Asked Questions About RRSPs	117

PART IV
APPENDICES

APPENDIX ONE	A Comparison of Common RRSPs	121
APPENDIX TWO	A Comparison of Self-Administered RRSPs	135
APPENDIX THREE	A Comparison of Annuities and RRIFs	149
APPENDIX FOUR	Survey of Annual Fund Performance	155
APPENDIX FIVE	Survey of Fund Volatility and Compound Performance	165
APPENDIX SIX	The Future Value of a Single Deposit	177
APPENDIX SEVEN	The Future Value of an Annual Investment of $1,000 a Year	179
	Index	181

CHARTS

I	The Advantage of Investing in an RRSP	3
II	The Impact of Waiting Five Years to Start Saving $1,000 Annually	81

TABLES

I	Contribution Limits to RRSPs	9
II	Growth of an Investment	23
III	Average One-Year Rates of Return for Mutual Fund Groups	27

Introduction

RRSPs 1992 CONTAINS FOUR parts. The first includes a chapter explaining how RRSPs work and why they should be the cornerstone of your long-term savings program. The second chapter covers the rules and their limitations, showing the rule for 1991, and the rule for 1992 and subsequent years when appropriate.

The second part covers RRSP investment alternatives and strategies. An important section is material designed to help readers determine how much money they will have to save in their RRSPs by retirement to provide the income they will need. As a second step, it helps them determine how much they will have to contribute annually to their RRSPs (and in some cases save outside their plans) to reach their retirement income goals.

The third part of *RRSPs 1992* covers other RRSP topics such as group RRSPs and unwinding your RRSP.

The remainder of the book includes the tables that many readers have found useful in previous editions.

Like its nine predecessors, this edition is designed to help people determine which type of registered retirement savings plan is best for them. It demonstrates how to evaluate different types of plans as well as how to make RRSPs part of a total savings package that will maximize after-tax rates of return without increasing risk.

About the author

Steven G. Kelman is an investment counsellor and one of Canada's foremost experts on registered retirement savings plans and other aspects of personal financial planning. He has acted as a financial planner for individuals and as a consultant in the mutual fund industry. Mr. Kelman is a vice-president of Dynamic Fund Management Ltd., a subsidiary of Dundee Capital Inc., formerly Dynamic

Capital Corporation. He is consulting editor with the *Mutual Fund Sourcebook,* the mutual fund information guide used by fund professionals in Canada, and is an advisor on the Mutual Fund Sourcedisk, both published by Southam Business Information and Communications Group Inc.

Mr. Kelman is the author of *Understanding Mutual Funds* and co-author of *Investment Strategies* – both produced by the *Financial Times.* His articles have appeared in the *Financial Times,* in magazines and on the business pages of daily newspapers from coast to coast. He has lectured on financial planning, RRSPs and mutual funds across the country. For several years, Mr. Kelman taught a course on applied investments to MBA students at the Faculty of Administrative Studies at Toronto's York University. Mr. Kelman is a chartered financial analyst and a member of the Toronto Society of Financial Analysts. After graduating in 1969 from York University with his MBA, Mr. Kelman worked as an analyst, then portfolio manager, for a major insurance company before becoming a senior analyst with an investment dealer. In 1975 he joined the *Financial Times* as a staff writer; he became investment editor in 1977. In April 1985 he joined the Dundee Group of Companies.

Acknowledgements

As I noted in previous editions, there are literally dozens of people whose views and advice are reflected in *RRSPs 1992.* I would like to thank my colleagues at Dundee Capital Inc. for their support and advice, especially my assistant Leslie Murray for keeping track of my research notes. I would like to thank Elaine Wyatt at the *Financial Times of Canada* who was responsible for producing this book and the others in the series.

I would also like to thank my wife Barbara for her continued support.

Steven Kelman
October 1991

PART I — THE ADVANTAGES AND THE RULES

CHAPTER 1

More Than Just a Tax Break

EACH YEAR THOUSANDS OF Canadians rush out just before the March 1 deadline (February 29 in 1992) to make hasty contributions to registered retirement savings plans. They're confronted by a bewildering choice of plans and bombarded with advertising campaigns that make it sound as though contributing to RRSPs is a national duty. Indeed, RRSPs are essential retirement tools for most Canadians.

Hundreds of RRSPs are available. Banks, trust companies, stock brokerage houses, mutual fund management companies, insurance companies and credit unions are trying to lure RRSP shoppers through their doors. What's more, many employers and professional groups offer their own plans. In the end, it's easy to see how taxpayers, smitten with RRSP fever in late February, often find that in their haste they have great difficulty choosing plans that suit their financial needs and their retirement goals.

There are enough stories of disaster to compile a catalogue of woes. In some cases, individuals have purchased plans that require continuing payments – only to find that one missed annual payment can mean the loss of part, or even all, of the money paid into their plans. Then there are those whose funds are put in jeopardy by the misfortunes of less-than-stable financial institutions.

The other side of the coin is missed opportunity. Many investors, rushing to make a decision close to the yearly deadline, ignore RRSP vehicles such as the stock market. While not for everybody, stock-oriented RRSPs have their place for those whose age and finances justify some higher-risk investments. The penalty for not exploring this route is lost opportunity for longer-term, superior gains.

For others, especially those near retirement age, a hasty decision to invest in stocks may mean losing out during times of poor stock market performance. Confident that their dollars were piling up in an equity plan, they may awake one morning to find their nest egg depleted. Yet when carefully chosen and tailored to an individual's age, temperament, financial needs and the economic environment, an RRSP provides one of the best means of deferring taxes and saving for a comfortable retirement.

But make no mistake: RRSPs are far from perfect. Wise investors will use them as handy devices for retirement savings. They will not lose sight of the risks that are involved in a long-term savings program, and they will be prepared to make changes if the economic environment calls for a shift in strategy.

The power of RRSPs

The RRSP was established by the federal government in 1957 to encourage Canadians who were not members of pension plans to save for their old age. By contributing to an RRSP, not only would you avoid paying taxes on some of your income – until you withdrew the money when you retired – but your savings would grow free of tax until retirement as well.

Why should you save inside an RRSP?

The first decision you have to make is whether you should save inside an RRSP. The answer is yes, and it's easy to see how appealing an RRSP can be by making a quick calculation. Let's say you contribute $1,000 a year to a plan for thirty years at an average annual return of 10 percent. At the end of the thirty years you will have $180,943. Of course, if you contributed more, say $7,500 a year, you would end up with $1,357,076 – enough to provide you with an annual income at age sixty-five of about $163,000 in today's dollars.

But let's say you decide to ignore the RRSP and save outside the plan instead. In the first place, you won't have $1,000 because you'll pay tax on the money. If your combined federal-provincial tax rate is 39 percent – the approximate rate on taxable income of between $28,784 and $57,588 in 1991 – you would have about $610 after taxes (the actual rate you'll pay depends on your province or territory of residence and ranges from about 37.5 percent to 42 percent, excluding surtaxes).

If you invest this $610 a year for thirty years at 6.1 percent – don't forget you pay tax on interest income earned outside your RRSP so your 10 percent return would also be reduced by 39 per-

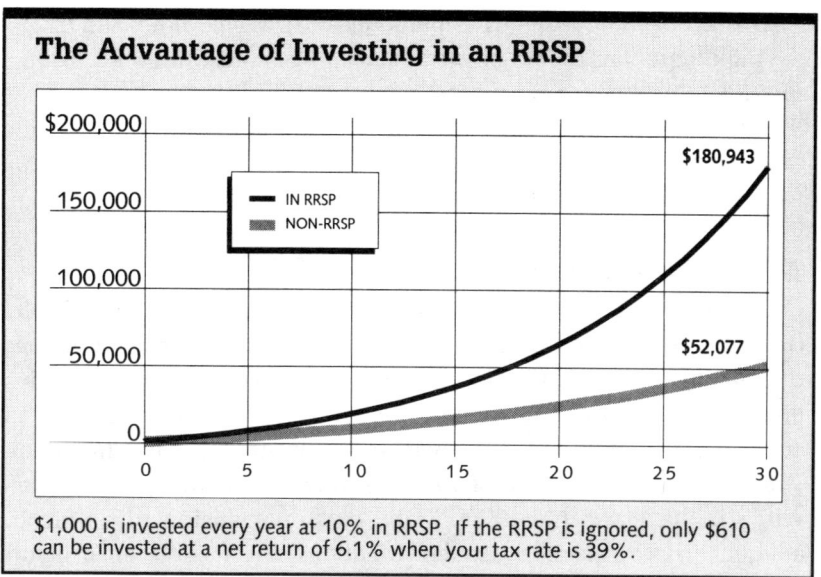

CHART I

cent – you would have $52,076 at the end of the thirty years, less than one-third of what you would have with an RRSP.

Of course, if you cashed in your RRSP at the end of thirty years you would pay tax on the proceeds. But even if you did, and paid the top tax rate of about 44 percent (depending in which province you live) on the proceeds, you would still end up with more than $99,500, almost double the amount you would have if you were to save outside your RRSP. And remember, you don't have to cash in your RRSP at retirement. You can move your RRSP into a RRIF which will allow your earnings in the plan to continue to grow untaxed while you are withdrawing income, which will be taxed, to finance your retirement.

The greatest advantage in using an RRSP for deferring income taxes is enjoyed by people in the highest tax brackets. Someone with taxable income of more than $57,588 has a marginal tax rate of about 44 percent. If he or she chooses to save outside an RRSP, $1,000 a year invested at 10 percent over thirty years would build to even less – about $43,588, or one-quarter the amount saved inside an RRSP. On the other hand, someone with taxable income of less than $28,784 would have a marginal tax rate of 25.5 percent. The taxes on $1,000 of earnings would be about $255, leaving about $745 for investment. With a 10 percent rate of return reduced to

7.45 percent after taxes, this person would have about $82,023 by saving outside an RRSP, or less than half that accumulated through an RRSP.

While the benefit is greatest for people paying the top marginal tax rate, there are clearly benefits for others. An RRSP is not simply a tax break for the wealthy.

An RRSP can supplement your pension

Ottawa's program of pension reform includes higher contribution limits for RRSPs and better protection for people who are members of pension plans. Undoubtedly, it will help people who are just entering the work force to provide themselves with adequate income when they retire. However, most employers don't have pension plans. Even for most people over thirty years of age, the system will still have shortcomings. Many existing pension plans are inadequate. If you are in a pension plan you may wish to ensure your financial security in retirement by also having an RRSP since even the best pension plan may not give you enough.

The most a pension plan can pay an individual is $1,722.22 a year for each year of pensionable service. But to get that amount the average of your best three years' earnings would have to be $86,111. Even then you would have had to work for the same employer for many years to get an adequate amount. If you had changed jobs several times during your career, pensions from previous employers' would not be based on your income with your current or most recent employer.

The maximum pension for someone earning less than $86,111 is 2 percent of the average of the best three years' earnings times the number of years of service (the new rules remove a restriction which limited the number of years' service to thirty-five). However, many pension plans are structured so that the maximum annual pension payment is far less than 2 percent.

Government plans inadequate

Adding to the need for an independent source of retirement income is the inadequacy of government pension plans. The current maximum, including Canada Pension Plan payments, is about $1,000 a month. Don't look at this as an inflation-indexed supplement to your company plan. Some company pension plans have a proviso whereby the benefits that the plan pays are reduced by the amount of government benefits received. Moreover, the "claw back" reduces some benefits for some higher-income individuals.

An RRSP is also good insurance for people who work for firms that are on a precarious financial footing. It is possible for a firm to fail and have substantial unfunded pension liabilities, which means that employees can end up with less pension money than expected.

In today's mobile job market an RRSP can be essential. While pension reform will make pensions portable and vested after two years' service, nearly 60 percent of the work force is still without the benefit of pension plans.

Some drawbacks to RRSPs

Keep in mind that your RRSP is a tax break given to you because the federal government wants you to be able to finance your own retirement. Consequently, the purpose of an RRSP should be to save for retirement. To ensure we adhere to that purpose, Ottawa insists that we follow certain rules. To make the most of your RRSP, you too should consider it a long-term investment – something you won't touch until retirement age.

But no one can map out his life completely and there may come a time when you will need your RRSP money for an emergency. If you do, you could face a hefty tax bill. Your RRSP doesn't eliminate taxes; it only defers them until you withdraw income, usually through a RRIF or an annuity that allows you to soften the tax bite. You can take out your money at any time, but you will pay tax on the proceeds. In some cases, this could push you into a higher tax bracket and erode or eliminate most of the advantage an RRSP has provided.

Even so, after several years the benefits of having RRSP assets grow and compound untaxed outweigh the tax burden on a lump sum. If an individual sets aside $1,000 a year at 10 percent, there would be $6,715 in the plan at the end of five years. If that investor had contributed $3,000 a year, he would have $20,147. If the investor cashed in that RRSP at the beginning of the sixth year, the tax paid would depend on his marginal tax rate. At the most, the tax would be $8,864. If he was paying the median tax rate, Revenue Canada would take $7,857. At the lowest rate the investor would lose $5,137 to taxes. He would still have more money in hand after the tax bill than if he had built his savings outside an RRSP.

Despite this catch, RRSPs are still the best route for retirement savings. They provide an easy way to reduce your taxes and at the same time build a comfortable nest egg. But that is not to say that an RRSP is for everyone. For some people, saving for things other than retirement must take precedence.

The dream of home ownership, for example, may be more important to many younger Canadians than retirement income forty years down the road. These people are often better to postpone their RRSPs and save outside an RRSP instead. The decision you make depends largely on your income level. If your marginal tax rate is 25.5 percent and you have limited savings, perhaps the down payment should be a priority. Your tax saving is only 25.5 cents for every dollar put in an RRSP. On the other hand, if your marginal tax rate is 44 percent, your tax saving is 44 cents for every dollar put in an RRSP. Someone who is paying the maximum tax rate and has substantial income available for savings would put money into an RRSP and put the tax refund toward a down payment on a home.

In the past, missing the opportunity to make an RRSP contribution meant it was lost forever. Beginning with the 1991 taxation year you will be able to carry-forward unused RRSP contributions. This will not be made retroactive; it will begin with unused portions of your 1991 contribution limit. If you don't make an RRSP contribution in one year you will be able to carry it forward for use in a later year, getting your deduction at that time.

CHAPTER 2

The Rules of the Game

IT IS IMPORTANT THAT PEOPLE investing in RRSPs understand the basic rules. While most are straightforward, some are rather complex. Moreover, some of the rules have changed over the years, in most cases for the better. For example, new rules implemented in 1986 gave Canadians more control of their RRSP assets during retirement. On June 27, 1990 Bill C-52 – amendments to the Income Tax Act which involve retirement savings – received Royal Assent and most of the changes to RRSPs proposed over the past five years finally became law.

Many of the changes, such as higher contribution limits, came into effect in 1991. There's a jungle of rules to fight your way through – the rules for the 1991 taxation year and the rules that will gradually come into force over the next five years. One word of caution: the RRSP rules will continue to change from year to year and you must keep up to date.

Who can contribute?

Any one who is seventy-one years old or younger and has earned income can contribute to an RRSP. There isn't a minimum age for establishing an RRSP – even a young child can have an RRSP as long as he or she has earned income.

What is earned income?

Earned income is income from employment, including taxable benefits such as the standby charge for a company car. Besides salary and wages, earned income includes:
- Supplementary unemployment benefits,
- Alimony and maintenance payments,
- Royalties,
- Research grants,

- Net business income,
- Net rental income, and
- Certain other types of taxable income stemming from employment, such as taxable sick or disability benefits.

These are the types of income which generally disappear when a person retires. Consequently, Ottawa holds the view that these are the only types of income which can be saved on a tax-assisted basis toward retirement.

This was not always the case. Prior to 1990, earned income included superannuation and pension benefits, including OAS, CPP and QPP benefits, retiring allowances, death benefits, and payments out of RRSPs, RRIFs and DPSPs. These are now excluded along with any income, or losses, while you're not a resident of Canada. Neither does earned income include:

- Family allowance payments,
- Unemployment insurance payments,
- Adult training allowances,
- Payments from an income-averaging annuity,
- Scholarships, bursaries or payments from a registered education savings plan,
- Dividends from Canadian corporations, interest, income from limited partnerships, capital gains and other investment income.

In calculating earned income, you must deduct any union or professional dues as well as alimony or maintenance payments you must make.

Calculating earned income is relatively simple for anyone whose income is from salary and wages alone. Anyone who earns more than $63,888.88 of earned income and doesn't belong to a pension plan or DPSP can contribute the maximum $11,500. Others might want to make a detailed calculation using Revenue Canada's Pension and RRSP guide.

The contribution deadline

For the 1991 taxation year, you can make your RRSP contribution anytime during 1991 or the first sixty days of 1992 – until Saturday, February 29, 1992. The deadline for the 1992 taxation year is March 1, 1993. If you turn seventy-one in 1991 you must contribute to your plan before the December 31 maturity date.

Contribution Limits to Tax Shelters

Year	RRSP	DPSP	Money Purchase
1990	$ 7,500	$3,500	$11,500
1991	11,500	6,250	12,500
1992	12,500	6,750	13,500
1993	13,500	7,250	14,500
1994	14,500	7,750	15,500
1995	15,500	7,750	15,500

TABLE I

The contribution limits

A new set of rules came into effect with the 1991 taxation year along with higher contribution limits. While the definition of earned income remains the same, your maximum 1991 contribution will be 18 percent of your earned income in 1990 – not your income in 1991 – up to $11,500, less any pension adjustments. For people who are not members of pension plans or deferred profit sharing plans, the pension adjustment will be zero. The RRSP limit will then grow by $1,000 a year until it reaches $15,500 in 1995. After 1995, the limit will rise with the national rise in wages.

For most people who are members of pension plans, the pension adjustment to be used in their 1991 RRSP calculation will be the contributions they and their employers make to a pension plan in 1990 or contributions made by an employer to a DPSP for the 1990 taxation year. The exact figure can be found in box 52 of your 1990 T4 slip which you received before the end of February 1991.

For some members of pension plans RRSP contribution limits might be reduced by past service pension adjustments (PSPAs). PSPAs are benefits provided to employees under a defined benefit registered pension plan for past service. PSPAs will be adjusted to reflect any withdrawals by the taxpayer.

Because pension contributions are noted in your T4 slips, calculating RRSP contributions will be as simple as in previous years for most people, although anyone affected by PSPAs may find it more difficult. However, Revenue Canada will issue individual statements toward the end of 1991 informing people of their contribution limits for 1991. It will still make sense to make RRSP contributions as early in the year as possible to take advantage of tax-free compounding. If you overcontribute (within reasonable limits) you will carry-forward your overcontribution to the 1992 taxation year.

For the 1992 taxation year, your contribution limit will be 18 percent of 1991 earned income to a maximum of $12,500 less any pension, DPSP contributions and PSPAs, plus RRSP "contribution room" at the end of 1991. For most people RRSP contribution room, if any, will be unused contributions from 1991. Again, most people should have little difficulty calculating their 1992 contribution limits.

If you are a member of a defined benefit pension plan your employer should be able to provide you with your pension adjustment figure or at least with your benefit entitlement from which you can determine your pension adjustment. You can then make an RRSP contribution early in 1992. You can, however, calculate the figure on your own. This is done in several steps.

First, determine what is called your "benefit entitlement" by multiplying your earned income by your "unit benefit" or "benefit accrual rate" which your employer can supply. The benefit accrual rate is a percentage of your previous year's earned income and cannot exceed 2 percent. For 1992 contributions, the maximum 1991 earned income for this calculation is $69,444. Consequently, the maximum benefit entitlement is $1,389. Next, multiply your benefit entitlement by 9 (the figure you get should not exceed $12,500) and from this subtract $1,000. Even if your pension plan makes the maximum pension contributions you will still be able to make an RRSP contribution of at least $1,000.

Many employee organizations representing groups such as teachers and municipal employees will almost certainly provide their members with information about maximum RRSP contributions.

Carry-forward of unused RRSP contributions

It's true. The earlier you start your RRSP contributions, the more money you will accumulate. In reality, many people aren't able to make RRSP contributions every year and, in the past, if you missed the opportunity to make a year's contribution you lost it forever. Beginning in 1991, that will change. If you haven't contributed the maximum to an RRSP for a given taxation year you will be able to make up the missed contributions in the years to come. The carry-forward begins with unused contributions from 1991.

Unfortunately, the contribution room you can carry-forward is not infinite. There are limits that will kick-in in 1998. The amount you can carry-forward cannot exceed the maximum RRSP contributions you could have made in the previous seven years. To protect those people who leave the work force for a few years or who have retired and whose contribution room could fall to zero, there is a second rule. Under this rule, the carry-forward limit is 7/2 of the RRSP dollar limit for the year.

Although the carry-forward gives you greater flexibility, making up six or seven years' contributions in one year could trigger alternative minimum tax in some circumstances.

Eligible investments

Only certain types of investments can be used in RRSPs but this is not a concern for the vast majority of people. These eligible investments include:
- RRSP savings accounts, guaranteed investment certificates, term deposits,
- shares of Canadian companies and some foreign companies listed on a recognized Canadian stock exchange, shares of foreign companies listed on specific exchanges, shares of some over-the-counter U.S. and Canadian companies, shares of some small businesses,
- certain types of bonds such as treasury bills, Canada Savings Bonds, Government of Canada bonds, provincial government bonds, Crown corporation bonds, bonds issued by Canadian corporations listed on a recognized stock exchange, and stripped bonds,
- certain types of mortgages, including your own.
- covered call options, warrants and rights issued by companies listed on a Canadian stock exchange,
- mutual funds that invest in eligible securities,
- foreign investments to a maximum of 14 percent of the value of the specific RRSP in which the foreign investment is held. The February 20, 1990 budget included a proposal to raise this limit from 10 percent to 12 percent for 1990 and to increase it by two percentage points a year to a maximum of 20 percent by 1994.

This proposal, while not yet passed, will almost certainly be made retroactive.

There are a few investments that you cannot hold in your RRSP. Most of them are tangible assets such as gold bullion or coins, precious metals, real estate or collectibles such as stamps, coins, art and antiques. However, you can hold mutual funds that invest in precious metals or real estate.

Contribution and substitution of securities

You do not have to contribute cash to your RRSP. You can contribute eligible investments at fair market value. If you own shares of a Canadian public company, for example, you can contribute these to a self-directed RRSP. There are tax implications if you do this; they're discussed in chapter nine. You can also withdraw assets from your RRSP, replacing them with cash or other securities of the same value.

RRSP transfers

Transfer between RRSPs: You can transfer from one RRSP to another without triggering any tax implications provided the transfer is made directly between plans. If you decide to move from plan A to plan B, the administrator of plan B will provide you with the proper form to complete.

Transfer of pension to RRSPs: Effective 1990, you can no longer make tax-free transfers of pension income to your RRSP. Once you start to receive pension income, it is taxable and you cannot defer tax on it using an RRSP. It is important to realize that this restriction applies only to periodic payments. It does not apply to lump-sum payments made from a pension plan when you change jobs. In that case, you can transfer your pension to your RRSP tax-free, provided the transfer is made directly between the plans.

Roll-overs are a routine action for people who take early retirement but some people might be better off keeping the pension – especially those who want the freedom to name anyone as a beneficiary. If you die, the person named as the pension beneficiary will receive a pension, on which he or she will have to pay tax as income is received. With an RRSP, the commuted value of the plan is taxed unless it is rolled over into a plan for a spouse or common-law spouse.

Locked-in RRSPs: An RRSP stemming from the transfer of a pension generally includes a provision locking it in until retirement age, which prevents it from being prematurely collapsed. Such RRSPs can be managed the same as other RRSPs. However, at retirement the RRSP must be used to purchase a life annuity. (Provincial and federal regulators have been reviewing this requirement.)

Transfer of pension income to spousal RRSPs: Under the old rules, many retired people built spousal plans by contributing 20 percent of their pension income to a spousal plan. However, pension income is no longer earned income. Recognizing that it is difficult for people in retirement to change their financial planning, the federal government is allowing a tax-free transfer of up to $6,000 a year of registered pension income or income from a DPSP to a spousal RRSP. OAS, CPP and QPP income does not qualify. This went into effect in 1989 and expires after the 1994 taxation year. If you have excess pension income and are married, you would be wise to look at the spousal transfer as a means of deferring taxes now and splitting income down the road.

Transfer of retiring allowances: Prior to 1989 you could transfer to your RRSP up to $2,000 of a retiring allowance for each year that you were a member of a registered pension plan or DPSP and up to an additional $1,500 a year for each year you did not have these benefits. In 1989, the limits were replaced with a single limit of $2,000. The old limits remain in effect for service before 1989.

If you are leaving an employer and a portion of your severance or retirement package is retiring allowance, arrange to have the retiring allowance paid directly into your RRSP by your employer using a Revenue Canada form "Tax Deduction Waiver In Respect Of Funds Being Transferred." This way you can avoid withholding tax. If you receive the funds directly, contribute them to your RRSP as a retiring allowance, declare them as income and claim an offsetting deduction on your tax return.

Transfer to a spouse: An RRSP can be transferred tax-free to your spouse in two circumstances only:
- on death and only then if the spouse is named as beneficiary,

- on marriage breakdown provided the couple is no longer living together and a court has ordered a division of the RRSP.

Transfer of an RRSP to a common-law spouse: Common-law spouses are eligible, and have been since the beginning of 1988, for survivor benefits and for the transfer of RRSP assets on a breakdown of a relationship. At the time, the definition of spouse was changed to "a person of the opposite sex who is married to the individual or has been living with the individual in a conjugal relationship and has so cohabited for a period of at least one year, or is a parent of a child of whom the individual is a parent." Homosexual relationships remain excluded.

This means a common-law spouse can be named as a beneficiary for benefits under an RRSP annuity or a RRIF and the RRSP, annuity or RRIF will be transferred tax-free. The new definition also allows transfers of RRSP assets from one spouse to another when a common-law relationship ends, subject to a written separation agreement or court order.

If you are in a long-term common-law relationship you should consider naming your significant other as beneficiary for your RRSP and adjusting your will so your common-law spouse can benefit from the tax-free roll-over to his or her RRSP or RRIF should you die.

Spousal RRSPs

A spousal RRSP is a plan registered in the name of your spouse to which you make contributions based on your income. Although the plan is not owned by you, you get the tax deduction for the contribution. You can make contributions to both your RRSP and your spouse's, as long as your total contributions do not exceed your yearly limit.

Spousal plans allow a couple to build a pool of funds that will give both husband and wife a stream of income in retirement – an important tax planning strategy. The taxes paid on two incomes is usually much less than the taxes that would be paid if all the income flows to one person. Also, both spouses will then be eligible for the federal pension income tax credit which begins at age sixty-five for payments stemming from an RRSP through a RRIF or a life annuity.

A spousal plan also gives you the ability to continue making RRSP contributions past age seventy-one. You simply make the contribution to the RRSP of a younger husband or wife. Contributions to the spousal plan must stop and the plan must be deregistered in the year in which the younger spouse turns seventy-one.

Once a spousal plan is set up, it becomes the property of the spouse in whose name it is registered. It does not belong to the contributor. (Some financial advisors refer to spousal plans as "prepaid alimony.") Although federal law allows RRSPs to be split upon divorce or legal separation, couples should look closely at the stability of their marriages before using spousal RRSPs.

Another a word of warning. Couples should not set up a spousal plan and withdraw the money after a few days or months in hopes of paying tax at a lower rate. Revenue Canada frowns on this ploy. The money taken out of a spousal plan within the year in which the contribution was made or the next two years is seen as income of the contributing spouse and taxed at his or her marginal rate.

The federal government does not recognize common-law relationships for spousal contributions, although it does recognize them for survivor benefits under RRSPs, RRIFs and annuities and for tax-free transfers on marriage breakdown.

Excess RRSP contributions

Revenue Canada doesn't like it when you put more in your RRSP than you're entitled to. Not only will they hit you with a penalty of 1 percent a month on any excess contribution for as long as it remains in the plan, but also if you don't withdraw the money within two years, it will be taxed when you do take it out. You end up paying taxes on the same income twice – not a good idea. To withdraw the money you must use Revenue Canada form T3012 or you'll have to pay a withholding tax.

Prior to 1991, some people intentionally overcontributed to their RRSPs to bring their contribution up to $5,500 and withdrew the money within the two years. Any interest earned on the overpayment during that time remains in the plan to compound untaxed; as a result, a practice of overcontributing can create substantial tax-sheltered gains. However, this strategy could be viewed by Revenue Canada as a tax avoidance scheme. Moreover, changes to the rules in 1991 have reduced the benefits of overcontributing.

These limits and penalties will continue to be applied to over-contributions made in 1990 and previous years. For over-contributions made in 1991 and subsequent years, the 1 percent monthly tax will be applied to contributions that exceed your "cumulative excess amount." This is the amount you are allowed to contribute to your RRSP plus $8,000. This $8,000 cushion should provide an adequate margin for error in calculating RRSP contributions. However, the $8,000 cushion is not available to people who are under eighteen years of age at the beginning of the year. This eliminates the so-called "kiddies RRSP" which some people used in past years as an income-splitting and tax avoidance gimmick. The "kiddies RRSP" was an RRSP opened for a young child with a non-deductible contribution. The funds were allowed to grow untaxed until age eighteen when they were withdrawn, generally with little tax payable.

If you overcontribute unintentionally and take reasonable steps to eliminate the excess, Revenue Canada may waive the 1 per cent monthly tax.

Maturing your RRSPs

Your RRSP must mature no later than December 31 of the year in which you turn seventy-one. Before that date you must choose one of the RRSP maturity options – a registered retirement income fund or annuity. If you're older than seventy-one you cannot contribute to your own RRSP. However, you can contribute to a plan in your spouse's name provided he or she is under seventy-one or the contribution is made before December 31 in the year your spouse turns seventy-one.

Using your RRSP assets as loan collateral

It is possible that you may have to dip into your RRSPs before you intend. Before you cash in, investigate an alternative. While Ottawa prohibits using RRSPs as collateral for a loan, it does allow borrowing against the assets in your RRSP. It's complicated, but it can be done.

It works like this: a trust company, usually the trustee of your plan, will lend you money against certain RRSP assets such as treasury bills or guaranteed investment certificates issued by that trust company. You pay tax on the value of the assets taken out of the plan and when you restore them to your RRSP you will get a corresponding deduction. Restoring those assets will not infringe on the RRSP contribution you will be able to make that year, even if it causes your total contribution that year to exceed your dollar limit.

Withholding tax

The federal government requires that a withholding tax be deducted when money is pulled out of an RRSP. The rates, other than for Quebec, are 10 percent on the first $5,000, 20 percent on $5,001 to $15,000 and 30 percent on anything higher. Quebec residents face higher levels because they are also subject to a provincial withholding tax. The combined rates for Quebec are 18 percent on the first $5,000, 30 percent on $5,001 to $15,000 and 39 percent on amounts greater than $15,000.

Keep in mind that the withholding tax may not be what you ultimately pay. If your income level in the year that you cash in is low, you may get a refund; if your income is high, you may end up paying more when you file your tax return. Of course, if you transfer the money directly to another RRSP or convert to a RRIF or annuity, no withholding tax will be deducted.

RRSPs and death

If you die, the money in your RRSPs will be included in your income for the year of your death and taxed. There are steps that can be taken to reduce the burden of taxes on your death.

Your last RRSP contribution: An RRSP contribution can be made on behalf of a deceased person in the year of death. This would be done to reduce the estate's tax liability and to increase the RRSP amount that would be rolled over into the surviving spouse's plan.

Name a beneficiary: It is important that you name a beneficiary for your RRSP. This should be done in your will. If you live outside Quebec, you can also name your beneficiary on your RRSP application form. However, the named beneficiary should be the same in both your will and on the RRSP application. If not, the will takes precedence. If you have not named a beneficiary, the proceeds in the RRSP are paid to your estate if you die.

Most people name their spouse as beneficiary when they set up an RRSP. This ensures that upon death the plan can be rolled into an RRSP for the spouse if he or she is seventy-one or younger. If the surviving spouse is older than seventy-one, the RRSP can be rolled into annuities and RRIFs. You can also name a common-law spouse as beneficiary with the same rollover provisions.

If you do not name your spouse as beneficiary, consider naming your estate and giving instructions in your will for disbursement. Before you do this make sure you seek legal advice and understand the potential tax consequences.

RRSP roll-over to a child: If you don't have a spouse at the time of death, the money in an RRSP can be paid to a dependent child or grandchild, in whose hands it would be taxed. However, the proceeds can be used to buy an annuity for the child with a term not exceeding eighteen years minus the child's age. This allows the RRSP to be brought into income over a number of years and could result in less tax being paid.

A parent or grandparent of a dependent disabled child or grandchild should seek legal advice from a person experienced in structuring estates to avoid loss of provincial family benefits.

RRSPs and U.S. citizens

Finally, individuals whose circumstances differ from the norm should seek professional advice in structuring their retirement savings as well as other financial matters. For example, an RRSP may not be the best retirement savings vehicle for a U.S. citizen living and working in Canada. An American living in Canada would be required to file tax returns in both countries, and while RRSP contributions are deductible in Canada, they are not in the U.S. However, non-residents can transfer funds from a registered pension plan or DPSP to an RRSP tax-free.

RRSPs and bankruptcy

Your RRSP can be seized by creditors if you go bankrupt. Until recently, most advisors believed that the only way to protect your RRSP from creditors is to establish a plan that is an insurance policy, with certain dependants named as beneficiaries. A decision in a Saskatchewan court has many financial planners questioning whether such plans are, in fact, creditor-proof. This type of RRSP may be of interest to people who are personally liable for their business debts. Most insurance companies offer RRSPs that are very similar to plans offered by banks, trust companies and mutual fund management companies, except that the insurance company plans are considered policies with beneficiaries and appear to be "creditor-proof."

A word of caution. Your insurance company RRSP won't be creditor-proof if it is opened after it became obvious that you were in financial difficulty.

A spousal plan of any type seems to be creditor-proof, as well, provided that the spouse has not guaranteed any of the contributor's obligations and the contributions were made a reasonable amount of time before the contributor became insolvent.

RRSPs and the GST

The goods and services tax introduced at the beginning of 1991 has had virtually no impact on RRSPs. It is, however, too early to tell whether there will be a significant long-term impact. Contributions are not taxed because they are capital. Similarly, withdrawals and payments from RRIFs and annuities are exempt. Income earned in an RRSP is also not affected.

However, management fees of mutual fund RRSPs are subject to the tax, as are RRSP trustee fees. Both cases affect only a minority of RRSP investors. GST will raise the management expenses of the average equity mutual fund by about 0.14 percent, not a significant amount at first glance. Nevertheless, over a period of years the reduction in rate of return that will result from GST will reduce the amount available for a RRIF or annuity significantly, perhaps by 2 percent to 3 percent over thirty years. The actual amount will depend on the average rate of return earned, the age of the plan and amounts contributed annually.

And while interest rates paid by financial institutions are GST exempt, an institution has to pay GST on its GST-taxable expenses. These costs will undoubtedly be reflected in the rates it pays on RRSP contributions. For an individual choosing an RRSP, even though the GST has a long-term impact on the amount of money accumulated it should have no bearing on an investment decision.

PART II — INVESTMENT STRATEGIES

CHAPTER 3

Risk, Reward and Essential Strategies

GETTING AN RRSP IS AN EASY enough task. Virtually every bank and trust company offers a full complement of plans ranging from RRSP savings accounts to RRSP mutual funds. Life insurance agents, credit unions, mutual fund dealers, stockbrokers and financial planners all carry a variety of plans. Your employer may offer a group plan that gives you an immediate tax break and various investment choices. Engineers, physicians, dentists and teachers can pick among plans sponsored by their professional associations. If these off-the-shelf plans aren't enough, you can tailor-make your own RRSP using self-directed plans offered by investment dealers, many trust companies, a few banks and some mutual fund dealers.

With several hundred off-the-shelf plans available plus the option of creating your own, choosing a suitable RRSP may seem to be a difficult task – one you might prefer to leave to an expert. Yet, most investors don't have an investment counsellor.

If you don't have this expertise at your fingertips, there are steps you can take to ensure that you get the best possible RRSP, or RRSPs since you are allowed more than one. First, you should consider three important points:

1. How flexible should the plan be to meet your financial needs in case of an emergency? Flexibility in an RRSP is the ease with which you can make contributions and the ease with which they can be cashed or transferred to another plan or company.
2. How much risk are you willing to take?
3. How compatible will your plan or plans be with your other savings and financial plans?

Most RRSPs are one-shot affairs. Once you've made your contribution, you are under no obligation to contribute more money each year. However, some plans are contracts under which you must make monthly payments. If you're offered one of these plans, find out what will happen if you need to withdraw your money or must miss a payment because of an emergency. You'll want to avoid plans in which hefty portions of early payments go toward commissions and administrative costs. If you have to collapse your plan, you could face heavy penalties and lose much of the money you have already deposited.

Therefore, it's best to avoid any RRSP that locks you into a rigid payment schedule. You should also avoid any plan that locks you into a specific investment until retirement. There are many alternatives, including plans that allow you to make monthly payments but do not impose any penalty if you can't meet the payment schedule. In the same vein, consider the liquidity of any investment you purchase for your RRSP. The liquidity of an investment is the ease with which you can sell it for a fair price; think carefully before committing yourself to any investment that cannot be easily sold.

Weigh the risks

The second point to consider is risk. In investment plans, risk is the volatility of an investment – how much it will rise and fall in value from day to day or week to week. Guaranteed plans offered by banks, trust companies and credit unions probably carry the least amount of risk. With these investments you know in advance how much you will earn over a specific period. You also know that at the end of that period you will have a certain amount of money, consisting of your original capital plus interest.

For example, if you had put your money in a guaranteed five-year RRSP in June 1984 your average compound return would have been about 11.5 percent. If, however, you had locked in your money for five years in June 1988 your annual return to June 1993 will be about 7.5 percent. The trade-off in a guaranteed plan is the likelihood that you will earn a lower rate of return over time than you would with a less predictable investment.

At the opposite end of the spectrum are equity funds. Equity funds are mutual funds that invest primarily in a diversified portfolio of common stocks. Your return depends on the performance of the stock market. Some of the benefits of mutual funds include diversification of stock investments, professional management and liquidity, since most mutual funds can be redeemed at any time.

Growth of an Investment

HOW AN INVESTMENT OF $1,000 A YEAR CAN GROW OVER TIME AT DIFFERENT RATES OF RETURN

Year	8%	10%	12%	14%	16%	18%
1	1,080	1,100	1,120	1,140	1,160	1,180
2	2,246	2,310	2,374	2,440	2,506	2,572
3	3,506	3,641	3,779	3,921	4,066	4,215
4	4,867	5,105	5,353	5,610	5,877	6,154
5	6,336	6,716	7,115	7,536	7,977	8,442
6	7,923	8,487	9,089	9,730	10,414	11,142
7	9,637	10,436	11,300	12,233	13,240	14,327
8	11,488	12,579	13,776	15,085	16,519	18,086
9	13,487	14,937	16,549	18,337	20,321	22,521
10	15,645	17,531	19,655	22,045	24,733	27,755
11	17,977	20,384	23,133	26,271	29,850	33,931
12	20,495	23,523	27,029	31,089	35,786	41,219
13	23,215	26,975	31,393	36,581	42,672	49,818
14	26,152	30,772	36,280	42,842	50,660	59,965
15	29,324	34,950	41,753	49,980	59,925	71,939
16	32,750	39,545	47,884	58,118	70,673	86,068
17	36,450	44,599	54,750	67,394	83,141	102,740
18	40,446	50,159	62,440	77,969	97,603	122,414
19	44,762	56,275	71,052	90,025	114,380	145,628
20	49,423	63,002	80,699	103,768	133,841	173,021

TABLE II

In theory, an RRSP invested in equities should provide a higher long-term rate of return than other types of RRSPs as the value of the underlying stocks grows. Indeed, this has often been the case. In the ten years ended June 30, 1989, many funds recorded average compound returns greater than 13 percent. These compound returns assume all of the profits are reinvested. For example, a 10 percent rate of return for two consecutive years would give you a total return over that period of 21 percent if you reinvest the interest earned. Money market funds that hold short-term instruments, such as government-guaranteed treasury bills, earned an average of 11 percent during the same period.

Much also depends on the periods measured. If we take the ten years ended June 30, 1991, the average ten-year rate of return was just over 8.5 percent. But for the shorter term, it is a different story. Over the twelve months ended June 30, 1991, the range of returns for RRSP-eligible mutual funds that invested primarily in stocks was -19.3 percent to 27.1 percent, with an average of 4.3 percent. If we look at the twelve months ended June 30, 1989, the average return was just over 10 percent while looking at the twelve months ended June 30, 1988, shows that the range of returns for RRSP-eligible mutual funds that invest primarily in stocks was -31.4 percent to 16.2 percent, with an average of -4.2 percent. In the previous twelve-month period the range was -12.8 percent to 93.5 percent, with an average return of 18.5 percent.

How your returns are affected

The rate of return you earn on your RRSP determines the amount of money you can roll into RRIFs or annuities at retirement time. Small differences in the rate of return can make a big difference in the size of your retirement pot. An individual who contributes $3,000 annually for thirty years to a plan and earns an average of 5 percent compounded annually would accumulate $209,282. For a sixty-five-year-old man, that would be enough to purchase an annuity paying about $2,400 monthly.

However, if that person earned 9 percent on his annual contributions, he would have $445,725 at retirement time, which would buy an annuity paying about $5,000 a month. An average return of 13 percent would lead to a total of $993,945 and an annuity that would pay $11,300 a month. An average return of 20 percent over thirty years – although it is highly unlikely – would result in a total of $4.2 million, enough to buy an annuity that would provide a monthly income of $47,700.

Should you take more risk? While small differences in the rate of return lead to substantial differences in the wealth that builds up, to get higher returns you must take more risk. This is not advisable for many individuals, especially those approaching retirement age or already retired with just enough retirement funds. In fact, anyone whose lifestyle could be affected adversely by a drop in the value of their retirement assets should avoid risk. On the other hand, someone who is approaching retirement or who is retired with a comfortable retirement nest egg may decide to invest at least a bit in growth investments as a hedge against inflation.

Many investors who had invested in stocks either through RRSPs or other channels got a rude shock between August and October 1987 when the Toronto stock market lost about 31 percent of its value. However, people who bought at the October lows saw their investments, as measured by the Toronto Stock Exchange total return index, rise 24 percent by the end of June 1988, 40 percent by the end of June 1989. However, over the next twelve months, the market hardly moved. Despite shocking drops like the 1987 crash, returns from the stock market usually exceed those of guaranteed investments over time.

Your choice of strategies

There are four basic investment strategies from which to choose, with a myriad of variations of each. The first alternative is to put everything in guaranteed investments. The advantage is that your returns will always be positive; the disadvantage is that other investments have traditionally produced significantly higher returns. The term "guaranteed" stems from the fact that the interest rate is guaranteed by the financial institution involved. You are a creditor of the institution, and RRSPs on deposit with banks and trust companies are insured by the Canada Deposit Insurance Corporation. Insurance company plans are not covered by deposit insurance but by the Canadian Life and Health Insurance Compensation Corporation.

The interest rate on a guaranteed plan depends on the term for which you agree to tie up your funds. A savings account or variable rate RRSP gives investors a rate of return that moves up and down with general interest rates. If interest rates move higher, your return increases; if rates fall, so does your return. A similar vehicle is the money market mutual fund. It invests in short-term bonds, treasury bills, savings certificates and the like. Because it is usually able to secure higher rates than those offered individuals, returns are higher.

The second type of guaranteed RRSP ties up your money for one to five years. The rates paid on these plans – an RRSP GIC or term deposit – are generally, but not always, higher than on variable rate plans to compensate for locking in your money for a fixed term (variable rate plans were paying higher rates than fixed-term plans in 1989 and 1990). The risk here is that interest rates could move higher while you are locked in, so you could lose the opportunity for higher returns. This choice is appropriate for those investors who value certainty.

Another fixed income option is to invest in a mutual fund that holds top-quality bonds or mortgages. The advantage is that mutual funds are managed by investment professionals who vary holdings in portfolios to reflect expected changes in interest rates and to give investors more stable, and often higher, returns than they would earn if their money was tied up in conventional guaranteed investments.

Because of the safety of this type of mutual fund, it is ideal for those who plan to purchase a life annuity or a guaranteed RRIF at retirement age. The second alternative is to invest everything for growth. The advantage is that over the long term you are likely to earn a significantly higher return than you would if you put your money in a guaranteed investment. The disadvantage is that you could suffer financially over the short term if you had to cash in your plan or withdraw funds when share prices are low.

A third strategy is to invest in both guaranteed and growth investments in a mix determined by your age. This strategy assumes you can afford more risk when you're young and would gradually reduce the portion of your investments in growth investments as you get older and closer to retirement. The portfolio mix between guaranteed and growth investments might be as follows:

- If you're in your twenties, you have at least three or four decades of investing ahead of you. As a result, you can accept volatility. Consider putting all of your RRSP assets into equities.
- If you're in your thirties, you still have a fair amount of investment time ahead of you, so you can put most of your assets into equities. Nevertheless, you might want to keep a portion in a more stable area of the market. Consider putting 80 percent of your money into equity funds and the remaining 20 percent into fixed income securities or fixed income mutual funds.
- If you're in your forties, you should consider a more conservative stance by putting about 60 percent of your assets into equity funds and the remainder into fixed income investments.
- If you're in your fifties, your equity holdings should be reduced to about 40 percent and your fixed income holdings raised to 60 percent.
- If you're in your sixties, consider having 80 percent of your retirement assets earmarked for fixed income and guaranteed investments and the remaining 20 percent in equities. A large por-

Average One-Year Rates of Return for Mutual Fund Groups

	1991	1990	1989	1988	1987
Equity mutual funds – RRSP-eligible	4.3	-0.5	10.1	-4.2	18.5
Equity funds – not RRSP-eligible	-1.6	7.7	8.7	-11.8	17.6
Bond and mortgage funds	12.4	4.2	9.8	7.2	7.8
Money market funds	10.8	11.3	9.5	8.2	7.5
Market indices					
91-day Canada treasury bill	10.9	12.8	11.1	8.7	8.0
Consumer Price Index	6.1	4.5	4.9	4.1	4.6
ScotiaMcLeod mid-term index	15.3	2.8	12.3	8.7	18.2
Standard and Poor's 500	3.7	11.9	18.9	-15.2	20.6
TSE Total Return	1.9	-2.4	13.5	-5.2	24.6

NOTE: For periods ending June 30

TABLE III

tion of the fixed income investment should be in guaranteed securities with maturities to coincide with retirement.

The advantage of a strategy based on age is that you hold a growth portfolio during the time you can most afford volatility and a conservative portfolio when you need to reduce risk. The age categories suggested above are guidelines that will vary with your circumstances. People who have pension plans they consider adequate might decide to put all their RRSP savings into equities with the intention of moving the money to a RRIF at retirement to provide rising income as a hedge against inflation. Or, if you plan to sell your home when you retire and invest the capital for income, you might decide that a larger portion of your savings should be invested in equities.

If you follow the strategy of weighing your mix of equity and debt assets according to your age, you should apply the ratio to all your investment assets, not just RRSPs.

Your fourth investment strategy alternative – and the one that makes sense for most people – is to invest your RRSP in a mix of fixed income and growth investments that you juggle with the changes in the economic and market environment. Preservation of capital would be your paramount concern. If you follow this strategy you would have a major portion of your investments, perhaps even everything, in growth investments when they offer excellent value. On the other hand, when stocks are expensive you would likely hold most, if not all, of your RRSP investments in fixed income instruments.

You can manage your portfolio yourself through a self-directed RRSP that allows you to make all the investment decisions. Or you can use a balanced, or "managed-asset-mix", mutual fund. This is probably the preferred alternative, unless you have a history of successful investment management.

You should give serious consideration to the managed or balanced approach to RRSP investing. By varying the asset mix to reflect anticipated market conditions, you, your investment advisor or the managers of the funds you own can take advantage of growth and income opportunities while at the same time structuring your portfolio to preserve capital.

The key benefit of the managed approach is stability. Rates of return of different types of investments – bonds, short-term investments such as treasury bills, Canadian common stocks, foreign common stocks and precious metals – can be very different at any one time. By emphasizing areas of the market that are the best values at a given time, you are likely to get a long-term rate of return that is higher, and more stable, than the rate earned by any single class of assets.

Table IV shows the average one-year rates of return for twelve-month periods ended June 30 of RRSP-eligible equity funds, including balanced funds, bond and mortgage funds, money market funds and foreign equity funds, which can be up to 14 percent of an RRSP. It gives an indication of the volatility of rates of return on different classes of assets over the past five years. The money market fund returns are about two percentage points higher than you would expect from a variable rate RRSP from a major financial institution. A more extensive table is included in the appendix.

The RRIF as an extension of your RRSP

When deciding which investment strategy to choose, it is essential that you take a long-term view of your investment. Until a few years ago, most people with RRSPs bought life annuities sometime between the ages of sixty-five and seventy-one to finance their retirement. The annuity paid a fixed amount of money each month for life, generally with some minimum guaranteed payment period, and you prayed that inflation would not leave you destitute. At the time, the RRIF option wasn't acceptable to most people because the federal government restricted withdrawal options. This changed in 1986, and the RRIF is now the sensible option for most people.

A RRIF is an RRSP in reverse. You withdraw money from your RRIF to finance your retirement. You can take out as much as you want each year, so you are in full control. However, you must take out a minimum amount, which is the amount held in your RRIF at the end of the previous year divided by the difference between your age and ninety, or your spouse's age if she or he is younger. If you are seventy-one, you must withdraw 1/19th of the plan, if you are seventy-two you must withdraw 1/18th, if you are seventy-three you'll have to withdraw 1/17th and so on.

Keep in mind that your money has to provide adequate income for as long as you live, which is why the life annuity still appeals to people who have a family history of longevity and expect to live beyond age ninety.

Regardless of which strategy you choose, be conservative with your RRSP. Too many people have destroyed the likelihood of a financially worry-free retirement by speculating with their RRSP funds. The RRSP should be the most conservative portion of your portfolio; it is not the place to speculate on mining exploration, unproven technologies or high-risk real estate developments. There is nothing wrong with speculation, but it has no place in retirement savings. The amount of tax-assisted funds you can contribute to an RRSP is limited; if you lose it, then the advantage of tax-free growth on that money is gone forever. Remember, a contribution of $1,000 a year earning twelve percent will be worth about $270,000 at the end of thirty years, while the value of a single contribution of $1,000 at twelve percent is $32,000 in thirty years. With that type of growth available from conservative investments there is no reason to speculate in your RRSP.

Your total financial package

You should consider your RRSP as part of your total financial package and structure your investments to pay as little tax as possible. Inside your RRSP, all investment income grows untaxed. But it is fully taxable at your marginal tax rate when it is withdrawn through a RRIF, an annuity or simply cashed in. It doesn't matter whether it is interest, dividend income or capital gains. Outside your RRSP, interest is taxable at your marginal tax rate, while dividends and capital gains are taxed at lower rates. In fact, your first $100,000 of capital gains is exempt from tax.

This means that if you are investing in a mix of interest and growth investments both inside and outside an RRSP you should keep the interest-paying investments inside your RRSP and the growth investments outside your RRSP. You'll pay less in taxes.

Too many people pay more tax than necessary. If you hold $50,000 of top-quality growth mutual funds in your RRSP and have $50,000 in Canada Savings Bonds and guaranteed investment certificates outside your plan, you'll pay tax on the interest earned on your CSBs and GICs as well as on the capital gains earned in your RRSP when that money is withdrawn. You're better off switching your investments: Move the CSBs and GICs into the RRSP and the equities out.

This is relatively easy to do. It involves setting up a self-directed RRSP, which is explained in detail in Chapter Seven, then substituting your growth investments for your interest-paying investments.

This is feasible if you've chosen a fixed ratio of income versus growth investments for your overall portfolio. If you are taking a managed-asset view you may find that constantly moving your assets around is a difficult task, particularly if you are investing using a managed-asset-mix or balanced mutual fund. If that's the case, the switching of assets is really beyond your control.

If the decision comes down to saving on taxes or having the most suitable investment policy possible, choose the investment policy over the tax savings. Look at tax savings as icing on the investment cake.

Guarantees versus growth

Although you have two broad investment options to consider – fixed income and growth – there is a wide variety of choice within each. If you want guarantees, you can walk into any bank, trust company or credit union and get an RRSP that pays a specified rate of return for a specific period. If growth is your desire, you can choose from several hundred mutual funds. Mutual fund management companies offer these through independent sales forces, and several major financial service organizations offer funds through their own sales forces. In addition, many insurance companies offer funds or RRSP-eligible insurance policies that are similar to mutual funds. All major banks and trust companies, and some of the smaller ones, offer funds.

Some RRSP-eligible mutual funds invest primarily in Canadian common stocks for long-term growth. Others invest in bonds, mortgages or both for high current income and a secondary objective of growth. An increasing number have a mix of growth and income assets that varies with market conditions. There are also real estate funds, precious metals funds and funds that invest outside of Canada. The funds that invest internationally are generally not RRSP-eligible, although they can be used to constitute the foreign property portion of an RRSP.

If an off-the-shelf plan doesn't appeal to you, you can start a self-directed plan. Perhaps the rates paid on guaranteed investments seem tame, and you're not concerned about safety; you can go out and buy a piece of the high-yielding, high-risk mortgages that appear on the market from time to time. You may get double the rate of return that you could get from a financial institution. Just remember, that rate, which may exceed 20 percent, reflects the risk. You also lack the protection of deposit insurance with such investments, and if the borrower defaults you have to look to the asset that has been put up as security. The time to determine the value of the security is before you invest, not afterward.

Diversify

A final point: diversify your investments. Unless you have a crystal ball, or a fantastic investment record, spread your risk. If you invest in guaranteed RRSPs, choose a range of terms so all your RRSPs don't come up for renewal at the same time. No one can predict where interest rates will be several years from now and by staggering investments you avoid the possibility of having to reinvest all your funds when rates are low.

If you opt for growth, diversify your investments through one or more mutual funds, or by spreading your money among a number of individual stocks within your self-directed RRSP. A portfolio of six stocks doesn't give you as much diversification as a fund, but it is an acceptable compromise. Just remember not to concentrate your holdings in one industry; that would defeat your intention to diversify.

CHAPTER 4

Guaranteed Plans: Playing it Safe

GUARANTEED FUNDS OFFER one of the safest havens for retirement money. Because they pay fixed returns and offer the security of deposit insurance, they are by far the most popular RRSP alternative available. In fact, they are the only suitable choice for people who are unwilling to accept any of the risk associated with marketable securities, such as stocks or bonds. They also make sense for anyone who cannot afford to take risks. If you are approaching retirement, or are retired and have limited savings, stay with guaranteed plans that are similar to guaranteed investment certificates (GICs) and term deposits.

During retirement, when preservation of capital is paramount, guaranteed plans are also a good RRIF choice for those who have reached the point where inflation is not a threat to lifestyle.

In addition, guaranteed plans are well suited as temporary havens for RRSP savings. For example, you may intend to eventually put your money in a mutual fund but would prefer to wait until prices settle. You could temporarily deposit your RRSP cash in a financial institution's variable rate guaranteed plan with the intention of switching later to one of its mutual funds.

Under a guaranteed plan, you are lending your money to a bank, trust company or other financial institution which agrees to pay you a guaranteed rate of interest for a specified period of time. After that period expires, you can renew the plan, probably at a different interest rate, or move your money into another investment. The big advantage of a guaranteed plan is that you know what the value of your RRSP will be at the end of the investment period. It will equal the amount that was in the plan at the beginning of the period plus the guaranteed interest.

Rates offered by institutions on guaranteed plans rarely vary by more than one-quarter to one-half of a percentage point. Any investment offering higher rates, such as floating rate debentures, may not be as secure. If the rate quoted seems high, verify that the investment offered is as secure as money deposited with a bank, trust company or credit union.

Guaranteed safety

Guaranteed funds with these institutions are safe, not only because the holders know their rates of return in advance but also because there is little danger of a Canadian bank, trust company, credit union or insurance company failing and being unable to meet obligations to depositors or policyholders. This theory has been tested as recently as 1985, when two western Canadian banks failed. There were delays, but obligations to depositors were met in full.

Government agencies are supposed to monitor closely deposit-seeking institutions to ensure depositors' funds are always protected. In addition, most of these institutions are members of the Canada Deposit Insurance Corp., a federal agency that insures depositors at each institution against losses. This insurance covers up to $60,000 principal and interest on deposit with banks and trust companies not exceeding a term of five years. RRSP accounts are treated separately from personal accounts, so an individual with $60,000 in a savings account and another $60,000 in an RRSP with the same institution would be fully covered. Deposit-taking institutions in Quebec benefit from a similar system, set up under the auspices of the Quebec Insurance Board.

The $60,000 limit applies to deposits at a particular bank or trust company. You cannot circumvent this limit by opening several accounts at different branches of the same institution. But you will have complete coverage if you limit your RRSP holdings with any one bank or trust company to $60,000. Even so, many investors have much more than $60,000 on deposit with major banks and trust companies. Their view is that no government would allow a major bank or trust company to fail – a view shared by most investment professionals. However, the same unwritten guarantee is unlikely to apply to smaller institutions.

Deposits in credit unions are covered under legislation that generally provides for unlimited coverage, except in Quebec and Ontario. The province of Ontario insures up to $60,000 in each account, so complete insurance coverage at an Ontario credit union can be had only by a series of RRSPs that are less than $60,000.

Investors who plan to put their money into guaranteed RRSPs should make sure the institution they intend to deal with is covered by deposit insurance and that their RRSPs will qualify. Plans that invest in mortgages, bonds and equities are not covered.

Investors should also realize that deposit insurance doesn't mean they will receive full interest on guaranteed deposits for the entire term of their contract. If an institution fails, you'll get your principal back, plus interest only up to the day the institution folds. If this is a major concern, stick with the larger banks and trust companies. You won't earn as much interest as you would with some of the smaller institutions, but you'll probably sleep better.

Guaranteed RRSPs offered by insurance companies are not covered by Canada Deposit Insurance but by the Canadian Life and Health Insurance Compensation Corporation. Coverage on RRSPs and RRIFs is up to $60,000.

The two types of plans

There are two basic types of guaranteed RRSPs. The first requires a commitment by an investor to tie up funds for up to five years. Because the financial institution involved knows how long it is likely to have use of the funds, it can in turn lend the money to other customers. For instance, money put into a five-year trust company RRSP certificate would allow the trust company to lend an equivalent amount in five-year mortgages.

The second type of guaranteed plan is similar to a bank or trust company premium savings account, where interest paid changes with general interest rate trends.

If you go for a plan that guarantees an interest rate for a fixed period, you may not have access to your funds in the case of an emergency. Usually, the five-year term is not a disadvantage for most RRSP investors because the funds put into the plans are earmarked for retirement and in most cases aren't needed earlier. The five-year interest rate is based on the general interest rate structure of the economy and is comparable to rates on trust company five-year GICs.

At least one trust company offers a guaranteed RRSP in which investors' deposits are converted to U.S. funds. Such plans are designed for people who intend to retire in the U.S.. However, the interest rate paid is much lower than the rate paid on Canadian funds. Consequently, the usefulness of this alternative seems limited. Because these accounts are denominated in a foreign currency they are not protected by CDIC insurance.

On the other hand, variable rate guaranteed RRSPs pay a rate that moves with inflation. From the mid-1970s to the summer of 1981, they provided a rate of return superior to that of fixed-term guaranteed plans. The rates they paid have since tumbled and will continue to fall as long as interest rates move lower. Once the inflation rate increases, variable rates will move higher once again. Indeed, in 1989 and during the first half of 1990, variable rates were higher than five-year rates as the Bank of Canada kept short-term rates high to cool the economy and to support the Canadian dollar.

The term of a variable rate RRSP can be as short as one month and as long as six months, depending on the plan and its issuer. Some pay daily interest, so in theory the rate can change at any time. Variable rate plans make sense for people who are worried that inflation is going to get worse and want RRSPs in which rates adjust fairly quickly.

You can collapse a variable rate plan at any time but it can take as little as a few days or as long as six weeks to get your money, depending on the financial institution involved. This is generally of little concern to the majority of RRSP holders who rarely, if ever, switch plans. But it is something that should be considered by those approaching retirement. They must give adequate notice to obtain the funds necessary to buy an annuity or other retirement option. The length of time required to get at funds should also concern those who use guaranteed plans as a temporary investment.

The self-directed alternative

Recently, many investors have reaped higher returns from guaranteed investments by placing them in self-directed RRSPs. During June 1991, banks and trust companies were paying about 5.5 percent on variable rate RRSPs. But individuals with self-directed plans could hold treasury bills purchased from major investment dealers that yielded about 8.7 percent. Many people also use self-directed plans to hold Canada Savings Bonds. Others hold medium-term Government of Canada bonds, which sometimes pay a higher return than trust company GICs.

Because the annual cost of a self-directed plan is generally about $125, it is an alternative that should be considered by investors who have $10,000 or more in RRSP savings and are willing to monitor interest rate trends in hopes of realizing superior returns.

Mutual funds

Another alternative is a money market fund RRSP. These are mutual funds that pool the savings of many small investors to invest in treasury bills, bank deposits and, in some cases, commercial paper. They are safe because of the quality of their holdings and because of their diversified portfolios. Also, money market funds pay as much as two percentage points more than variable rate guaranteed plans because the size of their investments allows them secure higher rates.

Money market funds, as well as variable rate RRSPs, are suitable for individuals who are within a few years of retirement and intend to purchase an annuity when they retire. Similarly, they are good choices for anyone who requires a high degree of flexibility and does not want to be locked into a plan for a long period.

Avoid withdrawal fees

Regardless of whether you choose a guaranteed savings account RRSP or one with a lock-in period, you can save yourself some money by shopping around. In addition to differences among interest rates, the registration, administration and withdrawal fees vary widely among institutions. These fees can make a difference to total return, especially in those few cases in which withdrawal or closing-out fees are substantial. Rarely, however, do these exceed $100 and they can be avoided entirely.

Most banks and trust companies and some insurance companies have done away entirely with administration and management fees on their guaranteed RRSPs. However, there are a number that still levy charges – usually no more than 0.25 percent, with maximums of $12.50 to $25, depending on the institution. The tables in appendix one, appendix two and appendix three show fees charged by a number of institutions.

Some financial planners, insurance agents and annuity brokers act as agents for smaller banks and trust companies and can solicit RRSP deposits. They shop the market for you. Just remember that the rates you want to compare are the net rates, after all fees.

Watch the compounding period

There is another point to consider when choosing a guaranteed RRSP – the way interest is calculated. For example, a trust company offering 11.5 percent compounded annually would pay $115 interest on principal of $1,000 at the end of the year. A trust company offering the same rate compounded semi-annually would pay $57.50 interest after six months and an additional 5.75 percent on $1,057.50, about $60.81, six months later.

Semi-annual compounding has the effect of raising the rate of return in this case to about 11.83 percent. Although the difference may seem small, it can make a significant impact on the amount of income you will receive at retirement. Some financial institutions compound interest monthly, so it pays to shop around.

Of course, you should also pay attention to general interest rate trends. Rates in Canada have been extremely volatile during the past decade. The banks' prime lending rate – the rate at which they lend to their most credit-worthy customers – moved from 12.75 percent in November 1980 to a high of 22.75 percent in the summer of 1981. It subsequently retreated to a plateau of 11 percent in the spring of 1983, then moved up again in 1984 to 13 percent. In September 1985 it was 10.25 percent, it hit 13 percent in January 1986, fell to 8.75 percent by March 1987 and gradually rose to 14.75 percent in March 1990. The prime began to fall in August 1990 and was 14 percent at the end of that month. In June 1991 it was 9.75 percent.

It is difficult to predict which way interest rates will move. If they increase, individuals who tie up their funds for the next five years at today's rates may end up shortchanging themselves. In the fall of 1982, for example, investors were getting 14 percent on five-year guaranteed RRSPs; little more than a year earlier they were getting 19 percent. Yet in the mid-1970s, 10 percent was considered a good rate.

Read the fine print

Be wary of rates offered during the height of the RRSP-buying season. Banks and trust companies tend to get involved in price wars for variable rate RRSP money in January and February, only to cut rates in March. As a result, you should ask to see a list of rates that were in effect over the past 12 months and consider these rates when making your RRSP decision.

If you choose to invest in a guaranteed plan, read the fine print. While most institutions have straightforward presentations, a few do not. Some institutions apply a guaranteed rate only to the principal, with a floating rate paid on interest earned in the plan.

Be suspicious, too, of advertising that promotes returns that seem to be much better than average. For example, a few years ago, one issuer claimed that it paid an "average yield" of 16 percent on its guaranteed plan over a period of several years. A close examination of its figures indicated that its 16 percent average yield was equivalent to 13.5 percent compounded. This RRSP product was not as attractive as the issuer had suggested.

Caution should also be exercised when considering plans offered by life insurance companies to compete with bank and trust company guaranteed RRSPs. They are known as flexible-premium guaranteed-interest annuities or, in some cases, single-premium deferred annuities. Unlike many other insurance company products they do not require ongoing contributions. They are similar to many bank and trust company guaranteed RRSPs in that they guarantee a rate of return for up to five years so holders know in advance what rate of interest the company pays. The difference is that there is often an initial fee, or front-end load, of up to 5 percent on insurance company plans. Some may charge a back-end load, or surrender fee. While interest rates quoted may seem higher than trust company or bank rates, that premium disappears when investors consider that only ninety-five cents out of every dollar put into the plan goes to work for them.

Where to go

If interest rates are your main consideration, your first choice for savings account RRSPs should be from the trust company group. However, you should shop around and look at the rates offered by all financial institutions and money market funds at the time you want to invest your money. If you don't have time to shop, stick with one of the major trust companies or banks. In banking and finance, big is often best when it comes to safety. If you are ultraconservative, stick with one of the five major chartered banks.

CHAPTER 5

Using Mutual Funds in Your RRSP

WHILE GUARANTEED RRSPS are the first choice of most people, between $25 billion and $35 billion of RRSP investments are held as mutual funds.

A mutual fund pools the savings of many individual investors. The pool is invested in a portfolio of securities. Investors hold shares or units of the fund. Each share or unit has a value called the net asset value per share or unit which is equal to the total value of the portfolio – net assets – divided by the total number of shares or units outstanding. The number of shares or units will change at the end of each business day depending on the number of units purchased and redeemed that day.

The type of securities in the portfolio reflects the specific objectives of the fund. For example, if a fund's objective is long-term growth of capital tied to the Canadian economy, the capital would be invested in a portfolio primarily of Canadian common shares. If a fund's objective is interest income tied to the bond market, the capital would be invested in a portfolio made up of bonds and debentures.

There are several types of RRSP-eligible mutual funds – funds which can be held without limit in an RRSP. These include:
- Canadian equity funds;
- Bond funds;
- Mortgage funds;
- Bond and mortgage funds;
- Money market funds;
- Balanced funds, which hold both equities and bonds;
- Real estate funds;
- Certain specialty funds, such as precious metals funds and energy funds.

You can also hold international funds in your RRSP. But, because their investments are foreign securities, their value at the time of purchase cannot exceed the foreign property limit set by Ottawa.

Mutual funds offer advantages that should be important to any investor, including those who are trying to build a pool of wealth within their RRSPs. These advantages are:

- Diversification. Your risk is spread among many securities; if one turns sour it will have little impact on the total value of the portfolio. A mutual fund allows investors with limited assets to achieve a diversity they could not reach investing on their own.
- Liquidity. You can purchase or redeem most mutual funds on short notice, usually locking in the price set at the close of business on the day in which the fund receives your order, less any acquisition or redemption fees that you might have to pay.
- Professional management. The selection of securities in a mutual fund is made by a professional investment manager who is trained and experienced in investment decisions. The management fee charged by mutual funds ranges around 2 percent a year with fees for equity funds generally higher than for fixed income funds. Other costs include acquisition and redemption fees, if applicable.

Watch your costs

Mutual fund RRSPs are offered by banks and trust companies, mutual fund dealers, financial planning organizations, stockbrokers, some credit unions and insurance companies. Banks, trust companies, insurance companies and some financial planning organizations may offer only their house brand of mutual funds. Others will offer funds managed by several organizations. Most banks and trust companies generally sell their funds directly to the public and do not charge an acquisition fee or redemption fee. These are called no-load funds.

Mutual fund management companies, insurance companies and some financial institutions use sales forces, either their own or independents, to sell their funds. They may charge an acquisition fee of up to 9 percent in return for service and advice but this fee can be much lower if you're investing hefty sums of money in the fund. The fee is also usually negotiable.

Moreover, there has been a trend in the funds industry away from acquisition fees toward what are called deferred declining redemption fees. If you buy a fund that has this kind of fee, all your money is invested. If you redeem, you are charged a redemption fee which declines over time. For example, if you redeem within one year you might expect to pay a fee of 4.5 percent to 5 percent, depending on the fund. If you redeem after two years you might pay 4 percent. If you remain with the fund, or fund group, for six or seven years, you might not pay any fee when you redeem. If you decide to buy a fund available only upon payment of an acquisition fee or with a redemption fee, buy through a specialist who has the knowledge and experience to give you your money's worth.

Information widely available

All fund companies provide detailed information on their funds. Quarterly and annual reports will detail the fund's recent performance, list the securities held in the mutual fund and give an overview of the fund manager's economic outlook. In addition, each fund must issue what is called a simplified prospectus. This prospectus explains in detail the fund's investment objectives and all fees and charges, including commission and redemption fee schedules, if applicable.

The *Financial Times*, *The Globe And Mail Report On Business* and *The Financial Post* publish monthly performance tables. Southam Business Information and Communications Group Inc. produces the Mutual Fund Sourcedisk which provides performance information on a computer disk and allows users to rank performance of funds within various user-determined categories. In addition, Southam publishes the Mutual Fund Sourcebook which gives detailed information on more than 600 mutual funds.

CHAPTER 6

Income Funds: Better Returns, Little Risk

BOND AND MORTGAGE RRSPs provide a middle-of-the-road alternative to guaranteed and equity investments. By relying on bond and mortgage markets, these plans should provide a reasonable balance between the higher-risk, equity plan and the secure, guaranteed plan.

Bond and mortgage plans, also known as fixed income plans, are mutual funds that invest in portfolios of top-quality bonds, mortgages or both. The main objective of a bond fund is to provide high, current income; capital growth is of secondary importance. A manager of a bond fund will try to obtain some capital growth through astute trading, but most of the return stems from income. The objective of a mortgage fund is also high, current income, but the nature of this type of fund makes capital growth less likely. As a group, the difference in returns between mortgage and bond funds is not great, although the capital growth potential of bond funds gives them an edge over mortgage funds in periods of volatile interest rates. During periods of stable rates, mortgage funds should provide higher returns.

Because of the quality of the underlying assets and the fact that they are professionally managed, fixed income funds are an excellent alternative to guaranteed plans.

During periods of high but stable interest rates, when the rate of inflation is relatively constant, fixed income funds can be consistently good performers. But on average they underperform variable rate guaranteed funds when interest rates soar. Still, they have excellent track records when inflation and interest rates are falling. The conventional wisdom is that fixed income funds are suitable for individuals who are unwilling to accept the broad variations in return that can come with owning an RRSP invested in the stock market. These investors are willing to shoulder some fluctuation in the value of their investments over time as a trade-off for a better return than is available from guaranteed RRSPs.

The question of the suitability of fixed income funds becomes more critical when interest rates are volatile. With narrow spreads between returns on guaranteed plans and the yields available on some fixed income funds after deducting management fees, guaranteed plans may seem to be better bets much of the time, especially for investors who fear uncertainty.

However, fixed income funds – particularly bond funds – do offer some important advantages over guaranteed plans. First, a fund offers more flexibility than a fixed-term guaranteed plan because units (or shares) can be redeemed at any time and the proceeds switched into another type of investment. Second, a bond fund manager has a much broader choice of investments than do individuals. He or she can invest in Canadian bonds paying interest in foreign currencies, including U.S. dollars, Japanese yen, Swiss francs and Australian dollars. This allows the manager to hedge against declines in the Canadian dollar or to invest in markets with higher interest rate levels.

As well, a manager can shorten or lengthen the average term of the fund's holdings by varying investments in securities. For example, a few years ago some bond fund managers loaded their portfolios with twenty-year bonds paying as much as 18 percent. GICs paid comparable rates at that time, but five years was the longest you could lock in that rate. Bond and mortgage funds are excellent RRIF choices for those who are drawing substantial portions of their plans for income and who do not want to face the sometimes negative returns of equity funds.

How fixed income funds work

Bond and mortgage funds are a good alternative to guaranteed plans, but they are not well understood by many RRSP shoppers. For one thing, unlike guaranteed plans, they are not covered by deposit insurance. However, that should not be a problem, especially in the case of mortgage funds offered by major banks and trust companies. These hold mortgages that are guaranteed by a government agency or insured against default. Consequently, their assets are risk-free although the values of these assets will fluctuate with changes in interest rates. Similarly, the vast majority of bond funds offered as RRSP investments emphasize government or government guaranteed bonds and top-quality corporate debt securities.

Mortgage funds pay a somewhat higher interest rate than guaranteed plans. The major difference from an investor's point of view is that the rate of return of a mortgage fund fluctuates with market conditions. Therefore, you don't know in advance what your return will be for the next five years, although you would expect to do moderately better than you would by buying a five-year guaranteed RRSP. Because most mortgages have terms of five years or less, they are potentially less volatile than bond funds, which can hold bonds with maturities ranging up to 20 years or more.

Bond funds, while not covered by deposit insurance, are low in risk, as already mentioned. Bond portfolios are often heavily invested in government bonds, which guarantee payment. The other popular investments with these funds, corporate bonds, are generally secured by company assets. If a company defaults on its debt, creditors such as bondholders rank ahead of shareholders. In addition, any single corporate bond is only a small portion of the total portfolio.

When investors buy units in a fund, they become part owners of the bonds and mortgages in the portfolio. They pay the manager a fee to administer the assets and a share of any profits or losses goes to their accounts. Fixed income funds are available through many financial institutions and some investment counsellors. Shares in a fixed income fund are valued at the total worth of the portfolio, divided by the number of units outstanding. The number of units changes daily, weekly or monthly, depending on the fund, as new investors buy units and others redeem theirs. The value of a bond or mortgage fund unit changes with variations in interest rates.

It's easy to see how it happens by following this example: a bond maturing in twenty years, with a face value of $1,000 and paying interest at 10 percent, would sell in the bond market at $1,000 only if similar bonds were yielding 10 percent. But interest rates change from time to time and, if the general interest rate structure were higher and new bonds were available that paid 12 percent, the 10 percent bond would no longer sell at $1,000. Instead, other investors would be prepared to buy it only if the price were chopped so that the income on the bond would result in a 12 percent yield based on the new price. In this case, the 10 percent bond would yield 12 percent if the price were cut to about $833.

Yet interest rates can move down as well as up. If rates fell and bonds of similar term and quality to the 10 percent bond were available at 8 percent, then other investors would be willing to pay more than $1,000 for the bond. Because the bond pays a higher rate of interest than the going rate, its value would rise to about $1,250. If it were sold, it would yield 8 percent on the higher price. Unit prices of fixed income funds move in a similar manner.

Each fund unit represents part ownership in a portfolio that may contain hundreds of bonds or mortgages, which may differ from each other in quality, coupon rate and term of maturity. Each shift in interest rates or change in demand for bonds of specific quality or term will increase or decrease the value of the total portfolio. In turn, this will affect the price of a unit of the fund. Depending on the type of financial institution managing the portfolio, fund values are calculated daily, weekly or monthly. Generally, mutual funds determine unit values at the close of each business day, while trust companies and banks calculate unit values weekly or monthly.

Structuring portfolios

The rate of return earned on a fixed income fund depends largely on how managers structure portfolios using different maturities and securities with varying coupon rates. Recently, bonds with maturities of five years or less were yielding marginally less than bonds maturing in twenty years. A year earlier, five-year bonds were yielding more. The higher yield, a year ago, on the five-year bonds theoretically compensates for the likelihood that interest rates were poised to decline. Holders of longer-term bonds were willing to accept a slightly lower rate in return for the certainty of having a fixed stream of income for twenty years at what they expected would prove to be an attractive yield.

However, three years earlier, in June 1988, bonds with maturities of about five years were yielding less than bonds maturing in twenty years. The higher rate on a long-term bond compensates for the risk of a rise in inflation during the bond's life.

Because of this higher rate, a portfolio with a heavy weighting of longer-term bonds should provide a higher return than one with shorter maturities during a period of stable interest rates and inflation. But even in bond and mortgage portfolios, high-return securities can mean higher risk. As many investors learned in 1980 and 1981, when interest rates soared to record levels, RRSP fixed income plans with portfolios of longer maturities fell more in value than funds with portfolios of shorter maturities. The opposite occurred in 1982 and 1983, when interest rates plunged.

Shorter-term bonds are less volatile because their dates of maturity, at which money is repaid and can be reinvested, are closer than the due dates of longer-term bonds. A manager expecting volatile rates and higher inflation would probably include a high proportion of shorter-term bonds in the portfolio, shortening the average maturity of fund holdings. But a manager who expects stable or declining rates would generally go for longer maturities to maximize returns.

Bond fund managers who expected rates to drop sharply would project where they expect rates to move and structure their portfolios to emphasize those maturities which would likely provide the greatest capital appreciation.

Sometimes you win, sometimes you lose

Bonds have been a loser's game in much of the postwar period as interest rates have skyrocketed. In the late 1940s, Government of Canada long-term bonds were issued at rates of about 3 percent. But as inflation increased and eroded the value of money, lenders demanded higher coupon rates to compensate for inflation. Until 1981, it appeared that the peak had occurred between 1974 and 1976, when some Government of Canada bonds were issued with coupons in the 10 per cent range. But in 1981, rates soared to more than 17 percent. For buyers at that time, bonds have been a winner's game. For a period in 1989, and again in the first half of 1991, long-term interest rates fell sharply. Consequently, some bond funds outperformed equity funds during 1989 and in the year ended June 1991.

Bonds that were issued when rates were lower trade at substantial discounts to issue price. For example, a $1,000, 15.75 percent Government of Canada bond that is due February 1, 2001, traded in 1981 at about $890 to yield more than 17 percent. Buyers at this price receive $78.75 of interest every six months until 2001, when they receive the full $1,000 face value. The 17 percent yield reflects the combined return of the flow of interest payments and the present value of the $1,000 to be received in 2001 on the discounted $890 current market value. Ten years later, those bonds were trading at about $1,310 to yield about 10.5 percent.

Managers must choose

Managers who expect interest rates to be stable over long periods will usually hold large portions of their portfolios in high-coupon bonds. That way, they lock in a high income stream.

Managers who expect major declines in interest rates would go for portfolios weighted heavily with discount bonds. That way, they get substantial capital gains as rates fall and the spread between market value and face value shrinks. For example, managers who bought long-term bonds in September 1981 and held them for 12 months had total returns of income and capital appreciation approaching 40 per cent.

A manager who correctly anticipates the timing and direction of interest swings can increase a fund's performance substantially. But an error in judgment could prove costly to the fund's unit holders. In the twelve months ended August 31, 1981 unit values of many funds declined because their managers had incorrectly structured their portfolios in expectation of lower rates. Other managers took more cautious stands but, on average, their funds still underperformed guaranteed investment funds.

The best performers of the fixed income group were money market funds that invest almost entirely in short-term bonds and commercial paper with maturities of less than one year. These funds have rates of return that continuously reflect current interest rates. However, they will not generate capital gains for their holders in a period when rates are falling. The trend reversed in the twelve months ended August 31, 1982, when rates fell, making fixed income funds top performers.

The mortgage market

The rapid rise of interest rates during the 1960s led to a major change in mortgage markets. Institutions found themselves unable to continue setting residential mortgage rates for the life of a mortgage. Instead, they found it necessary to set rates for five-year periods only, at the end of which the rate would be adjusted. This was necessary because the funds invested by some financial institutions are borrowed on a five-year basis.

For the fixed income fund with mortgages, the five-year renewal period is beneficial in periods of rising rates because the manager can revise rates upward after five years. But if rates are down at the end of five years, the mortgage rate charged at that time will also be lower. This means that if rates slide over the next five years, a bond fund with most of its assets in long-term bonds will do better than a mortgage fund that has its assets in shorter-term securities. This happens because the bond fund will continue to derive income from high-coupon bonds beyond five years.

While both types of funds will show gains as rates drop, the gain for the bond fund should be larger. If the opposite occurs and rates go up over the next five years, then mortgage funds with a mixture of one- to five-year mortgages in their portfolios will outperform funds invested heavily in long-term bonds. Mortgage funds attracted hundreds of millions of dollars of RRSP money during the second half of the 1970s because of good performance. But they suffered too during the surge in rates in 1981 before recovering in 1982 and 1983.

Mortgages usually pay slightly higher interest rates than bonds available at the same time. However, there has been little difference historically between well-managed bond funds and well-managed mortgage funds. The trading flexibility a bond manager has relative to a mortgage manager dealing in poorly marketable mortgages offsets the benefits of higher mortgage rates. There are exceptions, of course, and some bond funds have performed substantially better than mortgage funds over the past five years.

Lower management fees

Management fees for bond funds, generally in the range of 0.5 percent to 1 percent of net assets, are below the 1 percent to 1.25 percent of net assets many mortgage funds charge. The difference at least partially offsets the higher interest rates usually available on mortgages.

Besides rearranging their portfolios to make the most of expected interest rate swings, bond fund managers have other ways of increasing returns. One such method is to include higher-risk bonds. While Government of Canada bonds may yield 10 percent, some bonds issued by corporations that could have trouble meeting their obligations might trade at prices to yield a return as high as 16 percent. However, such risky securities would be ill advised for most investors saving for retirement. Consequently, few fund managers buy high-risk bonds for retirement portfolios. The majority of bond fund managers restrict their purchases to Government of Canada bonds, debt securities of major banks and trust companies and bonds issued by the provinces, municipalities and corporations with the best credit ratings. They will trade these constantly to improve yield or upgrade quality.

Investigate first

Most mortgage fund managers invest in guaranteed or insured first mortgages rather than lower-quality vehicles. Unfortunately, there can be exceptions, so any investor considering fixed income RRSPs should read the prospectus to determine what is in the portfolio and whether the investments are conservative. The volatile interest rates of the past decade have taken their toll on bond and mortgage fund performance.

The *Financial Times of Canada* survey of investment fund performances for periods ended June 30, 1991, notes that annual compound rates of return from fixed income funds for five years ranged from 5.9 percent to 10.8 percent, averaging 8.6 percent. For three years, the range was 0.5 percent to 11.9 percent, with an average of 8.7 percent. Over one year, performance ranged from 5.2 percent to 19.2 percent, with an average of 12.4 percent.

The vast majority of funds had returns clustered around the average return for each period covered in the survey. In fact, most fixed income funds will have similar rates of return over relatively long periods of stable interest rates.

If you assume rates are going to be stable over the next few years and decide to invest in fixed income RRSPs on that basis, narrow your search by rejecting any fund that has consistently ranked below the average performance in the group. Don't just use the period ended June 30, 1991. Look at how the funds performed over different twelve-month periods.

It also makes sense to examine the size of the fund. Be suspicious of top-performing funds with assets of only a few hundred thousand dollars. Managers of such funds might not be able to sustain top performance if their funds' characteristics change through growth in the assets under management.

Investors who are looking for fixed income RRSPs because they expect interest rates to move lower have to go through a somewhat different process. In addition to searching for good performance, they must examine the individual prospectuses and latest quarterly reports of the funds, looking for portfolios fully invested in longer-term bonds. Dynamic Strip Bond Fund, for example, invests primarily in strip bonds which are, in effect, bond coupons payable at some specified future date. The fund will do well in periods when rates fall and poorly when rates rise relative to other bond funds.

Don't put all your eggs in one basket

Such a portfolio would have substantial capital appreciation if rates were to decline. In contrast, some managers are holding substantial portions of their portfolios in short-term notes and other cash equivalents. While well protected if rates move higher, these portfolios will have only limited capital appreciation if rates decline.

Of course, investors who expect rates to move higher should choose guaranteed savings account RRSPs, money market funds or fixed income funds holding bonds with relatively short-term maturities. If you do choose a fixed income RRSP, remember the adage about putting all your eggs in one basket. It is best to hold your retirement savings in more than one RRSP to reduce the risks of placing all your savings with a manager whose luck turns bad or who proves to be incompetent.

You should also continuously monitor the performance of the fund and its manager, using the same criteria employed in choosing your funds. Managers and management philosophies change with time, and such changes may not be compatible with your investment objectives.

Consistently superior performance is difficult to find, as the tables of fixed income funds in Appendices D and E demonstrate. However, in periods of extremely volatile interest rates, such as the past seven years, funds that invested heavily in bonds and mortgages did well in those periods when rates declined, in particular in those years when they were falling from record levels. This is a reversal from 1981, when bond and mortgage funds fared poorly and money market funds did well.

Consider costs

Once you've narrowed the field to a handful or two, it's time to shop around for the best buy. As with guaranteed funds, registration, administration and withdrawal fees vary widely among institutions. These charges can make a substantial difference in overall return, especially on smaller RRSPs.

Don't forget to look at acquisition and redemption fees. Most banks and trust companies sell their funds directly to the public. Mutual fund management companies, insurance companies and some financial institutions use sales forces, either their own or independents, to sell their funds.

CHAPTER 7

Equity Funds: For Long-Term Growth

IF LONG-TERM GROWTH IS your objective, you should consider equity fund RRSPs. Historically, they have provided the best long-term returns, although prices tend to be volatile.

The performance of equity fund RRSPs depends primarily on the performance of stock markets – or segments of these markets. Although equity plans are favourites when stock markets are on a roll, they're not suitable for those who lose sleep when markets dive. For patient investors, the compensation, at least theoretically, is that over a long enough period of time equity funds can be expected to deliver a better rate of return than most other types of RRSPs. But remember, stock markets move in cycles.

Between July 1982 and August 1987 the Toronto Stock Exchange 300 composite index – the most widely used measure of Canadian stock market performance – rose 202 percent, attracting many people to RRSPs invested in equities. Many investors had been lured from guaranteed funds to equities with promises of 18 percent returns. But the market's fortunes changed. Between August and October 1987, the TSE 300 fell 31 percent, sharply reducing investors' savings. It subsequently recovered much of its loss, and between October 1987 and July 1988 gained 24 percent. In the twelve months ended June 1989 it rose another 13.5 percent. In the twelve months ended June 1990 it declined 2.4 percent. In the subsequent twelve months ended June 1991 it rose 1.9 percent.

No simple formula

Many investors and their financial advisors were shocked by the volatility of stocks. However, the big price swings did not surprise more experienced investors who remembered the cycles of the 1960s and 1970s.

Although it would be wonderful to accurately predict stock market performance, there is no simple formula for doing so because each cycle has its own underlying factors. The losses of 1980 and 1982 were largely the result of record interest rates, recession, falling gold prices and the impact of federal-provincial politics over the oil industry. In 1980, gains were largely triggered by soaring oil prices and the spillover effect on the prices of gold and other metals. The gains of 1982 to 1987 were largely fuelled by falling interest rates that eventually sent stock prices to unsustainable levels, setting them up for a fall, while the lacklustre performance of 1990 and 1991 could be tied to investor concern about the recession.

Since the Second World War, stocks have generally outperformed fixed income and guaranteed investments during periods when investors expected inflation to be stable or to decline. However, markets have been extremely volatile during the past decade because of changing inflationary expectations and their impact on profits. But if investors perceive that declines in inflation are part of a long-term trend that won't be destroyed by economic recovery, then stocks and bonds will form a relationship in which equities almost consistently outperform fixed income securities.

For investors who are willing to bet that stock prices will continue to rise, there are many equity plans on the market. Not only do stock and mutual fund brokers sell equity funds, so do most banks, trust companies and insurance companies as well as financial planning organizations. Even one department store offers a series of house-brand funds, some of which are RRSP-eligible investments.

Yet not all equity funds sold in Canada can be registered as RRSPs. To qualify, they must have no more than 10 percent of their assets in foreign securities (Ottawa has proposed raising this limit but it was not yet law in October 1990). Those funds that are not eligible for registration as RRSPs usually hold foreign investments that exceed the limit. However, they can be included in the foreign property holding within RRSPs as the 14 percent foreign property content, and many investors include them in self-directed plans for that reason. In fact, some mutual fund dealers and investment dealers offer low-cost self-directed plans specifically for this purpose. Some fund management companies also offer a similar service to clients who buy into their funds.

Your protection is in diversity

Equity funds, like bond and mortgage funds, are not covered by deposit insurance. Instead, your protection against permanent capital loss is diversification. Portfolio managers spread a fund's money among a large number of companies, so if one fails, it represents only a small portion of total investments.

Unlike guaranteed and fixed income plans, RRSPs invested in the stock market vary widely in performance. For periods ended June 30, 1991, the *Financial Times of Canada* monthly survey of investment funds reported wide variations in rates of returns for RRSP-eligible equity funds. Over a five-year period, the best-performing fund had an average annual compound rate of return of about 13.7 percent, while the poorest lost an average of 7.4 percent a year. The fund with the losses concentrated on risky venture-capital investments, while most others were more diversified. During the five years, the Toronto Stock Exchange total return index, the TSE 300 plus dividend returns, registered an annual compound rate of return of about 9 percent.

Over the past three years, the average annual compound rate of return for RRSP-eligible equity funds ranged from -17.3 percent to 21.2 percent. Over the past year, the range was -19.3 percent to 27.1 percent. These extremes in performance were achieved by the specialty funds.

However, June 30, 1991 is only one reference point. As any fund performance table will show, the results of performance yardsticks vary widely at different dates. If we use an ending date of June 30, 1987, the range of returns was -4.7 to 93.5 percent. Funds that are the best performers when the market is rising are often the poorest performers when the market is plunging. An examination of the performance table covering twelve-month returns in appendix four shows few funds are consistently good performers. In fact, if more than one ending date is considered for measurement, most funds have returns close to the average return of funds with similar volatility.

Pay attention to the manager

In the case of funds that are consistently at the ends of the performance spectrum, superior or inferior results can usually be attributed to the decisions of a single manager or a handful of individuals working together.

Some funds will disclose to shareholders the name or names of the individuals who buy and sell shares in the portfolio. But many will not, usually because a committee makes the investment decisions – and no committee has ever consistently outperformed the market. Because of this, over time the majority of equity funds will have returns comparable to those of stock market indexes. The reason is relatively simple: most fund management committees try to determine which segments of the market will outperform the general index and which segments will perform poorly. Then they buy and sell stocks to fit the model they've created. However, most fund managers are basing their decisions on the same information, so it's no wonder their results are similar. Because these fund managers' decisions result in a significant portion of total stock market trading, their results and those of the general market do not differ substantially.

High-risk stocks

Several equity funds have outperformed the general market over lengthy periods. During the stock market heyday of the 1960s, many mutual funds were marketed on a record of apparent superior performance. In fact, their higher rates of return stemmed from their substantial holdings of high-risk stocks. When the market slid in early 1969, these stocks fell more than the general market, pulling down the performance of the funds that held them.

Most of today's fund managers are unwilling to load their portfolios with high-risk stocks, since such a strategy has been unprofitable over the long term because of volatile share prices over the past few years. A more common strategy is to increase or decrease the portion of the portfolio held in cash, according to the manager's perception of the outlook for the market's direction. Again, because most institutional managers use similar information in arriving at their decisions, this strategy does not usually result in consistently superior performance.

A few portfolio managers have been able to outperform their competitors by adopting a strategy that avoids basing portfolios on market weightings. Instead, they concentrate heavily in specific groups of stocks for a year or so, then completely switch out of these into other types of stocks or into cash. As a result, they might be heavily invested in gold shares at one time and not hold any a year or two later.

Other managers ignore market weightings and prefer to buy individual stocks they consider undervalued by the market. Managers who employ this type of portfolio strategy usually outperform the market in most periods. Often, they have positive results even when stock prices are moving down, or, at least they decline less than the general market.

Spread your money among funds

The problem facing investors is that there are not enough managers generating superlative returns for RRSP-eligible funds. Neither is there a valid measure for determining future performance. Consequently, the best that investors can expect to do is to sort through funds' results and spread their money among two or three funds they consider to be better performers and whose investment objectives seem compatible with theirs.

The cost of acquiring units in a fund should be a major consideration when deciding which fund to buy. Some, such as most bank and trust company funds, can be purchased directly without paying commissions. Others must be purchased through a salesperson and involve payment of an acquisition fee or alternatively, a redemption fee. If you buy into a fund that involves payment of a commission, regard the fee as payment for advice and service. And to make sure you get full value, deal only with a specialist with significant experience in funds who can help you determine what products meet your needs.

The first step in choosing equity-based RRSPs is understanding that some funds are more volatile than others. An extremely volatile fund is one whose monthly rates of return, measured over a period of years, swing widely. In contrast, a fund with low volatility is one whose rates of return are fairly stable. The *Financial Times of Canada* monthly survey of investment funds ranks RRSP-eligible equity funds by volatility so investors can compare each fund (for which at least thirty-six months of data is provided) with other funds with the same objective. Specialty funds that concentrate on one area of the market, such as gold or energy stocks, tend to be among the more volatile. The least volatile funds are those with large portions of their assets invested in high-yielding securities, which tend to stabilize the portfolio. Balanced and managed-asset-mix funds, as a group, are among the least volatile funds. However, not all fall into that category.

These lower-volatility funds often appeal to investors who want some growth but who also desire stability. In addition, they are particularly suitable for those who want a growth component in their RRIFs. These funds should be among the first choices of investors who, while approaching retirement, want to maintain some equity participation.

Examine past performance

Once you have determined what level of risk you are willing to assume, the next step is to examine the past performance of funds. While historical results are not a perfect indicator of future performance, they are a fair indicator of how a fund may perform under certain market conditions. They are also among the few yardsticks available to small investors whose accounts are not large enough to justify demands for detailed information about portfolio managers' experience, size of research staffs and investment strategies. Such information is readily available only to giant corporate or union pension funds. Even so, large investors seldom get results that are significantly different from those of small investors.

Using the *Financial Times of Canada* mutual fund survey, reject any fund that consistently ranks below the average performance of the group. For this test to be valid, it should take into account several years of information. This way, you will be judging performance in all types of markets – rising, stable and falling. Once you've narrowed your choice to funds that at least match the market's performance, it's time to examine the size of the fund. As with fixed income funds, be suspicious of top-performing equity funds with few assets. Many fund managers have been unable to sustain top performance when their funds grew; the increased size forced them to broaden their choices of securities and led to average performance.

Investment objectives

The third step is to check the investment objectives of the remaining funds against your own. This can be done only by obtaining copies of prospectuses issued by funds. These are available from a salesperson or directly from the management company.

Most equity funds have similar objectives – long-term capital appreciation through prudent investment, with current income a secondary consideration. However, there are some specialty funds that concentrate on specific industries, while others concentrate on senior companies for dividend income. The higher-risk specialty funds have a place in sophisticated investors' RRSP portfolios, but only if their holders are willing to make adjustments as circumstances dictate. For example, precious metals funds have been among the best and worst performers of recent years, depending on gold price trends.

Once you've selected some possible choices, compare costs. As with other types of funds, published performance figures tell only part of the story. Fees for registration, administration and withdrawal vary widely among funds and can make a substantial difference in your overall return.

Stay away from any type of purchase plan that involves rigid contribution schedules; these schemes are simply too expensive. For example, one insurance company had a plan in which 45 percent of first-year contributions went to sales charges, while 11 percent of the subsequent year's deposits went to administrative fees. These charges could not be justified by performance. However, some insurance company plans have provisions that insure holders against losses in excess of 25 percent, provided the plans are held for ten years.

Some insurance companies sell their funds without commissions. They assume you'll remain a long-term shareholder, so they compensate the salesperson through a commission based on the annual management fee charged by the fund. However, if you do cash in within a short period, expect to pay a redemption fee. Virtually every "no-load" mutual fund sold without an acquisition fee charges a redemption fee if a holder redeems within a short period of time, usually within a year. This is to discourage short-term trading, which is expensive for a fund.

Any equity fund offers diversification by spreading money among many stocks. Even so, it's unwise to gamble on a single manager. It is best to spread your retirement savings among two or three funds to lower the chance of placing all your money in the hands of a manager who performs worse than the competition.

There isn't a single fund that can be considered the best. The choice of funds should be based on your needs and investment expectations; the final decision on what to buy or avoid is yours alone.

Some better performers

It is getting more difficult each year to choose funds that look as though they will continue to outpace the market – for good reason. Many funds with top-notch performance have grown from an asset base of a few million dollars to hundreds of millions of dollars. The management styles responsible for their long-term performance when assets were small may no longer work as well in a larger fund.

Moreover, several funds have changed managers, and, in some cases, poor performance in the past may not be indicative of what a new manager will do. In other cases, high performance may reflect the expertise of a manager who has moved elsewhere. It comes down to finding a manager with whom you feel comfortable.

No-load funds

If you consider yourself fairly disciplined about investment matters, have a proven track record of investing on your own, and plan to follow your investments closely, consider no-load mutual funds. These are sold directly by management companies, so you don't pay commissions. All your money goes directly to work for you.

Some trust companies and banks and a few mutual fund management companies offer no-load funds. And they keep their shareholders informed about investments with quarterly reports. If, however, you need ongoing advice, you may be better off buying a fund that charges a redemption fee if you redeem within a certain number of years or which involves paying an acquisition fee or commission of up to 9 percent. Acquisition fees are negotiable and many sales are made at rates below the maximum. These days, 4 percent to 5 percent is the norm for funds sold by investment dealers. Fees also decline with the amount of money invested.

If you buy a fund through a mutual fund dealer or stockbroker, determine in advance the level of service you can expect. As far as group performance is concerned, there is no difference in the longer term between load and no-load funds. Some fund managers work both sides of the fence, managing load funds for one client and no-load funds for another. In any case, performance should be monitored continuously, either by you or the person through whom you make your purchase.

CHAPTER 8

Balanced, Real Estate and Specialty Funds

IN THEORY, THE BEST INVESTment strategy is one that allows investments in different classes of assets – bonds, stocks, foreign property, precious metals and short-term investments.

By shifting the mix, you, your investment advisor or a fund manager can emphasize bonds when bond yields are at historically high levels, stocks when stocks are inexpensive, or cash and precious metals when both stocks and bonds seem inappropriate. Such a strategy should provide investors with high income when yields are high, excellent long-term growth because stocks are purchased when they are inexpensive, and preservation of capital. In fact, the long-term rate of return of this type of investment program should be higher and less volatile than that of a pure equity strategy. The trouble is such results are difficult to achieve.

The balanced approach became very popular after stock markets plunged in October 1987. It was apparent that of the funds whose objective was long-term growth, the best performing were those that took the managed-asset-mix, or balanced, approach. Indeed, since October 1987 virtually all fund groups added one or more balanced funds to their stables, although the performance of some suggests they are balanced in name only and are in fact primarily equity funds. While the investment policies of these funds allowed their managers to hold a mix of assets, the managers sometimes failed to take a balanced approach.

To determine whether a fund is truly balanced, examine closely its latest quarterly financial statement to determine whether it has a mixture of fixed income and growth assets. Even more important, at least when examining a fund with three or more years' history, determine how it performed during the market decline from August to October 1987. A truly balanced fund should not have suffered as severely as equity funds. In the case of funds that sell directly to the public, this information can be obtained from the fund management company; with funds that use salespeople, ask dealers for details. You should also look at how the fund has performed in the latest twelve months as well as over the past five or ten years, recognizing that both bond and stock markets were exceptionally volatile during 1990 and 1991.

For funds with several years' history you can also look at volatility rankings to see if in fact they are less volatile than equity funds.

Real estate funds

Real estate is the most popular investment in Canada – if you think of your home as an investment. And with the rise in housing prices in most major markets until recently, housing has become an increasingly important part of Canadians' financial lives.

You can't hold real estate directly in an RRSP but you can hold units of real estate mutual funds that invest in Canadian property. These funds are designed for the pension and RRSP markets. They usually buy into industrial and commercial income-producing properties and avoid residential properties because of rent controls.

There are only a handful of real estate funds currently available. Some funds which were popular in their day experienced serious difficulties and disappeared. The oldest real estate RRSP fund, District Trust Retirement Savings Plan Real Estate Fund, was liquidated after its sponsor, District Trust Co., ran into financial problems. Another fund, Real Property Trust of Canada, changed managers in 1985 because of a dispute between its trustees and former managers. Redemptions were suspended temporarily and sales were terminated. It was eventually liquidated. In September 1986, Canadian Property Investors Trust suspended redemptions after the Ontario Securities Commission expressed concerns about appraisals of two properties.

However, beefed-up regulatory requirements for real estate funds were introduced in 1988 to reduce the incidence of such problems. The new regulations set stringent investment standards as well as standards for appraisals and evaluation of shares.

The returns on real estate funds consist of income and capital appreciation. Because real estate markets fluctuate, the funds should not be looked upon as short-term investments. Instead, they should be considered a plausible investment only by those willing to hold them for as long as a decade or more.

Moreover, real estate is a commodity. Its value depends on such things as vacancy rates, the cost of mortgage money and confidence in the economy. Many financial advisors suggest that real estate funds be considered only by people who already have substantial RRSP assets, and then only for part of their RRSP portfolio.

Like other investment funds, the key to positive returns is the quality of assets in the portfolio and the management behind the fund. Consequently, managers are expected to stick with top-quality real estate, generally in major urban centres.

When choosing investments, fund managers assess such factors as the quality of construction, municipal plans, zoning restrictions, demographic trends, financing and lease maturities, price and cash flow. Because judgment has so much bearing on the success or failure of a venture, experienced management is a must, especially since a well-managed property has a better chance of appreciating or holding its value.

Returns are only estimates

Real estate funds aim at annual returns in the 18 percent to 20 percent range. As a group their performance over the twelve months ended June 30, 1991 ranged from about -4 percent to 10 percent. Investors should realize that the returns reported by real estate pooled trust funds are just estimates. The value of real estate is determined by independent appraisers whose assessments are only informed opinions of a property's worth. Real estate fund values are not based on actual market transactions, like the values of bond and stock funds.

Properties are usually appraised only on the anniversary of their purchase. Therefore, in periods of rapidly rising or falling real estate prices, the unit values of real estate funds may understate or overstate the true value. Also, because the properties are appraised annually, real estate funds give the appearance of having more stable returns than equity funds whose values change daily as the market values of underlying securities change. In contrast, real estate funds are priced quarterly or monthly, and aren't as liquid as other RRSP options.

The rocky history and complex nature of real estate mutual funds make them an investment that should be made only by individuals who are willing to spend the time necessary to examine and compare funds before a purchase is made. Once the investment is made, the performance of a real estate pooled trust fund should be closely monitored.

Specialty funds

Other RRSP-eligible specialty funds include precious metals funds, energy funds and "small-cap" funds that invest primarily in smaller companies. Such specialty funds are usually more volatile than more broadly based funds. Consequently, they are probably best suited for part of an RRSP fund portfolio rather than the core holding. A specialty investment, Working Ventures Canadian Fund, might be considered for part of an RRSP portfolio by investors who can afford risk in their RRSPs. This fund invests in small business ventures. While not a mutual fund, in the normal sense, its units are available for RRSPs. However, they cannot be redeemed on demand, reflecting the long-term nature of the underlying investment. Risk is reduced somewhat by government credits which reduce the cost.

There are also "green" funds, which restrict their investments to companies that have proven to be environmentally friendly, and "ethical" funds that avoid companies that are in such businesses as the manufacture of armaments, liquor or cigarettes.

CHAPTER 9

Self-Directed Plans: Are They Right for You?

SELF-DIRECTED RRSPS DIFFER from other types of RRSPs in that the planholder is responsible for making all the investment decisions. If you're the owner of the plan, you can tailor your portfolio to your needs, whims, preferences and hunches.

A self-directed plan can be as risky as you make it. Properly managed, it can offer the highest potential returns of all types of plans. But self-directed RRSPs are commonly mismanaged. Instead of bringing investors profits, they can lead to staggering losses. For RRSP growth portfolios, they are best left to sophisticated investors.

However, self-directed RRSPs can also be of use to conservative investors who would otherwise invest in guaranteed plans. Such people often use self-directed RRSPs to hold treasury bills or Canada Savings Bonds as an alternative to a guaranteed savings account RRSP. By doing so, they can realize a moderately superior return without any increase in risk. For example, during June 1991, guaranteed savings RRSPs were paying as little as 5.5 percent annual interest. Investors with self-directed plans could buy treasury bills yielding about 8.7 percent.

Many people put CSBs in self-directed plans. They get a rate that is competitive with treasury bills yet locked in for a full year. On top of that, in recent years the federal government has raised the payouts on outstanding CSB issues during periods of rising interest rates.

For those who don't want CSBs, a self-directed plan can be used to hold Government of Canada bonds as an alternative to guaranteed plans that lock in funds for periods of up to five years. In addition to competitive returns, a self-directed plan holding bonds gives you greater flexibility. For investors with guaranteed plans, changes in investments can take as long as six weeks. With a self-directed plan, changes can often be made the same day.

Self-directed plans can also be used to hold investments not available as off-the-shelf products. For example, many people buy a security called "strip bonds" for their RRSPs. Strip bonds are bonds, usually government bonds, which have been purchased by a dealer who "strips" the coupons (the interest to be paid in the future) and sells the bond and the coupons individually. An investor who believes current interest rates are high and likely to decline would buy a coupon to be paid in, say, fifteen years. The price paid for the coupon would be only a fraction of the value the investor would receive when the interest on that coupon is due.

Setting up a self-directed plan

Setting up a self-directed plan is relatively simple. Arrangements are made through a trust company, bank, brokerage house or mutual fund dealer – if you plan to hold just mutual funds. The company that holds your self-directed plan acts as trustee, accepting your deposits and receiving or delivering any securities you buy and sell through your broker. It then credits your RRSP.

The cost of a self-directed plan is usually about $125 annually, although some trust companies charge more. The $125 fees are considered loss leaders by many brokerage firms, which expect to make their profit from trading commissions on self-directed plans. There may also be transaction charges or additional fees, depending on what types of investments you hold in your RRSP. The table in appendix B lists some typical plans and their charges.

Contributions in shares

You do not have to make your RRSP contribution in cash – you can contribute securities you already own, particularly if you don't have enough cash to make your maximum contribution. Revenue Canada regards such transfers as dispositions of property if the securities are worth more when you contribute them than they were when purchased. As a result, you could pay tax on any capital gains. If you want to put your losers in your RRSP you're better off selling them and contributing the cash; if you contribute the securities you won't be able to use your capital losses to offset capital gains.

You should also pay administration fees directly to the trustee rather than having them deducted from your RRSP. By paying directly you can deduct these fees from income for tax purposes.

Many individuals jump into a self-directed RRSP because of their low cost. However, too many people end up losing their retirement savings because of inappropriate investments. If you decide you want a self-directed plan to hold growth investments, keep in mind that the objective of your plan is to finance retirement, not to take risks.

A self-directed plan requires some investment sophistication and should be considered as an alternative to professionally managed funds only by individuals with knowledge of at least some of the investment vehicles that qualify for inclusion in self-directed RRSPs. A self-directed RRSP is not the place to learn about the stock market.

What never ceases to surprise investment professionals is the number of people who invest through self-directed plans but who don't know what investments qualify. It's important that you know what is allowed in your self-directed RRSP because penalties for investing in ineligible securities are severe. The value of the nonqualified investment must be included in income for the year in which it was acquired. However, that amount can be included in the calculation of earned income to determine the maximum RRSP contribution for the year. When an ineligible investment is sold, the net proceeds or cost, whichever is lower, may be deducted from income. You must also pay a monthly tax of 1 percent on the fair market value of the nonqualified investment from the time you buy it to the time you remove it from your plan.

Investments that qualify

For those who decide to control their financial destiny through a self-directed RRSP, Revenue Canada allows a wide range of investments to qualify for RRSPs. The following are the more common types:

1. Shares of Canadian public companies traded on the Alberta, Montreal, Toronto, Vancouver and Winnipeg stock exchanges can be held without limit. Unlisted stocks that meet the Income Tax Act's definition of a public corporation also qualify for inclusion. Stocks of foreign companies such as International Business Machines Corp. or General Motors Corp. that trade on Canadian exchanges can also be held. However, no more than 10 percent of your RRSPs may be invested in foreign assets. Ottawa has proposed raising the foreign property limit to 12 percent for 1990, 14 percent for

1991, 16 percent for 1992, 18 percent for 1993 and 20 percent for 1994 and subsequent years. At the time of writing, this was not law and you should make sure it becomes law before increasing the foreign holdings in your RRSP.

2. You can hold shares of foreign companies – within the limit on foreign property – if they are traded on the following stock exchanges: Paris, London, American, New York, Boston, Chicago, Cincinnati, Detroit, Midwest, National, Pacific Coast, Pittsburgh, Salt Lake, Philadelphia-Baltimore-Washington, and Spokane. In 1989 Ottawa amended the RRSP rules to allow investors to include U.S. over-the-counter stocks that are quoted in the NASDAQ listings. It is important that your broker make sure that any foreign stocks recommended for your self-directed plan meet Revenue Canada's requirements. It is your responsibility to make sure everything is in order.

3. Bonds, debentures, notes and similar debt obligations of companies whose shares are listed on Canadian stock exchanges, or the debt of their subsidiaries.

4. Warrants or rights listed on Canadian stock exchanges that entitle holders to securities that qualify for RRSPs. These include listed call options.

5. Shares of companies that qualify as investment corporations under the Income Tax Act. This would be disclosed in their prospectuses or notes to their annual reports. Investment corporations are sometimes called closed-end funds and invest in a portfolio of securities. If the portfolio is primarily in foreign securities, the shares are considered foreign property. The exceptions are companies whose shares are listed on a Canadian exchange and which have not issued additional shares after December 4, 1985.

6. Shares of mutual fund corporations or trusts that meet the requirements of the Income Tax Act. Again, this information would be found in the funds' prospectuses.

7. Mortgages, including mortgage-backed securities, that are insured under the National Housing Act or by the Mortgage Insurance Corporation of Canada on property situated in Canada, provided the mortgages are at arm's length and are administered by an NHA-approved lender. In other words, the planholder and mortgagor must not be related or connected through a company that is controlled by a member of the family. If a mortgage is issued to a non-resident of

SELF-DIRECTED PLANS: ARE THEY RIGHT FOR YOU? 71

Canada, it is considered foreign property and is subject to the foreign property limit.

You can also hold mortgages or participations in mortgages which are not NHA guaranteed or insured, provided they are secured by real estate in Canada and are at arm's length. Be cautious about the quality of the security and make sure that the value of the property exceeds the value of the loan by a good margin. This is important because if your RRSP acquires an asset for an amount greater than its fair market value, you have to include the difference as income.

8. The mortgage on your own home, provided you adhere to some fairly rigid standards.

9. Guaranteed investment certificates issued by Canadian trust companies.

10. Money on deposit with Canadian banks, trust companies and credit unions.

11. Bonds, debentures, notes, mortgages and similar forms of debt issued or guaranteed by the federal, provincial or municipal governments. This includes Canada Savings Bonds and bonds issued in foreign currencies.

12. Forms of debt issued by a co-operative corporation or credit union that meet the requirements of the Income Tax Act.

13. Life annuities with guaranteed terms of less than fifteen years.

14. Certain life insurance policies.

15. Shares of certain small business "growth corporations." These are of more interest to pension funds since the minimum investment required puts them beyond the reach of most RRSP investors.

What doesn't qualify?

While investors have a broad choice of securities for self-directed RRSPs, they should also be aware of those that don't qualify. These include gold and other precious metals, gems, commodities, commodity futures contracts, art and antiques, employee options to purchase stock, undeveloped land and shares of private corporations.

If you doubt that an investment qualifies for a self-directed RRSP, get professional advice. The trust company or broker that administers your plan may not check each transaction for eligibility.

In any case, the responsibility for ensuring that each purchase qualifies for your self-directed RRSP is yours alone.

Sometimes, even qualified investments may present problems for your plan. Not all trust companies are geared to handle mortgages or the paperwork if you write options against your stocks.

Some brokerage houses have even occasionally discouraged clients from trading stocks listed on the Vancouver Stock Exchange in RRSP accounts (other than those they administer) because of share certificate delivery problems. During the market boom of late 1980 and early 1981, brokers found it was virtually impossible to have share certificates delivered within a reasonable time. Normal settlement on a stock transaction is five days after the trade, but a trustee will pay for the stock only on receipt of the certificate. Consequently, brokers found they were providing interest-free financing for clients' RRSP trading.

If you intend to trade stocks extensively or write options on your holdings, a brokerage-sponsored RRSP makes more sense. But some people have more than one self-directed RRSP – one for stocks and bonds with their broker and another with a trust company to hold investments such as mortgages.

Avoid severe penalties

Your vigilance does not end with the purchase of a qualified investment. The penalty for holding an investment that becomes nonqualified is severe, even if the security was qualified when purchased. Stocks can become nonqualified if the company moves outside Canada, goes private or if its shares are exchanged for nonqualified securities, as can happen in some mergers.

Your RRSP is subject to a monthly tax of 1 percent of the value of the ineligible security for as long as that security is held. (If the investment was acquired by the plan before August 25, 1972, this tax does not apply.) However, you could face a 1 percent monthly tax on your entire RRSP if the value of ineligible investments exceeds 50 percent of the total value of your plan.

Watch foreign holdings

A tax of 1 percent a month also applies to foreign property in excess of the percentage allowed in an RRSP. This tax does not apply to foreign investments held before June 18, 1971. It applies to any purchases after that date that boost the total foreign portion of the plan above the limit – calculated using the cost of the foreign acquisition as a percentage of the market value of the plan at the time the purchase was made. More than a few investors have been penalized by holding mutual funds invested in foreign property which automatically used dividends to purchase more units. If you hold such funds in your self-directed plans make sure you have the dividends paid as cash into your plan.

If you hold foreign shares you would be wise to have dividends payable in cash to your RRSP and converted to Canadian funds when received, rather than in shares through dividend reinvestment plans offered by some companies.

Some investors and their brokers don't seem to understand that companies with their head offices outside Canada fall under the foreign property restriction even if their shares trade on a Canadian stock exchange. In contrast, shares of Canadian incorporated public companies, even when foreign-controlled, can be held without limit.

Borrowing against your plan

An RRSP cannot be used as security for a loan, although assets in a plan can. When the assets are used as security, planholders must include the fair market value of these assets in their income for tax purposes. When the loan is paid back, they are entitled to deduct the amount from income, less any loss suffered by the RRSP as a result of being used as security for the loan. When the assets are restored to the RRSP, you will get a deduction that does not infringe upon your contribution for that year.

Before committing yourself, check whether the trust company that administers your plan will allow the assets to be used as security. If it does not, you may want to move your plan to another trustee. Usually, a trust company will accommodate your needs if the assets against which you are borrowing are a debt instrument of that trust company or a government guaranteed security such as a treasury bill.

Borrowing against assets in a plan is a measure that should not be considered lightly because it will reduce the returns that build an RRSP's value. But for some people, it is a preferable alternative to collapsing an RRSP to raise cash.

Manage wisely

Most individuals who take out self-directed RRSPs do so because they expect to earn higher rates of return than those available from professionally managed funds. They expect to do this either through their own acumen or the expert advice of their brokers, lawyers or accountants.

Those who consistently achieve better returns than those of pooled funds have a number of things in common. They usually concentrate on certain types of securities that do not constitute a large proportion of most professionally managed funds. They are diversified, but not overly so, and they invest in relatively high-risk securities. Planholders can offset the higher risk with greater trading flexibility. The small size of most self-directed plans, relative to the multimillion-dollar pooled funds, allows the portfolio mix to be switched at will.

Just what constitutes a successful investment for a self-directed RRSP changes according to market cycles. At one time, the biggest gains may be in high-return mortgages; during other times, they may be in gold shares, energy stocks or even discount bonds.

The long-term success of a self-directed strategy depends on how nimble investors are in selling and switching investments. Many people who attempt to make big money by concentrating on specific market areas fail because they invest too late, concentrate on too few stocks, or depend on the same advice available to every other player in the market.

To make the most of a self-directed plan which invests in stocks, create a diversified portfolio then monitor it constantly, adding new investments which seem to offer above-average potential and selling those that no longer meet your expectations. Be prepared to spend a lot of time reviewing your holdings and seeking out new opportunities. If you depend on a broker or investment counsellor for advice you can still expect to spend time monitoring results to ensure you are getting the superior performance that you expect.

If you plan on being your own investment advisor, learn some of the techniques investment professionals use in portfolio management. The most straightforward, yet most complicated, is the method developed by Benjamin Graham more than sixty years ago. It involves searching for "value," defined as a stock with a share price below the value of the underlying assets of the company net of its liabilities. The method does take into consideration the company's earnings trend but the key is buying value.

Another method involves timing your purchases against overall market trends so that you move into the market near the bottom of the cycle and sell out just as the cycle peaks.

There are dozens of methods of investment. But whatever method you choose, take a disciplined approach, always remembering that whatever you do should reflect your objective of building capital to finance your retirement.

Hedging against devaluation

In recent years, some sophisticated investors have used self-directed plans to hedge against devaluations of the Canadian dollar against other currencies by purchasing qualified securities denominated in foreign currencies. Many provinces issue bonds in the United States and overseas in U.S. dollars, West German marks, Swiss francs, Japanese yen and even Hong Kong dollars.

While values of these currencies fluctuate widely, a portfolio of foreign-currency, government guaranteed securities may be useful from time to time as a hedge against any fall of the Canadian dollar. People who plan to retire outside Canada may want to hedge part of their RRSP in this fashion.

Similarly, some investors may want to use gold and silver as a hedge against currency devaluation. These are commodities and can't be held in RRSPs. However, there are several companies whose shares trade on the Toronto Stock Exchange and which invest primarily in precious metals and gold mining stocks. They are eligible investments for RRSPs because they are listed stocks, even though they have gold as important segments of their portfolios. In addition, gold mutual funds are eligible for RRSPs.

Mortgages can have a place

Some investors may choose to hold high-yield mortgages in their self-directed RRSPs. Indeed, some high-return mortgages have been advertised as yielding more than 25 percent. Be prepared to take a great deal more risk if you go for these investments.

For example, high-yielding mortgages are often on commercial properties with marginal profitability. Or, they may be on properties in rural areas where the economy is sluggish, on unfinished projects or on raw land. Such properties could prove difficult to sell in the event of a foreclosure. If you consider a high-yielding mortgage, make sure you obtain an independent appraisal of the property to determine if, in fact, the value of the security exceeds the value of the loan.

Lately, second mortgages have become popular as RRSP investments with some investors looking for high returns. Again, do your homework and determine whether the security you receive is adequate.

Some individuals with self-directed plans have tried to swap mortgages on their homes with other planholders at lower-than-market rates. Revenue Canada considers these to be non-arm's length transactions, which makes the mortgages nonqualified RRSP investments. People who have such criss-cross agreements risk having their plans deregistered. If that happens, the fair market value of all the assets in the plan is included in income and becomes taxable.

Minimum amounts for self-directed plans

The minimum amount needed to justify a self-directed plan really depends on the mix of securities desired. Someone who plans to speculate in a narrow area of the stock market could start with $10,000 and divide the money among two or three stocks. But for a diversified portfolio holding ten to fifteen stocks, $75,000 might be more appropriate. For all types of portfolios – stocks, bonds, mortgages or a combination – it is advisable to diversify among several securities to avoid the risk of placing all your money in the shares of a company that falls upon hard times or in a debt instrument that goes into default.

For mortgages, the amount needed for diversification might be in the $20,000 to $30,000 range, although some experts recommend substantially higher amounts, even for insured mortgages. In theory, small portions of mortgages – perhaps as little as $2,000 – could be placed in a self-directed RRSP. In practice, most mortgage brokers, accountants and lawyers who deal in mortgages dislike dividing them into such small amounts because of the administrative costs involved. Instead, they prefer a minimum of $10,000; if you're investing less than this you're probably better off investing in mortgage fund RRSPs.

CHAPTER 10

Putting Your Mortgage in Your RRSP

MORTGAGES ARE A GOOD RRSP investment because they're usually quite safe and they pay a high rate of interest. The most common question people ask about mortgages and RRSPs is whether they should put their own mortgage in their RRSP. It's a good question. After all, if you are going to pay interest on your mortgage who better to pay it to than yourself. Even if interest rates are volatile and you're uncertain about whether to chose a six-month or five-year term, you'll sleep better knowing that even if you choose wrongly from a borrower's point of view, you'll benefit as the lender.

Despite the prohibition against non-arm's length investments in your RRSP – a rule designed to prevent people from making special arrangements to the detriment of their RRSPs – you can put your own mortgage in your RRSP, as long as you abide by the stringent rules.

First, the mortgage must be insured either through a mortgage insurance corporation or under the National Housing Act. Second, it must be administered by an approved lender such as a trust company. And third, the interest rate must be comparable to that available on similar mortgages in the general marketplace. If the RRSP mortgage interest rate is less than the going rate, the difference between the price paid and its fair market value must be included in the planholder's income for tax purposes. In other words, there can be no special deals. The institution where you've made all the arrangements will treat your mortgage the same as all others. If you default, the institution will seek the same remedies it would seek for its own money.

The expenses involved in meeting these criteria, plus legal fees, make an RRSP mortgage a costly proposal, particularly for relatively small amounts. It makes little sense to consider putting your mortgage in your RRSP if your mortgage is $150,000 and your total

RRSP assets are only $20,000, even if a bank or trust company financed the difference. For small amounts, say less than $50,000, the setup and legal costs will wipe out any perceived economic benefit or potential higher return.

Most institutions charge about $200 to set up the plan plus annual fees of about $175. Some investment dealers allow you to hold your own mortgage in a self-directed RRSP for a comparable fee.

Some caveats

Before you act, think of some of the difficulties that might arise in the future. For example, what will happen if you sell your house and the purchaser assumes the mortgage? Will having that mortgage in your RRSP still be acceptable to you?

More important, if market conditions change and you decide that you want your RRSP invested in some other type of investment you won't be able to switch it easily because your portfolio will consist of a single investment which cannot be disposed of quickly or inexpensively.

Even so, holding your mortgage in your RRSP is an option that can be considered under certain circumstances. An individual whose mortgage holder doesn't want to renew, might decide to lend the funds to himself through his RRSP since he already faces the legal fees of switching lenders.

If the homeowner doesn't have enough in his RRSP to take on the whole mortgage, some financial institutions will lend the difference so that the RRSP and institution hold the mortgage on the property.

Some people whose homes are mortgage free and who have substantial RRSPs have used a mortgage in their RRSP as part of a plan to free capital for investment purposes. The're able to deduct the interest they pay to their RRSPs from income for tax purposes. This strategy should be followed only by investors who can tolerate risk. Moreover, there can be negative tax implications for investors who have not used up their lifetime capital gains exemption.

Others use their mortgage to diversify their RRSP holdings by investing the interest and principal received by the RRSP in growth investments such as mutual funds or common shares.

CHAPTER 11

Making Your RRSP Work Harder for You

ASIDE FROM HAVING AN effective investment portfolio which suits your objectives and ability to handle risk, there are several other strategies you should consider to make your plan work harder for you:

Make your contributions early

Many people make their contributions in the January or February after the end of the tax year. They line up at banks and trust companies after taking money out of their savings accounts for an RRSP contribution. Don't wait. You'll be better off financially if you make your contribution as early in the year as possible. The funds in an RRSP grow untaxed while at least some of the interest you earn on the money in your bank account is likely to fall into the hands of Revenue Canada.

If you plan to put $5,000 in your RRSP and can earn an interest rate of 10 percent, your return between January and the following March will be around $585. If you keep that money in your savings account instead of an RRSP you would owe Ottawa $227 in taxes if you're taxed at the 39 percent marginal tax rate. If you have the cash on hand and are fairly certain about your potential contribution for 1991, put it into your plan as soon as you can and you will avoid the taxes until you retire.

Get your tax break early

If you put your contribution into your plan in January, you usually won't receive your tax refund until more than a year later. Instead, if your RRSP contribution is deducted from your pay each month, the deduction can be reflected in the tax withheld from each pay cheque – if your employer co-operates.

The employer must apply in writing to the district Revenue Canada office for a waiver. If you're self-employed, you should apply for the waiver. The letter should include your name and social insurance number along with the amount to be contributed each month. It must also include the name, business address and phone number of the individual in the firm who will forward the contributions to the RRSP. With an immediate reduction in income tax, you may be able to plan for an even larger RRSP contribution since your take-home pay will rise. Similarly, if you make your entire contribution early in the year, you can get a receipt or letter indicating that the contribution was for the current year and have your employer seek permission to reduce the tax withheld on your income to reflect the fact that you've made an RRSP contribution.

Start your plan early

Prior to 1957, the only Canadians who could deduct pension contributions from taxable income were those who worked for firms that sponsored pension plans. Obviously, by allowing only those taxpayers to deduct pension contributions, the system discriminated against those who set aside funds for their retirement years on their own. The initial RRSP legislation, by allowing all Canadians to deduct contributions from income and reduce that year's taxes, went a long way toward ending this inequality. The latest revisions though, put all taxpayers on an even footing.

To take full advantage of RRSPs, it's best to start early. The earlier in life a plan begins, the greater will be the impact of saving in an RRSP. Look at the difference a five-year wait can mean. Take the case of a person, age forty, who decides to start an RRSP. If he invests $1,000 a year for twenty-five years and earns 10 percent, he will have $108,182 at retirement. But what if he had started at age thirty-five? He would have $180,943 at retirement because of the effect of compounding on those early contributions to his RRSP. Time is money and nowhere is this more apparent than in an RRSP.

Use the carry-forward only if absolutely necessary

The new rules mean that someone who can't make those early contributions will be able to carry them forward for future use. That, of course, is good news. But it is no substitution for making the contribution as early as possible. A single contribution of $1,000 grow-

The Impact of Waiting Five Years To Start Saving $1000 Annually

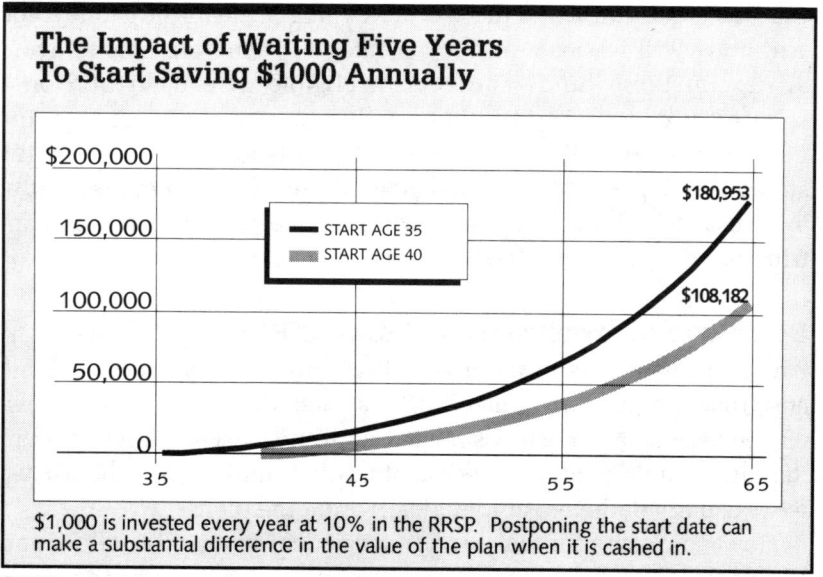

$1,000 is invested every year at 10% in the RRSP. Postponing the start date can make a substantial difference in the value of the plan when it is cashed in.

CHART II

ing at a 10 percent rate will be worth $17,449 at the end of thirty years. A five-year delay in investing that $1,000 cuts the amount to $10,835.

It makes sense to borrow

Interest on money borrowed for an RRSP contribution is not deductible from income for tax purposes. Still, it makes sense to borrow in many cases. If you don't have the cash for your contribution, borrow the money and pay off the debt out of your tax refund and your earnings. The longer money is left in a plan, the greater the impact of tax-free growth.

Short-term savings

Although RRSPs are intended to be long-term savings plans, there are times when they can be profitably used for short periods, provided funds are withdrawn during a year in which taxable income is low. That way, the tax burden that might be created upon closing out an RRSP is reduced. It is not uncommon for individuals to leave the work force to raise families and use the funds they have saved in RRSPs to provide income.

While nothing prevents people from closing RRSPs at any time, timing can be important. The simple act of waiting until January of the year after you leave the workforce might mean the money you withdraw will be taxed at a lower rate. It is even possible to avoid all tax on these funds and remain eligible as a deduction on a spouse's tax form. The key is to withdraw less each year than the maximum income the government allows before you begin losing status as a dependant. But remember, if you're taking money out of a spousal RRSP, deregistration within three years means the contributor will pay tax on the proceeds.

Don't take the trustee fee out of your RRSP

Any securities or deposits in your RRSP are held by a trustee. Bank and trust company guaranteed RRSPs generally don't charge a trustee fee because the costs associated with the trustee are reflected in the interest rate paid. In the case of mutual fund RRSPs, the trustee fee is usually deducted automatically from the plan.

However, some mutual fund management companies allow you to pay the trustee fee separately – an advantage because the fee is deductible from income for tax purposes. The trustee fee varies, but it is usually from $30 to $50. A single trustee fee may cover several funds within the same management group. Similarly, if you have a self-directed RRSP, pay the trustee fee separately so you can deduct it from taxable income.

PART III   SPECIAL RRSP CONSIDERATIONS

CHAPTER 12

Group RRSPs: Understand Your Choices

SOME INVESTORS HAVE AN alternative to the types of RRSPs we've dealt with so far. It's the group RRSP sponsored by their employers, unions or professional groups as an alternative or supplement to registered pension plans.

Professionally managed group RRSPs are usually made available to companies and their employees by trust companies, mutual funds, investment counsellors or insurance companies. They can be off-the-shelf, customized or self-directed plans, allowing groups with specific investment objectives a suitable RRSP alternative.

Group RRSPs will probably become more common in the future because of pension reform, which will increase the costs of pensions to employers. Many companies may decide that group RRSPs are the best way to provide a retirement savings vehicle for employees.

The most common group plan is the plain-vanilla group RRSP, which is simply a collection of individual RRSPs operated for members of a specific group. This type of plan is available to small and large companies, partnerships and sole proprietorships.

The primary benefit of a group RRSP over other RRSPs is the immediate tax saving that employees receive through payroll deductions. The employer seeks permission from Revenue Canada to reduce tax deductions to reflect the deductibility of the RRSP contribution. This means you get the tax break when the contribution is made instead of many months, or even a year, later when Revenue Canada deals with your tax return.

Benefits to employers

Group RRSPs are popular with employers because they are easily administered and can be less expensive to implement than pension plans. A group RRSP can usually be established without a set-up fee, although a customized self-directed group RRSP might involve some costs. A second advantage of group RRSPs may be fractionally lower management fees or trustee fees. A financial institution is usually willing to charge less to manage $1 million in a group plan than the same amount gleaned from hundreds of small accounts. Alternatively, there may be lower acquisition fees.

Before you sign

Many people plunge into a group plan simply because it's convenient or because their co-workers are signing on. Without a solid idea of what you're getting into, such action can prove expensive. Before you take part, examine all aspects of the plan. Is its investment philosophy flexible enough to suit your needs? Are its costs lower than, or at least competitive with, those of other plans?

With most group RRSPs, employees have the option to choose from a number of types of investments. Asset selection and mix is determined with the help of the plan's financial advisor. The choice of investments is generally wide enough to suit most people and usually includes growth, fixed income, guaranteed and balanced options. Some plans provide for investment choices within these categories and others even offer a choice of managers. As with any type of investment fund, investors should look closely at the investment record of the managers, comparing the performance record with published returns of RRSPs from trust companies, banks, mutual funds and insurance companies.

Examine all the costs

In addition to investment performance and suitability, you should also determine whether the plan allows switching from fund to fund, how often money can be deposited, and if there are any fees paid or penalties assessed when money is withdrawn.

Finally, examine all the costs involved in joining a group plan. The institution that manages the funds for the group may have several types of fees. Some have sales charges of up to 6 percent which are deducted from new money deposited. Others have declining redemption fees which range from 5 percent to 0 percent depending on the length of time you are with the plan.

Ongoing annual administration charges can range from $20 to $75 for each employee. Some employers will pay all or part of this cost, in which case such payments are considered by Revenue Canada as a taxable benefit to employees. In other cases, employees must foot the bill.

Management charges for investing the group plan's money vary widely, just as with individual RRSPs. They can range up to 2 percent for equity funds. Some managers also charge withdrawal fees.

It is important that the costs be spelled out in detail by the manager of the plan. If you are able to determine all your costs, including those charged by the group's sponsor or trustees, compare them with what you would pay for similar funds offered through trust companies, banks and other plan issuers. Enroll in the group plan only if it's to your financial advantage.

You should also look at the services you'll receive through the plan. Some group plans offer investment advice to help employees decide where to put their money. Others don't deal with individual investors.

Association plans

Another type of group plan is available only to members of a specific organization or association. For instance, the Canadian Medical Association offers several RRSP options to its members and their families. The association handles the administration of the plans and retains investment managers for the funds at fees much lower than those charged to individuals.

CHAPTER 13

DPSPs and Individual Pension Plans

IN ADDITION TO CONTRIButing to RRSPs, a high-income taxpayer who is a senior officer, but not a controlling shareholder, of a corporation might want to consider another type of tax shelter, the deferred profit-sharing plan. With a DPSP, the employer and not the employee makes a contribution. Prior to 1991, employees could make non-deductible contributions. The income earned on the employee's contribution grows free of tax until withdrawn from the plan and no tax is payable on the contribution when it is withdrawn.

Like the contribution limits for RRSPs, DPSP limits changed in 1991. For 1991, the contribution limit is 18 percent of wages and salary paid to the employee in that calendar year to a maximum of $6,250; for 1992 the maximum will be $6,750; for 1993 $7,250; and for 1994 and 1995 $7,750. After 1995 it will be indexed to inflation. Contributions must be made by the employer during its tax year or within 120 days after its tax year ends.

In a DPSP, money is allowed to accumulate tax-free for the benefit of employees in the plan. Each beneficiary shares in the contributions and income, which is taxed when the funds are withdrawn. Those proceeds can be sheltered from tax by transferring them on a lump-sum basis to another DPSP with at least five beneficiaries, to an RRSP or to a registered pension plan. However, employee contributions cannot be transferred.

DPSPs can be an important part of a compensation package because it is the employer, rather than the employee, who is putting up the funds for the employee's retirement. However, the plans are often overlooked because they seem complicated and can involve a great deal of paperwork for the employer. Moreover, the federal government no longer allows deductions for DPSPs if the principal owners of a company are beneficiaries. The rules were changed in November 1981 because at one time more than 90 percent of plans had no more than three beneficiaries, who in many cases were principal shareholders in the company.

DPSPs require minimum contributions to be made in years in which the company has profits. These contributions can take a number of forms: a percentage of profits, with a 1 percent minimum; a percentage of the employee's earnings, also with a 1 percent minimum; or a fixed amount, with a $100 minimum contribution for each employee each year. The amounts contributed can vary for each employee in the plan and the plan can be set up for selected employees. Companies can also structure their plans to include undistributed profits for prior years. This is an important alternative for companies whose earnings are volatile.

Vesting must take place no later than five years after allocation of amounts contributed before 1991. Beginning in 1991, vesting must take place immediately, except for employees with less than two years of continuous employment. All amounts must be vested at normal retirement age as defined by the plan. Similarly, amounts must be vested if an employee ends his employment because of permanent disability.

Company shares can be held

DPSP-eligible investments are the same as RRSP-eligible investments with a few major differences designed to prevent a DPSP from holding the employer's debt. Also, DPSPs can hold shares of the employer company if it is listed on a Canadian stock exchange, an investment which can provide an important incentive for employees.

Payments from DPSPs are taxable as income except when a portion of the payment includes employee contributions. These are exempt from tax. If the DPSP makes payments in instalments, employee contributions are considered to be withdrawn first.

If the distribution involves employer shares, another rule applies. The appreciation of the shares is taxable. However, the employee gets a special deduction equal to one-quarter of the difference which effectively taxes only 75 percent of the gain. For tax purposes, the employee's tax base is the cost of shares to the plan plus half the gain in value to the date of withdrawal.

Get expert advice

Some employers choose to set up and administer their own plans, either to save on administrative expenses or to get an investment portfolio mix more suited to the needs or risk preferences of employees in the plan than are available through mutual fund, trust or insurance company plans. Companies setting up a plan should hire advisors, not only to help establish the plan but also to provide advice over the years. There is more involved in running a DPSP than a self-directed RRSP.

First, employers must be familiar with the conditions which a plan must meet before it can be registered with Revenue Canada. The DPSP must have trustees who have sufficient authority to operate the plan and ensure that benefits are paid to employees. If the plan does not have a trust company as trustee, there must be at least three trustees, all of whom must be Canadian residents. For employers that are not public companies, at least one of the trustees must be neither a shareholder nor an employee.

When payments are made to the plan, they must be allocated to beneficiaries, along with any income earned. The plan must define normal retirement age and beneficiaries cannot lose their entitlements because of union membership or dismissal.

There are also strict rules on how long funds can be sheltered in a DPSP. The funds must be paid within ninety days of the employee's departure from the firm, the day in which he turns seventy-one, his death, or termination of the plan – whichever comes first. Also, any capital gains or losses by the plan must be allocated to the beneficiaries within ninety days of the end of the year in which they occur. Beneficiaries cannot borrow from the plan nor can their rights be surrendered or assigned.

DPSPs are also prohibited from investing any funds in the debt of the employer, related companies, or in the shares of a company that holds 50 percent or more of the employer's debt. The plan can borrow funds only to pay benefits and even then only if paying those benefits without borrowing would force the sale of assets at distress prices.

Employers planning to run their own DPSPs should also be well aware of the types of investments that qualify for the plans. These include government and government guaranteed bonds, government guaranteed mortgages, debt of public companies (excluding their own), shares of public companies, guaranteed investment certificates, mutual fund corporations as defined by the Income Tax Act and certain types of life insurance policies. Foreign investments are limited just as in RRSPS.

The qualified investments for DPSPs are similar in most cases to those listed for RRSPs. However, the rules for DPSPs are more detailed and the penalties for non-compliance are greater. If non-qualified investments are made, the plan is subject to a tax equal to the cost of the investment. Fortunately, the tax is refundable when that investment is sold.

Finally, anyone assuming the responsibility of managing other people's retirement savings should have some knowledge of portfolio management.

Individual pension plans

Individual pension plans, or IPPs, are the newcomers to the retirement planning world. They arrived on the scene in early 1991 but could not be registered at the time because the necessary regulations weren't in place. Ottawa released its proposed regulations governing such plans at the end of July 1991. With these on the table, accounting firms and some financial planners started fine-tuning their IPP products.

IPPs may be of particular interest to individuals who are forty years old or older, earn $100,000 or more a year and are senior executives of corporations, significant shareholders or owner-managers. An IPP is a "defined benefit" plan; the benefit the employee will receive is specified at the time the plan is established. Using defined calculations based on income, age and the employee's years of service - as well as actuarial assumptions about rate of return and inflation - the contribution level needed to achieve a specified retirement benefit is determined. This differs from an RRSP in which the contribution is defined but the eventual benefit depends on the rate of return earned as well as the amount of time the money spends in the plan; the pension benefit from an RRSP is generally not known in advance and has no limit.

They are an alternative to RRSPs yet, as presented by the companies which offer them, they allow more money to be sheltered than with an RRSP alone. The employee can contribute $1,000 to an RRSP even if the maximum pension contribution is made. Consequently, an IPP along with a $1,000 annual contribution to an RRSP will accumulate more than an RRSP to which maximum contributions are used. At retirement age, the IPP would be used to purchase a life annuity meeting the income specifications of the pension plan. Any surplus in the IPP over the amount required to buy a pension annuity would be taxed and paid in a lump-sum to the employee. As retirement draws near, the beneficiary of the plan could opt to transfer the portion of the IPP which would otherwise be used to purchase an annuity to a locked-in RRSP. This could further defer tax until age seventy-one when the locked-in RRSP must be used to purchase a life annuity.

The advantage provided by an IPP depends largely on age and, of course, the rate of return earned on the higher contributions.

However, it is still uncertain if the benefits that will be received at retirement from an IPP are substantially different than those that would be generated by an RRSP – a more flexible, less expensive and less complicated alternative. The regulations proposed by Ottawa require unisex actuarial tables to be used to calculate payments and place a 3 percent inflation index on the plans. These requirements reduce the attractiveness of the plans. IPPs are offered by several major accounting firms, at least one brokerage house, and by a few financial planning companies and actuaries. Costs of IPPs are very high relative to RRSPs. Set up fees can be several thousand dollars; the regular expenses for administration and actuarial valuations required every three years can be in the thousands of dollars as well. IPPs should be considered and examined on a case-by-case basis.

CHAPTER 14

Spousal Plans: A Second Stream of Income

BY REGISTERING AN RRSP IN the name of your husband or wife, you can obtain significant long-term savings, even if your spouse has received little or no earned income during the year. The objective of setting up a so-called spousal plan is to provide two streams of income during retirement. Depending on income levels at the time of retirement, the taxes you would pay as a family on the two streams could be much lower than on a single stream flowing to one person. Taxes would be further reduced when both of you become eligible at age sixty-five for the pension income tax credit for income stemming from an RRSP annuity or RRIF.

However, there are limits to spousal plans. They cannot be set up by just moving funds from an existing RRSP. And, while you can transfer lump-sum pension benefits to your own RRSP, you cannot transfer them to a spousal plan – with one important exception. In each year up to and including 1994, you can transfer up to $6,000 of pension income to your spouse's RRSP. This reflects the federal government's recognition that a transition period is necessary in the implementation of rules that prohibit the transfer of pension income to your own RRSP beginning in 1990.

Under tax regulations, there are only two other circumstances in which RRSP money can be transferred without tax to a spousal plan. The first is on the death of the taxpayer before the plan matures, provided the spouse is named as beneficiary. The second is on marriage breakdown if the couple is no longer living together and a court has ordered a division of the RRSP. Ottawa includes common-law spouses in its definition of spouse for the transfer of a plan on death or marriage breakdown. But, to contribute to a spousal plan, the couple must be married.

Because of these limitations, the best way to contribute to your spouse's RRSP is through a spousal plan. And the earlier the better, especially if the aim is to create two healthy income streams at retirement.

You can make contributions to a spousal plan even if you contribute to your own plan. However, the total amount of money you are allowed to contribute and deduct from your income for tax purposes cannot exceed the maximum you could normally contribute to your own plan. The total contribution to your and your spouse's plan for the 1991 taxation year can't exceed 18 percent of your 1990 earned income up to $11,500. In other words, you could contribute $1,500 to your own plan and you could put $10,000 into your spouse's RRSP if your contribution limit is $11,500. For 1992 and subsequent years, the total cannot exceed your new contribution limits.

A contribution to a spousal plan can be made regardless of whether the spouse is contributing to his or her plan. For example, in cases where the husband has substantial retirement savings and the wife has very little, both can make their contributions to the wife's plan. Furthermore, someone who is older than seventy-one – RRSPs must mature no later than December 31 of the year in which you turn seventy-one – can still contribute to a plan in the name of a spouse up until and including the year in which the spouse turns seventy-one.

Many couples want the same amount in each spouse's plan at retirement. This makes sense, provided both will withdraw the same income each year from a RRIF and both expect to have equal amounts of income from non-RRSP sources.

Spousal plans should generally be considered long-term savings programs designed for retirement. They should also be considered only by couples whose marriages are stable; once a plan is set up, it becomes the property of the spouse.

Tax liabilities

Cashing in a spousal plan can trigger some unexpected, and unwelcome, tax liabilities. Couples should not set up spousal plans with the intention of deregistering them within a few years to take advantage of one spouse's lower tax rate. Revenue Canada frowns on spousal plans deregistered within three years.

Under the Income Tax Act, if the holder of the spousal plan cashes it in during the year the contribution was made or in the following two years, the contributing spouse will have to pay the tax on the money withdrawn at his or her tax rate.

What's more, it makes no difference if the plans cashed in contain spousal contributions made more than three years ago. Ottawa will still determine whether contributions have been made during the past three years. If so, it will treat the withdrawal as the contributor's income and tax it accordingly. Even if the spousal plan contains contributions made by both husband and wife and the wife deregisters only part of the funds, the husband will still pay tax on the proceeds up to the amount of his contributions made during that year and in the previous two years.

Transferring a spousal plan to a registered pension plan, RRIF or annuity and then withdrawing the proceeds does not circumvent these rules. There are exceptions, however. You will not be caught by the tax rules if the RRSP is collapsed into a life annuity that cannot be commuted for three years or a RRIF from which the withdrawals in each of the three years do not exceed the minimum withdrawals required by law. Anything in excess will be considered income in the hands of the contributor.

If either spouse dies or is no longer a Canadian resident, these rules don't apply. Collapsing the plan will not trigger tax at the contributing spouse's rate.

There have been cases when one spouse receives a notice of reassessment from Revenue Canada and discovers that the other spouse, or former spouse, has cashed in a plan. Because the money belongs to the holder of the spousal plan, the permission of the contributing spouse is not needed to withdraw funds – but the contributing spouse may still face tax liabilities.

Only when there have been no contributions to the spousal plan for three years can the plan be cashed in and the proceeds taxed at the holder's rate. This allows some couples to use spousal plans as tax-effective savings vehicles for reasons other than retirement. The planholder can cash in the RRSP three years after the other spouse has stopped making contributions and the money is taxed at the planholder's lower rate. Nevertheless, by far the most common use of spousal plans is retirement savings.

CHAPTER 15

How Much Will You Have?

THE POOL OF WEALTH YOU are able to create in your RRSP will have a significant impact on the stream of income that will flow from your plans throughout your retirement years. The size of that pool depends on three factors:
- The number of years in which you contribute to your plans,
- How much you contribute,
- The rate of return you will have.

To take full advantage of RRSPs, it's best to start early. The earlier in life a plan begins, the greater will be the impact of saving in an RRSP because of the effect of earning interest on interest. Look at the difference a five-year wait can mean. If an investor contributes $1,000 a year to a plan for twenty-five years earning 10 percent annually, he will accumulate $108,182. If, however, he had started his program five years earlier, he will accumulate $180,943 in the RRSP over the thirty-year period. If he started his program at forty-five with the intention of retiring at sixty-five and contributed $1,000 a year earning 10 percent, he would accumulate only $63,002.

Another significant impact on your retirement nest egg is the return your RRSP earns each year. Relatively small differences in rates of return can make a substantial difference in the amount accumulated. If you earn 11 percent rather than 10 percent, the amounts accumulated after twenty, twenty-five and thirty years would have been $71,265, $126,999 and $220,913 rather than $63,002, $108,182 and $180,943.

For most people, particularly those decades away from retirement, it is impossible to accurately forecast how much you will have when you retire because it is impossible to predict how interest rates will behave over ten, twenty or thirty years, the impact of inflation or whether Ottawa will change the rules again.

Nevertheless, you should set targets for RRSP accumulation and monitor how well you are meeting them over time. If you find that you are falling behind, you can take appropriate action. If necessary, you can increase your RRSP contributions if you have room, save outside your RRSP or even adjust your expectations.

You should, of course, determine how much annual income you will need when you retire. Your expenses will likely be lower than they are currently. However, you will still pay taxes. The percentage you'll pay will depend on income and your tax deductions or credits. You can estimate a figure for taxes using your General Tax Guide. (If you need $25,000 after tax, you'll need roughly $30,000 pre-tax.)

Once you have your estimate of income needed, subtract $12,000 for Canada Pension and Old Age Security and any expected pension income, if applicable. You may want to lower this figure because of the "claw back" if your projected income exceeds $55,000. If you are a member of a pension plan, you should get a statement which projects your annual pension in current dollars. The remainder is the amount your RRSP will have to provide.

In general, $50,000 in an RRSP at age sixty-five will be enough to provide annual income of about $6,000. So, if your objective is $30,000 annual income, your accumulation target is $250,000.

But that's in today's dollars. If you are concerned about inflation – and you should be – and you are, say, fifteen years away from retirement, you will need a lot more than $250,000 to provide the same purchasing power that $30,000 provides today. If we assume 5 percent inflation, you would aim at accumulating $500,000 to provide annual income of $60,000. If you wanted to index that income against inflation and have the stream continue for twenty-five years you would need about $750,000 in your RRSP at age sixty-five. If you wanted to retire early, perhaps at age fifty, with an income of $60,000 a year you would need about $1 million in your plan.

After you've set your target, look at what you currently have in RRSPs. Appendix six is a table showing the future value of $1,000 using different rates of return. For example, at 10 percent $1,000 will grow to $1,100 after one year, $1,210 after two years and $1,331 after three years. You can estimate how much your RRSP will be worth at retirement using this table, the current value of your RRSPs and the number of years to retirement.

The rates of return you use should be reasonable and reflect your own investment results. Alternatively, use a 10 percent rate if you invest your RRSP in guaranteed investments; 12 percent is reasonable for growth investments. While you may be tempted to use returns which reflect recent high interest rates or the historic returns earned by some mutual funds you would be wise to be conservative. Otherwise, you could underestimate the amount you have to set aside each year to reach your retirement objective.

Let's work through an example. If you have $24,500 in your RRSPs and are twenty years away from retirement, multiply 24.5 by $6,727 – the value in twenty years of $1,000 invested at 10 percent. The future value of your current RRSPs will be $164,811.

Going back to your target, subtract the future value of your current RRSPs. If we assume your target is $500,000 and the future value of your current RRSPs is $164,811, then you will need to accumulate approximately $335,000 over the next twenty years.

To find out how much you will need to contribute each year to reach that goal, turn to appendix seven. The table in this appendix shows the future value of annual contributions of $1,000 for different rates of return. The value of annual contributions of $1,000 growing at a 10 percent return will be $63,002 in twenty years. Dividing $335,000 by $63,002 gives you $5,317, the estimated amount you will have to contribute annually to meet your goal.

You should review your holdings annually, updating your estimates to make sure you are on track.

CHAPTER 16

Unwinding Your Plan: RRIFs and Annuities

THE TIME WILL COME WHEN you must consider what you will do with the funds in your RRSPs. At the very latest, your RRSPs must be terminated by December 31 of the year in which you turn seventy-one – although you should certainly think about the action you will take long before then. (If you do nothing, Ottawa considers your entire plan as taxable income in the year you turn seventy-one.)

When it comes time to collapse your RRSP, you have four options. You can:
- cash in your plan and pay tax on the full amount,
- purchase a registered retirement income fund (RRIF),
- invest in a life annuity issued by a life insurance firm, or
- purchase a term-to-ninety annuity that provides payments until age ninety.

For most people, the choice narrows down to a life annuity, which provides a fixed monthly income for life, or a RRIF, which allows for variations in income until you reach age ninety. Annuities and RRIFs can both be structured to meet the needs of an individual or a couple. For example, payments under an annuity can continue upon the death of one spouse, and a RRIF can be scheduled to continue paying until the younger spouse reaches age ninety. Payments from either a RRIF or annuity to people sixty-five or older are eligible for the $1,000 "pension income amount" used in the calculation of tax credits.

There are good reasons for not waiting until the last minute to choose your retirement vehicle. Unless you plan to keep your RRIF with the same mutual fund management company, bank, trust company or insurance company that has your RRSP, you can't unwind your plan overnight. If you decide to move your money from one trustee to another, or to a company from which you intend to buy an annuity, the transfer can take a month or more. This delay could cause severe difficulties if left to the last minute by someone age seventy-one.

The new, improved RRIF

A RRIF is an RRSP in reverse. Like an RRSP, you have the same broad choice of investment alternatives. And like an RRSP, income earned in a RRIF grows tax-free – it is taxable only when withdrawn. A RRIF also gives you the flexibility to change investments should your needs change.

RRIFs have been popular only since 1986 when the federal government passed legislation to make them far more attractive. Until then, regulations regarding withdrawals from a RRIF were complex and inflexible, which limited the usefulness of RRIFs. Only small payments could be withdrawn from a RRIF in the early years of retirement, payments that grew gradually until much larger payments could be taken out in the few years before age ninety – beyond the life expectancies of most people.

The federal government recognized that these withdrawal regulations didn't give people the flexibility necessary for proper financial planning in retirement. As a result, Ottawa put an end to the RRIF's shortcomings and transformed it into a retirement option worthy of consideration.

With a RRIF you can now withdraw as much from your plan as you want, when you want. The ceiling on payouts has been removed, giving you the flexibility to withdraw funds to meet your needs. However, you must withdraw a minimum amount from your RRIF each year. This minimum is equal to the amount of money left in your plan at the end of the previous year divided by the number of years left until you turn ninety. So, if you are seventy and had $100,000 in your plan at the end of the previous year, you would have to withdraw at least $5,000 – $100,000 divided by twenty.

There isn't a minimum age for setting up a RRIF, although most people wait until they are retired and need the income. You can begin withdrawing income as soon as you establish your RRIF, although you can wait until the next calendar year if you wish. By using the rules creatively, you can take out a RRIF in December of the year you turn seventy-one and thus postpone the first payment until the end of the year you turn seventy-two.

You can also have more than one RRIF – another change from the old rules. This makes it easier for people to diversify their RRIF holdings through a variety of financial products. You could, for example, have one RRIF holding debt securities issued by a bank, a second invested in equity funds and a third in a bond or mortgage fund.

If you move into a RRIF and change your mind and decide you want an annuity, the funds in your plan in excess of the minimum payment for that year can be used to purchase a life annuity. However, the guaranteed payment term of the life annuity cannot be greater than the number of years to your age ninety or your spouse's age ninety.

Annuities also more flexible

The provisions for annuities have improved as well. Before the rules were changed in 1986, once you purchased a life annuity with an RRSP you were locked in for life. Now insurance companies are allowed to pay people the commuted, or remaining, value of life or term annuities. This means you can cash in your annuity contract for a lump sum that represents the value of the outstanding contract. You can take the money into income and pay tax on it, you can roll the money tax-free into an RRSP (assuming you're not too old to have an RRSP) or RRIF, or you can roll the proceeds into a new annuity with different payment arrangements. The third option may result in some financial penalties, depending on insurance company policy and interest rate levels at the time the first annuity was issued.

The main advantage of a life annuity is that it provides payments for as long as you live which gives you a security blanket during retirement. The disadvantage is that an annuity provides little protection against inflation. Although you can buy an annuity that will pay you an income that will keep pace with inflation, it usually provides much lower payments in the early years.

The RRIF looks best

If you are approaching retirement, look closely at a RRIF. It should be the choice for most people because it can be tailored to individual needs.

Consider setting up your plan using your spouse's age if he or she is younger than you. This allows payments to continue for more years. If you are seventy-one and your spouse is sixty-five, your

RRIF could be stretched over twenty-five years instead of only nineteen since the minimum payment in the first year would be the value of the plan divided by the difference between ninety and your spouse's age – sixty-five – instead of ninety minus your age – seventy-one. As with an RRSP, you would name your spouse, even a common-law spouse, as beneficiary. This allows the RRIF to roll tax-free into a RRIF or RRSP if you die. Any RRIF funds left on the death of your husband or wife would be taxed as income and go to his or her estate.

Buy from the same sources as RRSPs

RRIFs are available from the same sources as RRSPs – banks, trust companies, insurance companies, credit unions, investment dealers and mutual funds. In fact, buying a RRIF allows you to leave your retirement savings with the same institution that manages your RRSP or to manage your own plan by investing in the same kinds of securities that you hold in your self-directed RRSPs.

The same criteria for selecting an RRSP apply to choosing a RRIF. Avoid any RRIF that locks you into a specific company or manager. You'll appreciate the ability to move your money to another RRIF without penalty if you become dissatisfied with your RRIF's performance or if your personal situation changes.

Be cautious

When you choose a RRIF, exercise the same caution that is necessary when choosing an RRSP. Consider your assets and whether you can afford much risk. For those with limited wealth, a conservative strategy of investing in instruments that guarantee a specific rate of return for a given period of time is probably best. In this case, a guaranteed plan offered by an insurance company, bank or trust company would be a good choice. If you opt for guaranteed investments, make sure they are insured by the Canada Deposit Insurance Corporation or backed by the strongest financial institutions. Mortgage or bond funds are an alternative, but for the investor with less than $50,000 even these may be risky.

It is also possible to hold equity mutual funds within RRIFs, although these involve some risk and many are too volatile to be considered by people who depend on RRIF funds for retirement income. The age of seventy is not the time to be trying to make money on the stock market. If you feel you must use an equity fund for part of your RRIF, choose one of above-average stability.

If you have at least $200,000 or $300,000 in your RRSP and your strategy involves growth investments or a balanced or managed-asset-mix approach, you may want to continue using these same investments in your RRIF – at least in your early retirement years. Holding equities will help you to stay ahead of inflation – an important consideration since someone who retires at age sixty and faces 4 percent annual inflation will need double the income at age seventy-five to have the same purchasing power. By age ninety income needs will have doubled again.

RRIFs can also be self-directed. But just as most people should avoid self-directed RRSPs, they should also avoid self-directed RRIFs. However, if you are very conservative, a self-directed RRIF can be used to hold treasury bills and government bonds for higher returns than are available from off-the-shelf products.

Some RRIF strategies

The cornerstone of most retirement investment strategies is conservatism. By the time you invest in a RRIF, you are probably no longer in the work force; if you lose your money, you are unlikely to get it back. The idea, then, is not to do anything that could have dire consequences on your standard of living.

Unless you have a very rich nest egg to finance your retirement, you should limit your risk by keeping the bulk of your money in income-generating assets and the rest in growth assets as a long-term hedge against inflation. An 80 percent fixed income and 20 percent equity split is suitable for most people.

Alternatively, use the managed-asset-mix approach, which involves varying the percentages of income and growth investments to reflect market conditions. Even then, you may want to put as much as half of your assets in income-generating investments and use the managed-asset-mix strategy for the remaining half only.

If you have retirement savings both inside and outside a RRIF, remember that Revenue Canada taxes all investment income earned in a RRIF at full rates when it is withdrawn. Outside a RRIF or RRSP, dividend income from Canadian corporations is taxed at a reduced rate because of the federal dividend tax credit. Capital gains may go untaxed because of the lifetime $100,000 capital gains exemption. Because of this difference in tax treatment, you should put your interest income investments in your RRIF and hold your dividend income and capital growth investments outside your RRSP or RRIF.

Life annuities are an option

Until recently, the only retirement option most people considered was a life annuity from one of Canada's life insurance companies. Under these annuities, the insurance company promises to pay a specified monthly payment, which starts before the end of the year the annuitant becomes seventy-one and continues for life.

Most people choose plans with guarantees for ten or fifteen years. This means that if you die within the guarantee period, payments will continue to your beneficiary or your estate. Another option is a term-certain annuity, sold by trust companies and insurance companies. It provides income to age ninety.

The shortcoming of a life annuity is that you give up control of your assets in return for a fixed monthly or annual payment. The payment you receive is based on your age, the amount you invest and interest rates at the time the annuity is purchased. If you take out an annuity when rates are high, you'll get a larger payment than you would get when rates are low.

Annuity rates

Compared with other investments, annuity rates are low. In the summer of 1988, one broker discovered that the best annuity he could find for a seventy-one-year-old man with $100,000 who wanted an annuity with a fifteen-year guarantee paid $1,035 a month. In comparison, a mortgage amortized over fifteen years and yielding 11.25 percent would have returned about $1,150 a month in principal and interest.

Fifteen-year mortgage amortizations are extremely rare. But this demonstrates the spread between an annuity payment and the possible return from a potential RRIF investment. Also, unlike annuities, mortgage rates can change over the years, giving investors some protection against inflation but also exposing them to a drop in income if inflation, and consequently interest rates, decline.

A RRIF earning 9 percent compounded monthly with equal payments over fifteen years would pay $1,014 monthly. If the rate were 10 percent, the payments would be $1,074 monthly. Of course, someone facing retirement may choose a life annuity because of concerns over running out of money. But a RRIF is still the best choice because it allows adjustment of payouts to meet both income needs and the rate of return of the plan.

A difficult decision

The choice between a RRIF and an annuity can be difficult, particularly for someone who has decided safety is paramount and wants guarantees. If you fall into this category, do some comparison shopping. An annuity broker can provide you with details of insurance company annuities and RRIFs. You can compare these to determine which will provide you with the greatest income using any guarantee period you want.

It makes sense to visit several annuity brokers some months in advance of retirement to get their views on the best retirement alternatives for you and your spouse. An annuity broker can also speed up paperwork. This is important because some trustees can take weeks to transfer RRSP proceeds to an annuity issuer. Because annuity quotations are guaranteed for a limited time only, a slow trustee can cause problems.

Annuities aren't all alike

Brokers can help you sift through the maze of annuity rates — another important service because rates vary widely among companies. Finding the best rate can make a 10 percent difference or more in retirement income. To make choosing an annuity even more complicated, rates can change daily to reflect changes in the bond markets where insurance companies invest funds. Also, rates can change unexpectedly as insurance companies move to generate more annuity business by offering higher, more competitive rates.

If you have an RRSP with an insurance company, you can have your plan automatically rolled over into one of the company's annuities. Unfortunately, many people accept their life insurance agent's offer to do this without question, thinking all annuity rates are the same. The smart investor will obtain at least six quotes from other insurance companies. It's smarter still to visit an annuity broker who specializes in advising individuals and corporations on suitable annuities and their rates. You can see in Appendix Three the many different types of annuities and their rates.

It's your choice

There are several types of life annuities. Making the proper choice depends on your situation and your plans for retirement.

Like life insurance, annuities involve a pooling of risk. In the case of annuities, life insurance companies use annuity mortality tables that indicate the average life expectancies of individuals of different ages. For example, one widely used table estimates the life expectancy of a seventy-one-year-old man at 12.2 years. In other words, he's expected to live to be 83.2 years old. An insurance agent attempting to explain to a potential client the return on his investment from an annuity might calculate the return over the 12.2 years. However, such a calculation is not really valid. The tables are deliberately conservative to take into account the insurance company's cost structure and to compensate for its risk that life expectancy might increase.

Although life insurance companies recognize the impact of smoking on life expectancy and charge non-smokers lower premiums for insurance, they do not offer annuities with higher payments to smokers.

The highest rates

Straight life annuities pay the highest monthly income. For example, a seventy-one-year-old male might buy a straight life annuity paying $1,216 a month with $100,000. However, if he dies after receiving only one payment, his estate would not get any further payments. Conversely, if he lives to be 120, he would continue to receive his monthly annuity income.

Gender is another factor in determining the level of annuity payments. According to the annuity tables, a seventy-one-year-old woman has a life expectancy of 14.2 years – so a $100,000 straight life annuity that would give a man a monthly income of $1,216 would pay her only $1,156 a month.

Because payments stop at death, many people are reluctant to take out straight life annuities and many agents seem reluctant to sell them. However, they are suitable if you have no dependants or survivors and need as much income as possible.

To make straight life annuities more attractive, some companies guarantee a lump-sum payment to a beneficiary of the unpaid balance of the annuity if the annuitant dies before the original purchase price has been paid out. Monthly payments under such a plan are less than those of a straight life annuity.

Individual preference

The more common alternatives to straight life annuities are term-certain annuities. Like straight life annuities, payments are guaranteed for the life of the annuitant. But they are also guaranteed for minimum terms – usually five, ten or fifteen years – regardless of how long the annuitant lives. Because the income must continue for at least the guarantee period even if you die earlier, monthly payments are lower than those for straight life annuities. The longer the guaranteed payment period, the lower the monthly payment.

If both a husband and wife have retired, the joint-life-and-last-survivor annuity should be considered. Under these annuities, the insurance company agrees to pay income throughout the lifetime of both husband and wife – continuing payments after the first dies and stopping only after the death of the second. Monthly payments depend on the ages of both spouses. Joint-life-and-last-survivor annuities are also available with minimum-payment guarantees.

Another type of annuity is available for people who want to cash in their RRSPs before retirement, yet defer receiving annuity income. These deferred life annuities are suitable for individuals who believe annuity rates will decline in the near future and wish to lock in funds at a higher current rate. They are doing what the insurance company would do with their money – buying a long-term bond to fix the rate of return for twenty or more years. The alternative is an RRSP or RRIF holding long-term Government of Canada bonds.

Disclose your health problems

When shopping for annuities, disclose any health problems you might have. Many insurance companies offer what is known as an impaired annuity to individuals whose poor health has reduced life expectancy. Someone who is sixty-five and has a health problem may be quoted the same annuity rates that would be given to someone much older but in better health. Your alternative is a RRIF. If you have health problems you can withdraw more RRIF money in the early years of retirement.

Generally, people have little choice about when they retire and move their RRSPs into a RRIF or buy an annuity. However, most people can provide themselves with higher retirement incomes if they think about retirement well ahead of leaving work.

Start planning at least a decade before retirement. You'll probably be in your mid-fifties, your children will have finished school and your income will be near its peak. For many people, it will be the first opportunity to regularly deposit the maximum yearly RRSP contribution.

Snowbirds and RRSPs

If you're planning to escape Canadian winters by retiring to Florida or to some equally sunny location, you may want to investigate the tax advantages of giving up Canadian resident status and becoming a permanent resident of another country. But be warned: it isn't as simple as hopping on a plane to Miami. Changing your country of residence for tax purposes is complicated and in most cases requires professional advice. It makes sense to sit down with an experienced accountant several years in advance of retirement to plan your strategy and determine whether a change in status is advantageous. Of course, a look at the astronomical costs of U.S. health care may be enough to make you think twice.

If you become a resident of the U.S., or most other Western countries, and collapse your RRSP, it is subject to a withholding tax of as much as 25 percent. Instead, if it is to your advantage, you may elect to have the proceeds taxed as if you were a resident of Canada. If you choose to live in the U.S., any income from the day you give up residence until you collapse the plan would be taxable in that country.

CHAPTER 17

Gimmicks to Avoid

MOST PEOPLE USE RRSPS AS savings programs to finance their retirement. They make their contributions annually and at retirement use the wealth they've built to purchase a RRIF or life annuity. Others, however, look beyond the conventional and try to squeeze more benefits out of their plans.

"Tax-free" withdrawals

Some of the strategies these people try are actually gimmicks, such as the so-called "tax-free" withdrawal from an RRSP, which provide little, if any, real benefit.

In reality, there's no such thing as a tax-free withdrawal from an RRSP. Whatever you take out of an RRSP must be included in income for tax purposes, although you may not pay tax if you have deductions or investment losses that equal or exceed that income. What financial advisors are really recommending when they talk of tax-free withdrawals is the borrowing of funds to buy mutual funds or other investments outside your RRSP. In many cases, the loan is secured by a mortgage against your home. You then finance the interest expense by withdrawing money from your RRSP. Interest borrowed for investment purposes is tax deductible, so the interest expense offsets your RRSP withdrawal and your tax bill remains the same. The idea behind this strategy is to convert a portfolio that will be fully taxed when withdrawn to one that will be taxed at capital gains rates.

This strategy is far too risky for most people, particularly those approaching retirement and whose major financial assets are RRSPs and homes. It moves you out of a program designed to finance retirement into one that may have unpredictable financial consequences. In fact, in periods of high interest rates and low stock market returns, the value of your retirement savings would be eroded.

Overcontributions to RRSPs

Under the old rules some people overcontributed to their RRSPs. They would not get a deduction on their overcontribution; however, they could withdraw their overcontribution within two years, leaving any income earned to continue to grow untaxed. The new rules allow for a cumulative overcontribution of up to $8,000 without penalty; however, if you make an overcontribution, Ottawa will count it toward next year's RRSP contribution and tax deduction.

Let's look at an example. If you are allowed $11,500 for 1991 and contribute $19,500, your contribution room for 1992 will be $4,500, assuming a maximum contribution limit of $12,500 less your $8,000 overcontribution made the previous year. You could, of course, contribute $12,500 and maintain an $8,000 overcontribution. Just remember, you are contributing $8,000 of after-tax income and unless you can turn it into tax-deferred income by allowing it to be used as a subsequent year's RRSP contribution you will face double taxation when the money is withdrawn.

Some advisors recommend that their clients make an $8,000 overcontribution so that they get the benefit of the income which will be earned over the long term on those funds. The earnings on this money can be significant over many years. For instance, $8,000 earning 10 percent will grow to $53,816 over twenty years. However, it is difficult to predict your financial situation in the years ahead. In most cases, the overcontribution limit should be saved for its intended purpose – to act as a cushion should you inadvertently overcontribute as a result of a change in your circumstances. If you are fairly certain about your future income and choose to overcontribute, monitor your situation as well as the regulations in case Ottawa makes revisions.

A variation of this overcontribution strategy suggested by some advisors is for people who are members of pension plans and able to contribute $1,000 annually to their RRSPs. The gimmick involves making an $8,000 overcontribution, and thus benefit from the compounding of income. Just remember that the overcontribution, when withdrawn, is taxable. Alternatively, such people would make an $8,000 overcontribution but not make annual $1,000 contributions until they have rebuilt their overcontribution room.

Another gimmick or strategy would involve someone with limited RRSP and pension assets making an $8,000 overcontribution at age sixty-five. This individual would then receive his or her funds using a RRIF or life annuity at $1,000 a year and benefit from the pension income deduction. Their capital would be returned and the income earned on it would be received tax-free.

Before attempting this strategy, individuals should carefully work out the benefits, if any, which will result. For people with limited retirement income there may not be any benefit if their income is low enough to be tax-free without taking tax avoidance measures.

The $8,000 allowance for excess RRSP contributions will not apply to people under age nineteen and a tax of 1 percent a month will apply on overcontributions they do make. However a relative could give a gift of $8,000 to set up an RRSP to someone who turned eighteen in the preceding taxation year. The money would grow untaxed and could be used as a tax deduction when this individual has earned income – but is unlikely to be in a position to make RRSP contributions. An $8,000 RRSP contribution would grow to a value of more than $362,000 after forty years using a 10 percent rate of return.

Deferring contributions

Another gimmick claims to take advantage of the carry-forward of unused contributions scheduled to begin in 1991. It works like this: instead of making an RRSP contribution of, say, $6,000, you borrow $50,000 for investments and use the $6,000 to pay interest on the loan. At the end of seven years you would cash in your investment, pay off the loan and then make your past seven years of RRSP contributions out of profits. That way you would still be eligible for your RRSP deductions.

The $50,000 would grow to $125,100 at the end of seven years if it earned a 14 percent annual rate of return, giving you a pre-tax profit of $75,100. You would pay tax of about $24,500 on the capital gain if you have depleted or are unable to use your lifetime capital gains exemption. Out of this after-tax profit of $50,600, you make seven years of RRSP contributions, which in this case is $42,000. Depending on your circumstances, you could get back about $18,300 in tax money, so you would have $42,000 in your RRSP and about $26,900 outside your plan. If you cashed in your RRSP, the value of your total investment would be about $50,600.

Now let's see what would have happened had you simply made your $6,000 contribution each year. If that money earned an annual 14 percent return, you would have $73,398 at the end of seven years. That amount would be taxable if you withdrew it, giving you $41,470 after taxes.

Clearly, the strategy of borrowing provides a better return. However, it entails much more risk because you have no way of predicting whether you will cover the costs of your interest expense. Indeed such a strategy, if in place during the past few years when borrowing costs exceeded market returns, would have lost money.

Using an RRSP for short-term savings

Some people have used RRSPs as short-term savings vehicles – to save for a down payment on a home, for example. When they have saved the money they need, they cash in their RRSPs, pay tax on the proceeds and use the money left. This strategy has marginal benefits, if any. In some cases the amount cashed in may even move the planholder's marginal tax rate from 39 percent to 44.5 percent, decreasing the benefit further.

Insuring your RRIF

When the holder of a RRIF dies, the funds remaining in the plan are usually moved tax-free into the RRIF of the surviving spouse. On the death of that spouse, the balance is taxable as income. Therefore, some financial planners recommend that people with substantial RRIFs who want to leave an estate to children consider term insurance to cover the taxes that could be due when the second spouse dies. The amount of insurance would diminish as the value of the RRIF is whittled down. Look closely at the costs of such a scheme relative to the income you intend to withdraw. You may find the cost of the insurance a significant portion of your income. While the gimmick may benefit your survivors, the cost could diminish your standard of living.

CHAPTER 18

A Capsule Review

LET'S REVIEW SOME OF THE recommendations and strategies contained in this book.

Once you've decided to invest in RRSPs, the first step is to decide how much risk you want to take. You can choose among guaranteed RRSPs, fixed income plans, balanced plans and equity plans. Guaranteed RRSPs are low in risk and suitable for individuals nearing retirement who cannot afford to have the value of their savings fluctuate widely. However, the rates of return on these plans barely stay ahead of inflation.

At the opposite end of the scale are RRSPs invested in equity mutual funds. Their values depend on stock market movements and the investment skills of the fund manager. In addition, the risks associated with equity-invested RRSPs vary widely, so they are best for individuals who can accept some ups and downs in their retirement savings. People in their thirties and forties could put a substantial portion of their total savings into such plans. So could older people who have substantial assets built up inside and outside RRSPs. Alternatively, a mixture of different types of assets, managed for growth, income and preservation of capital, makes sense.

People who are approaching retirement but who decide to invest in the stock market should emphasize lower-risk, RRSP-eligible equity funds or balanced funds in their savings programs. Remember, if you have savings both inside and outside RRSPs, try to keep the interest-income investments inside your retirement savings plan and the growth and dividend investments outside. All three types of investment income are fully taxed when withdrawn from an RRSP as RRIF or annuity payments, but capital gains are given preferential tax treatment outside an RRSP or RRIF.

RRSPs that invest in fixed income instruments such as bonds and mortgages have returns that are less predictable than returns from guaranteed plans but that will almost certainly be more stable than returns from equity funds. In theory, they should provide higher returns than those of guaranteed plans, as they have in the past. However, because interest rates have been extremely volatile in the past decade, these investments should be closely monitored.

The higher potential returns from bonds and mortgages may not be high enough to justify the greater risk for people who have limited RRSP assets and cannot tolerate volatility in their investments. However, they are suitable for individuals with enough expertise to capitalize on interest rate swings. They also make sense for investors who are confident they can pick a mutual fund manager who can preserve capital while maximizing return by investing in fixed income instruments.

Investors who choose mutual funds for their RRSPs will find that some are sold over the counter at banks and trust companies and through investment counsellors. Others are sold by mutual fund dealers, stockbrokers and insurance agents – and you will probably have the option of paying an acquisition fee that can be as high as 9 percent or buying with the condition that you will pay a redemption fee if you redeem the fund within a specified period, generally six or seven years. The redemption fee generally ranges from 5 percent to 0.5 percent, reflecting how long you've held the fund.

If you choose a fund that is sold only through brokers or dealers, make sure the salesperson with whom you deal is an expert. The sales fee you pay is for service and, one hopes, independent advice. The salesperson should be able to help you decide which plans are suitable for your needs and help you choose an appropriate fund.

If going it alone is more your style, you might consider self-directed plans. With a self-directed RRSP you make the investment decisions. Forget about these if you have a history of losing money in the stock market. Retirement savings are too important for speculation.

No matter what your investment, monitor it carefully. Your financial circumstances change as you grow older and the investments that may have been suitable five years ago may be too risky or too conservative for today. Consider your RRSP as part of your total financial package. Invest in spousal plans if your marriage is stable enough to warrant them. Above all, make sure the plans you choose are flexible enough to allow you to change strategies without incurring severe penalties. The Canadian economy and individual fortunes are too changeable to justify plans that are stagnant.

CHAPTER 19

The Most Often Asked Questions About RRSPs

Q. How much can I contribute to my RRSP?
A. Your contribution depends on your earned income, earnings from salary and wages, business income and rental income.

For 1991 the maximum contribution is 18 percent of 1990 earned income to a maximum of $11,500 less contributions made on your behalf to a pension plan or deferred profit-sharing plan in 1990.

For 1992 the maximum contribution is 18 percent of 1991 earned income to a maximum of $12,500 less pension or deferred profit-sharing plan contributions in 1991, plus any carry-forward from 1991. Ottawa will provide you with a statement each autumn which will tell you how much you can contribute to your RRSP for that taxation year. However, it is to your benefit to contribute to your RRSP as early in the year as possible so you may wish to estimate your maximum RRSP contribution. If you are a member of a pension plan, your employer should be able to provide you with your pension adjustment figure or at least with your benefit entitlement from which you can determine your pension adjustment. To calculate your pension adjustment, multiply your benefit entitlement by nine, then subtract $1,000.

Q. Can I have more than one RRSP?
A. Yes. It is quite common for people to have more than one plan, in particular, guaranteed plans with different maturity dates. However, you can often get a higher interest rate by consolidating several plans.

Q. I'm not working but I have pension income and investment income. Can I contribute these to an RRSP?
A. No. Pension and investment income are not part of earned income. You can, however, contribute up to $6,000 a year of pension income to a spousal RRSP.

Q. Can I contribute to both my own RRSP and my spouse's plan?
A. Yes. But the total you contribute cannot exceed your contribution limit.

Q. Can I transfer funds from my RRSP to my spouse's plan?
A. Generally, no. The exceptions are on death and on the dissolution of a marriage, including a common-law relationship provided there is a court order.

Q. What are the age limits for having RRSPs?
A. There is no lower limit, as long as you have earned income. Your RRSP must mature no later than December 31 of the year in which you turn seventy-one. If you are older than seventy-one you can still make a contribution to a plan for a spouse who has not yet reached the age limit. You get the deduction but your spouse owns the plan.

Q. Can I cash in my plan before I retire?
A. Yes. However, the proceeds will be taxable.

Q. Should I pay down my mortgage or contribute to my RRSP?
A. The answer depends on your tax bracket, your mortgage rate and the rate of return earned on your RRSP. In theory, you might be better off paying down your mortgage first, then contributing to your RRSP using the carry-forward and saving for retirement outside your RRSP as well as inside. A compromise solution and one which many financial planners recommend is contributing to your RRSP and using the tax savings to reduce your mortgage.

Q. Should I borrow to make my RRSP contribution?
A. Yes. Use your tax refund to reduce the loan and pay the remainder out of income over the next year. The future value of your contribution will far outweigh the borrowing costs.

Q. Can my spouse cash in the spousal plan in the year in which I make the contribution? My spouse has no income.
A. While your spouse can cash in a spousal plan at any time, Ottawa will consider the income yours and tax you on it if the plan is cashed in in the year the contributions are made or in the subsequent two years. This three-year rule is designed to discourage tax avoidance using spousal plans.

Q. I am a member of a pension plan. Should I bother contributing to an RRSP?

A. The answer depends on the size of pension you can expect relative to your estimated income needs. Generally, you should have an RRSP to supplement your pension. The unfortunate facts are that few people work for the same firm long enough to get full pensions. As well, many pension plans simply do not provide adequate retirement income.

APPENDIX ONE

A comparison of common Registered Retirement Savings Plans offered by major banks, trust companies and credit unions.

Variable Rate RRSPs
Term Deposit RRSPs
Fixed Term Cashable RRSPs
Fixed Term Non-Cashable RRSPs

These tables were prepared exclusively for the Financial Times of Canada by Fiscal Agents, Oakville, Ontario.
Data current as of August, 1991

RRSPs – Variable Rate

Institution/ Interest Compounds	Interest Calculation Base	Rate May Be Adjusted	Minimum Deposit	Annual Fees	Other Fees
BANK OF MONTREAL					
Semi-Annually	MMB	Daily	$50 Subsequent deposit $25	None	Full or partial withdrawal or transfer $25.00 Fees waived if senior
Monthly	DCB	Daily	$50 Subsequent deposit $25 TDL $5,000 $25,000	None	(As above)
BANK OF NOVA SCOTIA					
Semi-Annually	DCB	Daily	None TDL $5,000 $25,000	None	Full or partial withdrawal or transfer Fee $25
CANADIAN IMPERIAL BANK OF COMMERCE					
Semi-Annually	DCB	Daily	$50 Subsequent deposit $50	None	Termination fee $25 if closed within a year. Partial withdrawal or transfer $25
HONG KONG BANK					
Semi-Annually	DCB	Daily	None TDL $5,000 $50,000	None	None
LAURENTIAN BANK					
Semi-Annually	DCB	Daily	None TDL $5,000 $15,000 $25,000	None	Full or partial withdrawal or transfer fee $20
Semi-Annually	MMB	Monthly	$100 Subsequent deposit $25	None	If opened before Nov. 1,1989: Full withdrawal or transfer $20 Partial withdrawal or transfer free. If opened after Jan. 1, 1988: Full or partial transfer to another institution $30

DCB: Daily Closing Balance. MMB: Minimum Monthly Balance. TDL: Tiered Deposit Levels

RRSPs – Variable Rate

Institution/ Interest Compounds	Interest Calculation Base	Rate May Be Adjusted	Minimum Deposit	Annual Fees	Other Fees
NATIONAL BANK					
Semi-Annually	MMB	Daily	$25 Subsequent deposit $25 TDL $5,000 $10,000	None	Termination fee $15 if plan is withdrawn upon maturity but prior to holder's retirement. Transfer fee $15 between institutions.
ROYAL BANK					
Semi-Annually	DCB	Daily	$100 Subsequent deposit $15 TDL $5,500 $25,000-$50,000	None	External transfer fee $10
TORONTO-DOMINION BANK					
Monthly	MMB	Daily	None TDL $5,000 $25,000 + $60,000	None	Full withdrawal or transfer to another institution $15
CANADA TRUST					
Semi-annually	DCB	Daily	None	None	On withdrawal or termination within six months $100, subsequent withdrawal or termination $25. One free per year if senior (60)
CENTRAL GUARANTY TRUST					
Monthly	DCB	Daily	$25 TDL $10,000 $25,000 + $50,000	None	None
CONFEDERATION TRUST					
Monthly	DCB	Daily	None	None	None

DCB: Daily Closing Balance. MMB: Minimum Monthly Balance. TDL: Tiered Deposit Levels

RRSPs – Variable Rate

Institution/ Interest Compounds	Interest Calculation Base	Rate May Be Adjusted	Minimum Deposit	Annual Fees	Other Fees
CO-OPERATIVE TRUST					
Semi-Annually	DCB	Daily	$100 Subsequent $100	None	None
FIRST CITY TRUST/MORTGAGE					
Annually	DCB	Daily	None TDL $5,000 $20,000	None	None
GENERAL TRUST					
Monthly	DCB	Daily	$100 TDL $10,000 $50,000 + $100,000	None	None
GUARDIAN TRUST					
Monthly	DCB	Daily	$50	None	None
LAURENTIAN TRUST					
Semi-Annually	DCB	Daily	None	None	None
MONTREAL TRUST					
Semi-Annually	MMB	Daily	None	None	None
Semi-Annually	DCB	Daily	None TDL $5,000 $25,000	None	None
NATIONAL TRUST					
Monthly	DCB	Daily	$100 Subsequent deposit $50 TDL $3,000 $10,000 $25,000 $50,000 Portion over $100,000	None	After the first year, 1 free transfer or termination annually, thereafter $25 each. $100 if closed within one year

DCB: Daily Closing Balance. MMB: Minimum Monthly Balance. TDL: Tiered Deposit Levels

RRSPs – Variable Rate

Institution/ Interest Compounds	Interest Calculation Base	Rate May Be Adjusted	Minimum Deposit	Annual Fees	Other Fees
PRENOR TRUST					
Monthly	DCB	Daily	None TDL $1,000 $5,000 $25,000 + $50,000 + $100,000	None	None
ROYAL TRUST					
Semi-Annually	DCB	Daily	$100 Subsequent deposit $25	None	One free withdrawal per year, thereafter $50 each
CUNA CREDIT UNION					
Annually	DCB	Daily	None	None	Transfer fee $25
FIRST CALGARY FINANCIAL SAVINGS & CREDIT UNION					
Quarterly	DCB	Daily	$100	None	If closed within 90 days, $25
VAN CITY CREDIT UNION					
Semi-Annually	DCB	Daily	$100	None	None
Semi-Annually	DCB	Daily	TDL $10,000	None	None

DCB: Daily Closing Balance. MMB: Minimum Monthly Balance. TDL: Tiered Deposit Levels

RRSPs – Term Deposit Type

Institution/ Interest Compounds	Rate May Be Adjusted	Minimum Deposit	Annual Fees	Other Fees
HONG KONG BANK				
At term deposit annual average rate	At chosen maturity date (180 - 364 days)	$500 TDL $25,000 $50,000 $100,000	None	If redeemed early rate reduction rmay apply
LAURENTIAN BANK				
At term deposit annual average rate	At maturity (180 days)	$500	None	Full/partial withdrawal or transfer $20 (Non-redeemable)
ROYAL BANK				
At term deposit annual average rate	At chosen maturity date (180 - 364 days)	$500	None	External transfer $10
TORONTO DOMINION BANK				
At term deposit annual average rate	At chosen maturity date (90 - 364 days)	$10,000	None	Full withdrawal or transfer to another institution $15
CANADA TRUST				
At maturity of term note rate set at time of issue	(91 Days) At chosen maturity date	$5,000	None	One free termination per year if over age 60. Termination fee $100 if closed within 6 months, $25 if closed after 6 months
GENERAL TRUST				
At term deposit annual average rate	At chosen maturity date (30 - 364 days)	$500	None	None
GUARDIAN TRUST				
At term deposit annual average rate	At chosen maturity date (30 - 364 days)	$3,000 TDL $25,000	None	None
LAURENTIAN TRUST				
At term deposit annual average rate	At chosen maturity date (30 - 365 days, multiples of 30 days)	$1,000 TDL $2,500 $5,000 $20,000 $60,000 - $100,000	None	None

RRSPs – Term Deposit Type

Institution/ Interest Compounds	Rate May Be Adjusted	Minimum Deposit	Annual Fees	Other Fees
MONTREAL TRUST				
At term deposit annual average rate	At chosen maturity date (32 - 364 days)	$5,000 TDL $10,000 $100,000	None	None
PRENOR TRUST				
At term deposit annual average rate	At chosen maturity date (30 - 364 days)	$1,000	None	(Non-redeemable)
ROYAL TRUST				
At term deposit annual average rate	At chosen maturity date (30 - 364 days)	$500	None	One free withdrawal per year, thereafter $50 each
WELLINGTON TRUST				
At term deposit annual average rate	At chosen maturity date (60 - 364 days)	$5,000	None	Full transfer to another institution or termination fee $50
CUNA CREDIT UNION				
At term deposit annual average rate	At maturity (180 days)	$500	None	None (Non-redeemable)
FIRST CALGARY FINANCIAL				
At term deposit annual average rate	At maturity (180 days)	$5,000	None	None
RICHMOND SAVINGS CREDIT UNION				
At term deposit annual average rate	At chosen maturity date (30 - 364 days)	$1,000 TDL $5,000 $25,000 $100,000	None	None
VAN CITY CREDIT UNION				
At term deposit annual average rate	At chosen maturity date (180 - 364 days)	$500	None	Transfer to another institution $25

RSSPs – Fixed Term – Cashable

Institution/ Terms Offered	Interest Credited/ Compounded	Interest Reinvested	Minimum Deposit	Fees
BANK OF MONTREAL				
12 - 60 months	Annually on Dec. 31 (pro-rated)	At initial offering rate	$500	Prematurity redemption interest rate reduction agreed to at time plan is taken out. Withdrawal/transfer fee $25
BANK OF NOVA SCOTIA				
12 - 60 months	Annually	At initial offering rate	$500	Withdrawal or transfer fee $25. Early redemption 50% reduction of issue interest rate excepting for purchase of Bank of Nova Scotia registered product
CANADIAN IMPERIAL BANK OF COMMERCE				
9 - 36 months	Annually, or at maturity if under one year	At initial offering rate	$500	No interest paid if cashed within 90 days. 5% per annum paid after 90 days.
HONG KONG BANK				
6 - 60 months	Annually, or at maturity if under one year	At initial offfering rate	$500 TDL $25,000 $50,000 $100,000	Prematurity interest rate reduction. External transfers prior to maturity, rate reduced to 5%
LAURENTIAN BANK				
1 - 5 years	Annually	At initial offering rate	$500	Prematurity redemption interest rate reduction to 4%. Full or partial withdrawal or transfer fee $20

RRSPs – Fixed Term – Cashable

Institution/ Terms Offered	Interest Credited/ Compounded	Interest Reinvested	Minimum Deposit	Fees
NATIONAL BANK				
1 - 5 years	Annually	At initial offering rate	$500	Transfer fee $15. $15 fee if plan is withdrawn upon maturity but prior to holder's retirement. Prematurity redemption interest rate reduction agreed to at time plan is taken out.
ROYAL BANK				
1 - 3 years	Semi-Annually	At initial offering rate	$500	Prematurity redemption interest rate reduction to 4%. External transfer fee $10

RRSPs – Fixed Term – Non-Cashable

Institution/ Terms Offered	Interest Credited/ Compounded	Interest Reinvested	Minimum Deposit	Fees
BANK OF MONTREAL				
6 - 60 months	Annually or at maturity if under one year	At initial offering rate	$500	Termination fee $25
6 - 84 months	Annually or at maturity if under one year	At savings account at time of crediting	$500	Termination fee $25
BANK OF NOVA SCOTIA				
12 - 60 months	Annually	At initial offering rate	$500	Termination fee $25
CANADIAN IMPERIAL BANK OF COMMERCE				
2 - 4 months 9 - 60 months	Annually or at maturity if under one year	At initial offering rate	$500	None
LAURENTIAN BANK				
1 - 5 years	Annually	At initial offering rate	$500	Full/partial withdrawal or transfer fee $20
NATIONAL BANK				
1 - 5 years	Annually	At initial offering rate	$500	Full withdrawal or transfer fee $15
ROYAL BANK				
1 - 5 years	Annually	At initial offering rate	$500	Transfer to another institution fee $10
1 - 5 years	Annually	At savings rate at time of crediting	$500	

RRSPs – Fixed Term – Non-Cashable

Institution/ Terms Offered	Interest Credited/ Compounded	Interest Reinvested	Minimum Deposit	Fees
TORONTO-DOMINION BANK				
1 - 5 years	Annually	At initial offering rate	$500	Full withdrawal or transfer to another institution $15
1 - 5 years	Annually	At savings rate at time of crediting	$500	(As above)
CUNA CREDIT UNION				
1 - 5 years	Annually	At initial offering rate	$500	None
FIRST CALGARY FINANCIAL				
1 - 5 years	Annually	At initial offering rate	$500	None
VAN CITY CREDIT UNION				
1 - 5 years	Annually	At initial offering rate	$500	None
1- 5 years	Annually	At savings rate at time of crediting	$500	None
CANADA TRUST				
1 - 5 years	Annually	At savings rate at time of crediting	$500 TDL $25,000 $50,000 $100,000 $250,000	Withdrawal or transfer $25 One free withdrawal or termination per year if over age 60.
1 - 5 years	Annually	At initial offering rate	$500 TDL $25,000 $50,000 $100,000 $250,000	(As above)
CENTRAL GUARANTY TRUST				
1 - 5 years	Annually	At initial offering rate	$500	None
1-5 years	Annually	At savings rate at time of crediting	$500	None

RRSPs – Fixed Term – Non-Cashable

Institution/ Terms Offered	Interest Credited/ Compounded	Interest Reinvested	Minimum Deposit	Fees
CONFEDERATION TRUST				
1 - 5 years	Annually	At initial offering rate	$1,000	None
FIRST CITY TRUST				
1 - 5 years	Annually	At initial offering rate	$500	None
1 - 5 years	Annually	At savings rate at time of crediting	$500	None
GENERAL TRUST				
1 - 5 years	Annually	At initial offering rate	$500	None
1 - 5 Years	Annually	At one year GIC or savings account rate	$500	None
GUARDIAN TRUST				
1 - 5 years	Annually	At initial offering rate	$1,000	None
18, 30, 42 & 54 months	Semi-Annually	At initial offering rate	$1,000	None
LAURENTIAN TRUST				
1 - 5 years	Annually	At initial offering rate	$500	None
1 - 5 years	Annually	At savings rate at time of crediting	$500	None
MONTREAL TRUST				
1 - 5 years	Annually	At initial offering rate	$500	None
1 - 5 years	Annually	At savings rate at time of crediting	$500	None

RRSPs – Fixed Term – Non-Cashable

Institution/ Terms Offered	Interest Credited/ Compounded	Interest Reinvested	Minimum Deposit	Fees
NATIONAL TRUST				
1 - 5 years	Annually	At initial offering rate	$500	One free withdrawal per year, thereafter $25 each
1 - 5 years	Annually	At savings rate at time of	$500	(As above)
PRENOR TRUST				
1 - 5 years	Annually	At initial offering rate	$1,000	None
ROYAL TRUST				
1 - 5 years	Annually	At initial offering rate	$500	One free withdrawal per year, thereafter $50 each
SUNLIFE TRUST				
1 - 5 years	Annually	At initial offering rate	$1,000	None

APPENDIX TWO

A comparison of self-administered Registered Retirement Savings Plans offered by major banks, trust companies, and investment dealers.

These tables were prepared exclusively for the Financial Times of Canada by Fiscal Agents, Oakville, Ontario.
Data current as of August, 1991

Self-Administered RRSPs

	Bank of Montreal	Bank of Nova Scotia
Annual Fee	$100	$100, plus $50 if holding mortgage in plan
Special provisions if holding only CSBs, GICs, T-Bills, etc.	None	None
Transaction fee	$20 each; waived for Nesbitt Thomson and Investor Line clients	$20 each; waived for ScotiaMcLeod or Scotia Security clients
Closing fee	None if transferred internally Withdrawals: $25 Transfer out: $50	$50 each. None if transferred with-in a Scotia RRSP or RRIF
Uninvested balances	Interest credited monthly calculated daily $0 - $4,999 $5,000 - $24,999 $25,000+	Interest calculated on daily closing balance, credited monthly at tiered savings account rates; 0-$4,999.99 $5,000-$24,999.99 $25,000+
Mortgage investments	Annual administration fee $200 Set-up fee (non-arms length) $100	Annual administration fee $175 Set-up fee $100
Mutual funds and options	Allowed Call options Not allowed	Allowed
Statements	Monthly if transaction, otherwise quarterly	Monthly if transaction otherwise quarterly

Self-Administered RRSPs

	C.I.B.C.	**Laurentian Bank**
Annual Fee	$100	$125
Special provisions if holding only CSBs, GICs, T-Bills, etc.	None	None
Transaction fee	Four free transactions, thereafter $15 each	None
Closing fee	One free partial per year, thereafter $50 each	None if transferred internally Full or partial withdrawal/transfer $100
Uninvested balances	Interest calculated on daily closing balance, credited monthly at tiered savings account rates: 0-$4,999.99 $5,000-$24,999 $25,000-$49,999.99 $50,000 and over	Interest credited monthly, calculated on daily savings account rate
Mortgage investments	Non-arms length mortgage: Annual administration fee $150 Set-up fee $100	Not allowed
Mutual funds and options	Mutual funds only	Not allowed
Statements	Quarterly Additional $15	Monthly if transaction, otherwise quarterly

Self-Administered RRSPs

	National Bank	Royal Bank
Annual Fee	$100	$100
Special provisions if holding only CSBs, GICs, T-Bills, etc.	None	None
Transaction fee	None	$15 on non-security items. Cdn.$40/U.S.$45 if valued under $2,000
Closing fee	Redemption fee $25 Transfer fee $50	$100
Uninvested balances	Interest calculated on minimum, daily balance of $300, credited savings account rate	Interest credited monthly, calculated on daily closing balance at tiered savings account rate: 0-$5,499.99 $5,500-$24,999.99 $25,000-$49,999.99 $50,000+
Mortgage investments	Not allowed	Not allowed
Mutual funds and options	Allowed	Mutual funds only
Statements	Monthly if transactions occur, otherwise quarterly	Quarterly

Self-Administered RRSPs

	Toronto Dominion Bank	**Canada Trust**
Annual Fee	$100	$250
Special provisions if holding only CSBs, GICs, T-Bills, etc.	If holding only T-D's Greenline mutual funds fee is $50	None
Transaction fee	None	$20 each transaction $25 each U.S. transaction
Closing fee	$50	$50 No charge for transfer
Uninvested balances	Interest credited monthly, calculated on daily closing balance at savings account rate	Interest credited monthly, calculated daily at savings account rate or "Super Rate Account"
Mortgage investments	Annual administration fee of $150 Set-up fee of $100	Arm's length mortgages: Annual administration fee $150 Non-arm's length mortgages: Annual administration fee $150 Set-up fees $100
Mutual funds and options	Allowed	Allowed Covered call options only
Statements	Monthly	Quarterly or monthly if transaction occur, otherwise annually

Self-Administered RRSPs

	Central Guaranty Trust	**First City Trust**
Annual Fee	$150	$100
Special provisions if holding only CSBs, GICs, T-Bills, etc.	None	If holding only CSBs, annual fee reduced to $50
Transaction fee	$15 each; waived for Marathon Brokerage clients	None
Closing fee	Full or partial de-registration $50 Asset withdrawal fee $50 Cash withdrawal fee $25	None
Uninvested balances	Interest credited monthly, calculated on minimum daily balance at savings account rate. $10,000 and over related to T-Bill rate.	Interest credited monthly, calculated on daily closing balance at savings account rate
Mortgage investments	Arm's length mortgage and non-arm's length: Annual administration fee $200 Set-up fee $100	Arm's length mortgage: Annual administration fee $175 Non-arm's length mortgage: Annual administration fee $225 Set-up fee $250
Mutual funds and options	Mutual funds only	Allowed Covered call options only
Statements	Quarterly	Monthly if transaction. Quarterly asset statements

Self-Administered RRSPs

	Montreal Trust	**National Trust**
Annual Fee	$150 plus $50 per asset in dividend re-investment program (e.g. mutual funds)	$125
Special provisions if holding only CSBs, GICs, T-Bills, etc.	None	If holding only investment products issued by National, Victoria & Grey or Premier, transaction fee waived
Transaction fee	First 15 free, thereafter $25 each	First 4 free, thereafter $15
Closing fee	$50 Partial de-registration $25 Transfer out $50	$50 Partial transfer or withdrawal $25
Uninvested balances	Interest credited monthly, calculated monthly at 1/2 of 1% below savings account rate	Interest credited semi-annually, calculated daily at savings account rate
Mortgage investments	Annual administration fee $175 Set-up fee $100	Annual administration fee $200 Arm's length set-up fee $50 Non-arm's length set-up fee minimum $100
Mutual funds and options	Covered call options subject to $20 opening fee and $10 closing fee	Allowed Covered call options only
Statements	Quarterly. Monthly statement fee of $25 per annum	Semi-annually. Other periods upon request $25.

Self-Administered RRSPs

	Royal Trust	**Trust General**
Annual Fee	$100 to $250	$150
Special provisions if holding only CSBs, GICs, T-Bills, etc.	Annual fee $100 if purchased through Royal Trust	None
Transaction fee	$20 in Atlantic and Ontario region Otherwise none	None
Closing fee	Transfers out $50 Otherwise none	1% of plan value, minimum $100, maximum $200 Partial withdrawals or transfers $50
Uninvested balances	Interest credited semi-annually, calculated on minimum monthly balance at savings account rate	Interest credited monthly, calculated on daily closing balance at prime rate minus 7%
Mortgage investments	Non-arm's length mortgage: Annual administration fee $275 Set-up fee $200	Annual administration fee $175 Set-up fee variable
Mutual funds and options	Mutual funds only	Allowed
Statements	Semi-annually. Monthly asset statements $75. Quebec & Western region monthly if transactions occur, otherwise semi-annually	Monthly portfolio statement

Self-Administered RRSPs

	Burns Fry Ltd.	**L.O.M. Western Securities**
Annual Fee	$125 pro-rated	$100. First year free if transferred in from another carrier
Special provisions if holding only CSBs, GICs, T-Bills, etc.	None	None
Transaction fee	None	None
Closing fee	$100 Partial withdrawals $25	None Partial de-registration fee $25
Uninvested balances	Interest credited monthly, calculated daily at MoneyMax rate (an open-ended money market mutual fund)	Interest credited monthly, calculated on minimum monthly balance at 2.5% less than CIBC prime rate
Mortgage investments	Non-arm's length only Annual administration fee $175 Set-up fee $200	Arm's length mortgages: $175 Annual administration fee $175 Non-arm's length mortgages: Annual administration fee $225 Set-up fee $250 + $75 to MICC
Mutual funds and options	Allowed Covered call options only	Allowed
Statements	Monthly if transactions occur Otherwise quarterly	Monthly
Trustee	Royal Trust	First City Trust

Self-Administered RRSPs

	Levesque Beaubien Geoffrion	**Marathon Brokerage Security**
Annual Fee	$100 $50 if market value of plan is less than $5,000	Marathon Brokerage $95 First Marathon Security $100
Special provisions if holding only CSBs, GICs, T-Bills, etc.	None	None
Transaction fee	None	None
Closing fee	$100 Partial de-registration, transfer or withdrawal $50	None – First Marathon Securities Marathon Brokerage – $15 per security, max. $60 De-registration fee $25
Uninvested balances	Interest credited monthly, calculated on daily closing balance Up to $9,999.99 - 4.5% below prime $10,000 & over - 3% below prime	Interest credited monthly, calculated on daily closing balance at 2 3/4% below prime rate
Mortgage investments	Non-arm's length mortgages only Annual administration fee $175 Set-up fee $175	Not allowed
Mutual funds and options	Allowed	Allowed Covered call options only
Statements	Monthly if transaction, otherwise quarterly	Monthly
Trustee	National Trust In Quebec: Société Nationale de Fiducie	Central Guaranty Trust

Self-Administered RRSPs

	Midland Walwyn	**Nesbitt Thomson**
Annual Fee	$100 pro-rated	$125
Special provisions if holding only CSBs, GICs, T-Bills, etc.	Annual fee waived if over age 50 and $50,000 or more in equity	None
Transaction fee	None	None
Closing fee	$50 partial de-registration, otherwise none	Full transfer fee $50
Uninvested balances	Interest credited monthly, calculated on daily closing balance at prime minus 3%	Interest credited monthly, calculated on daily closing balance at 4% below prime lending rate
Mortgage investments	Non-arm's length mortgages only Annual administration fee $150 Set-up fee $100	Non-arm's length mortgages only Annual administration fee $175 Set-up fee $100
Mutual funds and options	Allowed Covered short or long options only	Allowed Covered call options only
Statements	Monthly if transactions occur, otherwise quarterly	Monthly if transactions occur, otherwise quarterly
Trustee	Royal Trust	Montreal Trust

Self-Administered RRSPs

	RBC Dominion Securities	Richardson Greenshields
Annual Fee	$117	$133.75 pro-rated
Special provisions if holding only CSBs, GICs, T-Bills, etc.	None	No fees if holding only debt securities with maturities over one year
Transaction fee	None	None
Closing fee	$50 Partial de-registration or transfer fee $25	None First partial de-registration free, thereafter $50
Uninvested balances	Interest credited monthly, calculated daily at savings account rate	Interest credited monthly, calculated on daily closing balance at 2.5% below Bank of Montreal's prime lending rate
Mortgage investments	Non-arm's length mortgages only: Annual administration fee $275 Set-up fee $100	Non-arm's length mortgage only Annual administration fee $150 plus annual fee $175 Set-up fee $100
Mutual funds and options	Allowed Covered call options only	Allowed Covered call options only
Statements	Monthly if transactions occur, otherwise, quarterly	Monthly if transactions occur, otherwise quarterly
Trustee	Montreal Trust	Investors Group Trust

Self-Administered RRSPs

	Wood Gundy
Annual Fee	$125
Special provisions if holding only CSBs, GICs, T-Bills, etc.	None
Transaction fee	None
Closing fee	Full transfer out $100 Full de-registration $50
Uninvested balances	Interest credited monthly, calculated daily on a daily floating GIC rate
Mortgage investments	Non-arm's length mortgages only Set-up fee $200 Annual administration fee 3/8 of 1% per annum charged monthly
Mutual funds and options	Allowed Covered call options only
Statements	Monthly if transactions occur, otherwise quarterly
Trustee	Royal Trust

APPENDIX THREE

Annuities and RRIFs

Comparison of Payout Annuities
Comparison of Variable Rate GIAs
Comparison of Fixed Term Cashable GIAs
Withdrawal Plan from a RRIF

These tables were prepared exclusively for the Financial Times of Canada by Fiscal Agents, Oakville, Ontario.
Data current as of August, 1991

Comparative Summary of Payout Annuities as of August 12, 1991
BASED ON $50,000 PURCHASE

SINGLE LIFE ANNUITY
MINIMUM GUARANTEE (10 YEARS)
Male age 65

Institution	Amount
NN Financial	$511.69
Security Life	510.34
Imperial Life	510.16
North American Life	508.68
Royal Life	508.58
London Life	508.35
New York Life	506.55
Industrial-alliance Life	506.53
Aetna Life	505.65
Empire Life	504.79

SINGLE LIFE ANNUITY
MINIMUM GUARANTEE (15 YEARS)
Male age 65

Institution	Amount
NN Financial	$488.20
London Life	487.51
North American Life	486.80
Royal Life	486.62
Imperial Life	486.36
Security Life	485.82
New York Life	485.55
Manulife Financial	484.35
Canada Life	482.62
Equitable Life	482.46

JOINT ANNUITY
MINIMUM GUARANTEE (10 YEARS)
Both Age 65

Institution	Amount
Security Life	$460.08
Imperial Life	459.62
NN Financial	459.18
Manulife Financial	458.65
North American Life	458.56
Royal Life	456.93
New York Life	456.61
London Life	456.53
Mutual Life	456.46
Canada Life	456.45

JOINT ANNUITY
MINIMUM GUARANTEE (15 YEARS)
Both Age 65

Institution	Amount
Security Life	$456.41
Imperial Life	456.00
NN Financial	455.85
North American Life	455.63
Manulife Financial	455.48
Mutual Life	454.27
London Life	453.98
Royal Life	453.97
New York Life	453.88
Canada Life	453.32

Guaranteed Interest Annuities – Variable Rate

Institution	Interest Compounds	Interest Calculation Base	Minimum Deposit	Surrender Fees
Canada Life Assurance	Daily	Daily	$1,000 Subsequent $500 or $50 monthly	None
Confederation Life Insurance	Daily	Daily	$100 subsequent $100 or $50 monthly	None
Crown Life	Annually	Daily	$200 or $25 monthly	None
Great West Life Assurance	Monthly	Daily	$300 subsequent $100 or $32 monthly	None
Imperial Life Assurance	Daily	Annually	$500 or $30 monthly	None
London Life Insurance	Daily	Daily	$300 or $25 monthly. If initial deposit is less than $300 fee is $20	Surrender or withdrawal fee $25
Metropolitan Life	Daily	Daily	$100 or $30 monthly	None
Mutual Life Assurance	Annually	Daily	$250 or $20 monthly fee $10	Partial surrenders under $500: Fee $10
Standard Life Assurance	Monthly	Monthly	$1,000 subsequent $250 or $50 monthly	.0075% plus possible market value adjustment
Sun Life Assurance	Annually	Daily	$500 subsequent $250 or $50 monthly	None

Interest rate may be adjusted daily at all institutions.

Guaranteed Interest Annuities – Fixed Term Cashable

Institution	Interest Compounds	Interest Calculation Base	Rate May Be Adjusted	Minimum Daposit	Fees
Canada Life Assurance	30 days, up to 10.5 years	Annually	At initial offering rate	$1,000 TDL: $20,000 $50,000	Discounted to current contract rate plus 1%.
Confederation Life Insurance	3, 6, 15 mos. 1 - 5, 5.5 & 10 yrs	Annually	At initial offering rate	$500 TDL: $25,000 $100,000 $250,000	Market value adjustment plus 1% if greater than guaranteed rate, otherwise no charge
Crown Life	1, 3 & 5 yrs	Annually	At initial offering rate	$500	Adjusted to market conditions plus 5.5 % fee first year reducing to 0 in 5 years
Great West Life Assurance	1 - 20 yrs (And any month between 1 - 20 yrs)	Annually / Annually	At initial offering rate / At savings rate at time of crediting	$1,000 TDL: $25,000 $50,000	Adjusted to market conditions
Imperial Life Assurance	1 - 5 & 10 yrs	Annually	At term deposit rate	$500 TDL: $25,000	Adjusted to market conditions
London Life Insurance	1 - 5 yrs 182 - 364 days	Annually	At initial offering rate	$2,500 if under 2 years. $1,000 if over 2 years. TDL:$50,000	Adjusted to market conditions (minimum $1,000)
Metropolitan Life	1 - 10 yrs	Annually	At initial offering rate	$1,000 TDL: $25,000	(Non-cashable)
Mutual Life Assurance	1, 2, 3 & 5 yrs	Annually	At initial offering rate	$1,000 TDL:$5,000 $50,000 + $100,000 + $250,000	Adjusted to market conditions

Guaranteed Interest Annuities – Fixed Term Cashable

Institution	Interest Compounds	Interest Calculation Base	Rate May Be Adjusted	Minimum Daposit	Fees
Standard Life Assurance	15, 21 & 30 mos. (1, 3 & 6 mos. Min. $5,000)	Annually and/or at maturity	At initial offering or savings rate	$1,000 TDL: $50,000 $100,000 + $250,000	Adjusted to market conditions
Sun Life Assurance	1 - 10 yrs	Annually	At initial offering or savings rate or current rate	$1,000: compounded $5,000: Annual pay $10,000: Monthly pay TDL: $50,000	Adjusted to market conditions

The Income a $50,000 RRIF Will Provide

Withdrawing minimum required

Age	Monthly Income	RRIF Value On Jan. 1
65	$ 159	$50,000
66	175	52,927
67	193	55,925
68	213	58,994
69	234	62,120
70	258	65,281
71	284	68,455
72	313	71,612
73	345	74,716
74	380	77,725
75	419	80,587
76	461	83,242
77	509	85,621
78	561	87,637
79	618	89,195
80	682	90,178
81	753	90,453
82	831	89,863
83	918	88,226
84	1,015	85,329
85	1,123	80,922
86	1,244	74,715
87	1,382	66,363
88	1,539	55,451
89	1,727	41,468
90	1,977	23,736

The required minimum withdrawal rate is the value of the RRIF at the beginning of any year divided by the number of years left to age 90. Very small amounts are withdrawn in the early years, leaving the bulk of the RRIF to earn income. As a result the value of the RRIF grows and so do the payouts. The value of all withdrawals amount to $220,861.

Withdrawing $500 a month

Age	Monthly Income	RRIF Value On Jan. 1
65	$500	$50,000
66	500	48,737
67	500	47,291
68	500	45,699
69	500	43,949
70	500	42,024
71	500	39,906
72	500	37,576
73	500	35,014
74	500	32,195
75	500	29,094
76	500	25,683
77	500	21,931
78	500	17,804
79	500	13,264
80	500	8,270
81	231.42	2,777
82	00	00
83	00	00
84	00	00
85	00	00
86	00	00
87	00	00
88	00	00
89	00	00
90	00	00

The RRIF will deplete itself by age 80 and insufficient funds will remain to pay $500 each month in the following years. The total withdrawals amount to $92,906.40.

Each RRIF earns 10% a year. All pay-outs are subject to income tax.

APPENDIX FOUR

Survey of Annual Fund Performance

(for periods ending June 30)

Fund	1991	1990	1989	1988	1987	1986	1985	1984	1983	1982
Equity Funds- RRSP-Eligible										
20/20 Cdn Asset Allocation	8.9	5.8	....	....	....	....	....	....	....	....
20/20 Cdn Growth Fund	7.7	1.9	....	....	....	....	....	....	....	....
20/20 RSP Growth Fund	7.2	....	....	....	....	....	....	....	....	....
20/20 Sunset Fund	9.0	2.5	13.7	1.6	10.9	....	....	....	....	....
ABC Fully Managed Fund	17.7	5.3	22.5	....	....	....	....	....	....	....
ABC Fundamental Value Fund	27.1	6.2	....	....	....	....	....	....	....	....
AGF Canadian Equity Fund	-1.2	-9.1	9.2	-7.0	12.0	27.2	35.5	2.6	80.4	-31.5
AGF Cdn Resources Fund	-11.8	15.8	-6.1	-15.5	69.4	-15.4	-3.5	-11.3	70.9	-52.4
AGF Convertible Income Fund	3.4	-6.2	....	....	....	....	....	....	....	....
AGF Growth Equity Fund	2.4	-4.1	4.4	-17.0	20.3	33.2	21.5	-7.6	90.9	-49.8
AIC Advantage Fund	14.5	-8.0	11.7	-9.2	16.7	....	....	....	....	....
Admax Canadian Performance	-1.4	....	....	....	....	....	....	....	....	....
All-Canadian Compound Fund	3.3	2.7	7.0	-9.3	15.3	16.8	18.3	3.8	26.9	4.8
All-Canadian Dividend Fund	3.2	2.8	7.0	-9.3	15.3	16.7	17.6	3.0	24.5	4.8
Allied Canadian Fund	16.3	-4.6	4.1	-28.6	23.9	....	....	....	....	....
Altamira Balanced Fund	-0.9	-5.0	8.6	-14.3	12.5	21.3	....	....	....	....
Altamira Capital Growth Fund	3.2	6.3	12.0	-14.6	18.6	10.0	26.2	-8.9	61.3	-11.5
Altamira Equity Fund	13.7	18.0	32.7	....	....	....	....	....	....	....
Altamira Growth & Income Fund	10.8	3.5	12.2	12.6	12.3	....	....	....	....	....
Altamira Resource	8.7	....	....	....	....	....	....	....	....	....
Altamira Special Growth Fund	14.3	4.6	8.0	-14.9	12.5	....	....	....	....	....
Associate Investors	6.0	-3.6	15.0	-0.3	14.9	15.0	33.7	4.2	74.6	-30.6
BPI Cdn Equity Fund	-4.5	-1.3	5.3	....	....	....	....	....	....	....
BPI One Decision Fund	4.4	0.9	9.4	-4.6	10.3	....	....	....	....	....
Barrtor Canadian Fund	10.8	2.3	12.4	0.4	9.5	14.1	....	....	....	....
Batirente-Section Action	-1.4	-4.4	13.4	....	....	....	....	....	....	....
Batirente-Section Diversifiee	8.7	0.2	13.5	....	....	....	....	....	....	....
Bissett Canadian Fund	8.7	-1.3	12.2	-6.8	12.9	25.8	26.9	-1.2	....	....
Bolton Tremblay Cda Cum Fund	-0.9	-4.6	16.0	-7.7	10.7	19.4	11.7	-2.0	80.0	-32.4
Bolton Tremblay Cdn Balanced	6.1	-0.3	10.6	....	....	....	....	....	....	....
Bolton Tremblay Discovery	10.7	-9.8	3.4	....	....	....	....	....	....	....
Bolton Tremblay Optimal Cdn	5.0	-5.7	16.1	-5.2	10.3	....	....	....	....	....
Bolton Tremblay Planned Res	7.3	0.5	2.7	-14.0	25.0	5.9	4.0	-3.9	73.3	-33.8
Bullock Balanced Fund	5.6	0.7	9.3	....	....	....	....	....	....	....
Bullock Growth Fund	5.4	-8.5	7.3	-6.0	4.4	34.0	5.6	-14.2	75.3	-46.1
CDA RSP Balanced Fund	8.5	2.7	14.0	0.5	13.0	19.2	24.5	0.4	49.9	-22.7
CDA RSP Common Stock Fund	5.1	-1.7	16.2	-4.9	22.4	25.7	31.4	0.6	65.4	-21.5
CIBC Bal Income & Growth Fund	6.8	5.0	12.0	....	....	....	....	....	....	....
CIBC Canadian Equity Fund	1.4	2.8	....	....	....	....	....	....	....	....
Caisse de Sec du Spectacle	10.5	1.6	9.9	-0.4	7.9	19.4	26.3	-4.1	43.8	1.3
Cambridge Balanced Fund	12.7	2.3	8.4	6.9	10.3	29.4	26.7	0.1	26.5	8.3
Cambridge Growth Fund	6.3	4.4	12.2	-0.4	26.3	40.7	31.5	-0.3	47.9	-16.9
Cambridge Pacific Fund	1.4	12.1	-50.3	-15.9	1.9	19.5	16.9	7.5	....	....
Cambridge Resource Fund	-8.4	-7.8	-2.4	-7.7	27.5	17.9	10.6	-0.3	48.6	-13.5
Cambridge Special Equity	-19.3	-1.7	17.7	-7.1	....	....	....	....	....	....
Canadian Investment Fund	-1.4	0.4	15.4	-7.8	11.1	15.1	27.3	-5.1	66.4	-22.7
Canadian Protected Fund	7.0	6.4	5.8	8.8	5.9	22.3	....	....	....	....

Fund	1991	1990	1989	1988	1987	1986	1985	1984	1983	1982
Capstone Investment Trust	10.3	5.5	9.8	-10.6	10.1	24.6	26.9	-3.8	36.4	1.1
Cda Life Bal Eqty Income E-2	2.4	-4.8	15.4	0.3	14.3	26.9	33.9	-0.6	65.7	-25.7
Cda Life Cdn & Intl Equity S-9	0.7	-5.2	16.5	1.7	14.0	23.0	31.1	-1.0	64.3	-26.8
Cda Life Managed Fund S-35	6.1	-0.7	13.0	3.5	11.4	20.0	27.4	....	....	....
Cda Trust Inv Fund Equity	1.5	-0.1	12.7	-9.3	19.2	19.5	25.3	-9.5	67.3	-27.0
Cda Trust RRSP Equity	3.4	-0.1	11.2	-9.8	16.8	18.4	27.3	-8.1	70.2	-31.7
Cdn Anaesthetists Mutual Accum	1.7	0.6	11.9	-3.7	20.4	21.7	27.2	-2.6	59.5	-25.3
Central Guaranty Equity	1.4	-2.9	16.5	-8.0	11.9	19.8	31.0	0.7	65.5	-19.8
Central Guaranty Property Fd	2.3	8.3	15.6	11.4	6.8	....	....	....	....	....
Citadel Premier Fund	4.8	0.2	12.0	-6.2	25.0	12.5	22.4	-6.4	54.5	-11.8
Colonia Growth Fund	2.6	-3.9	3.2	....	....	....	....	....	....	....
Confed Growth Fund	-0.4	-7.0	14.6	-3.4	16.3	25.0	33.9	-2.6	74.6	-31.4
Corporate Investors Fund	1.7	-2.6	10.3	-2.0	22.3	2.4	27.7	3.3	63.0	-21.9
Corporate Investors Stock Fund	5.1	-8.0	-9.8	-31.4	13.9	43.0	26.4	-1.5	81.2	-45.5
Counsel Real Estate Fund	8.4	12.4	14.5	13.7	14.6	21.0	12.6	10.6	....	....
Crown Life Commitment Fund	2.6	-2.6	11.1	-4.7	....	....	....	....	....	....
Crown Life Pen Foreign Equity	0.7	2.9	16.6	-6.0	19.2	26.7	31.1	-5.9	30.9	4.8
Crown Life Pensions Balanced	8.0	3.0	12.0	2.4	11.0	....	....	....	....	....
Crown Life Pensions Equity	3.8	1.6	15.5	-3.6	18.2	26.9	36.0	-12.1	53.6	-28.1
Cundill Security Fund	-1.8	-4.5	9.7	2.1	22.6	10.3	23.9	3.4	56.7	-24.2
Dynamic Fund of Canada	2.4	1.2	12.5	-1.9	25.3	15.2	23.0	-6.5	65.2	-31.1
Dynamic Managed Portfolio	1.9	1.3	9.2	-2.3	30.0	....	....	....	....	....
Dynamic Partners Fund	5.9	4.1	....	....	....	....	....	....	....	....
Dynamic Precious Metals Fund	-3.6	3.1	-12.7	-7.2	73.2	-7.9	1.1	....	....	....
EIF Canadian Fund	12.9	-39.4	18.1	....	....	....	....	....	....	....
Elliott & Page Balanced Fund	9.0	-0.9	12.5	....	....	....	....	....	....	....
Elliott & Page Equity Fund	8.6	-6.4	20.7	....	....	....	....	....	....	....
Empire Balanced Fund #8	8.1	3.3	....	....	....	....	....	....	....	....
Empire Equity Growth Fund #1	3.0	-1.8	14.6	3.5	16.9	23.5	31.9	-9.4	85.9	-26.0
Empire Equity Growth Fund #3	6.1	-4.1	18.3	0.8	7.2	44.2	27.5	-9.0	86.0	-22.3
Empire Equity Growth Fund #5	1.2	-2.0	10.3	-13.7	17.0	24.2	43.9	0.7	66.0	-27.2
Endurance Cdn Balanced Fund	7.7	2.9	....	....	....	....	....	....	....	....
Endurance Cdn Equity	3.4	....	....	....	....	....	....	....	....	....
Ethical Growth Fund	7.3	4.0	16.0	13.9	9.1	....	....	....	....	....
Everest Balanced Fund	7.8	2.3	18.2	....	....	....	....	....	....	....
Everest North American	1.2	-2.0	11.9	-13.6	10.9	26.7	25.0	-5.7	85.3	-28.0
Everest Special Equity Fund	5.4	-2.4	15.7	-19.5	....	....	....	....	....	....
Everest Stock Fund	2.7	-0.2	....	....	....	....	....	....	....	....
F.M.O.Q. Omnibus	12.0	3.9	10.4	2.9	17.5	15.6	25.1	0.7	42.4	4.6
Fd Des Prof Du Que-Balanced	14.0	3.6	10.8	....	....	....	....	....	....	....
Fd Des Prof Du Que-Equity	4.7	-4.0	14.7	....	....	....	....	....	....	....
Fidelity Cap Balanced Fund	6.7	0.4	11.0	....	....	....	....	....	....	....
Fidelity Capital Builder Fund	13.9	1.3	14.3	....	....	....	....	....	....	....
First Canadian Balanced Fund	8.4	-0.6	10.1	....	....	....	....	....	....	....
First Canadian Equity Index	-0.5	-3.7	11.0	....	....	....	....	....	....	....
First City Growth Fund	3.3	-8.5	13.1	-9.7	....	....	....	....	....	....
First City Realfund	3.7	7.9	11.6	16.2	11.4	14.6	13.2	7.8	....	....
Fonds Desjardins Actions	3.2	-4.7	15.3	-11.0	8.7	16.2	24.9	-10.4	76.2	-29.0
Fonds Desjardins Equilibre	8.6	0.9	12.2	-0.6	....	....	....	....	....	....
Fonds Ficadre Actions	0.6	0.9	10.7	-23.7	13.0	31.0	....	....	....	....
Fonds Ficadre Equilibree	4.8	2.4	12.5	-10.0	11.3	....	....	....	....	....
Fonds SNF actions	-2.9	-15.0	-3.6	-20.5	....	....	....	....	....	....
Fonds SNF equilibree	5.4	0.9	9.2	-9.5	14.8	23.6	26.6	1.8	40.9	-3.4
FuturLink Cdn Growth	1.8	-1.0	15.2	....	....	....	....	....	....	....
FuturLink Select Fund	5.2	-0.3	12.6	....	....	....	....	....	....	....
GBC Canadian Growth	15.2	10.4	....	....	....	....	....	....	....	....
Global Strategy Americas	1.0	6.9	10.0	-18.0	....	....	....	....	....	....
Global Strategy Canadian	4.2	-0.2	13.0	....	....	....	....	....	....	....
Global Strategy Corp	13.5	7.5	4.3	-17.2	24.9	....	....	....	....	....
Goldtrust	-3.2	3.1	-18.3	-20.9	56.8	17.4	-7.1	-4.1	94.1	-34.1
Great-West Life Diversified RS	6.0	2.7	10.6	0.4	12.1	14.6	....	....	....	....
Great-West Life Eqt/Bond	8.8	1.9	10.8	....	....	....	....	....	....	....
Great-West Life Equity	3.7	1.8	9.9	-12.5	....	....	....	....	....	....
Great-West Life Equity Index	0.0	-3.9	11.2	-6.8	22.5	14.0	-18.4	40.5	....	....
Great-West Life Real Estate	-4.3	11.5	9.9	10.4	7.3	10.7	9.2	10.2	5.0	13.0
Green Line Cdn Balanced	6.6	-1.6	14.1	....	....	....	....	....	....	....
Green Line Cdn Equity	1.3	-5.6	19.0	....	....	....	....	....	....	....
Green Line Cdn Index	0.5	-3.5	11.6	-6.2	23.3	....	....	....	....	....

… APPENDIX FOUR 157

Fund	1991	1990	1989	1988	1987	1986	1985	1984	1983	1982
Guardian Balanced Fund	12.2	5.8	9.7	5.9	14.7	11.5	24.4	0.2	50.5	-8.8
Guardian Cdn Equity Fund	-2.4	-4.2	7.0	-7.6	14.5	34.5	23.6	-7.7	59.7	-24.4
Guardian Diversified Fund	6.9	8.9	....	....	....	....	....	....	....	....
Guardian Enterprise Fund	1.5	5.7	2.5	-1.9	8.9	24.4	24.4	0.2	86.9	-24.6
Guardian Growth Equity	4.2	6.5	....	....	....	....	....	....	....	....
Gyro Equity	-3.4	-0.7	9.0	-1.0	28.4	....	....	....	....	....
Hongkong Bank Balanced	5.0	....	....	....	....	....	....	....	....	....
Hongkong Bank Eqt Index	2.7	....	....	....	....	....	....	....	....	....
Hyperion Managed Trust	8.5	4.8	....	....	....	....	....	....	....	....
Imperial Growth Cdn Equity	3.0	-5.9	27.4	17.3	31.3	23.1	28.9	-5.0	71.3	-27.4
Imperial Growth Diversified	7.4	2.5	....	....	....	....	....	....	....	....
Industrial Dividend Fund	-8.7	-5.8	2.7	6.1	27.4	16.5	33.2	6.5	69.7	-21.4
Industrial Equity Fund	-12.5	-13.0	-2.9	-0.5	31.4	18.1	16.8	0.3	88.1	-25.4
Industrial Future Fund	-0.9	-2.6	11.0	....	....	....	....	....	....	....
Industrial Growth Fund	-1.5	-2.5	8.4	4.5	27.7	16.4	27.1	2.8	77.7	-17.1
Industrial Horizon Fund	0.4	-1.7	10.1	15.2	....	....	....	....	....	....
Industrial Pension Fund	-9.8	-7.9	3.5	4.3	23.4	20.8	30.6	0.6	84.0	-21.2
Integra Balanced Fund	8.6	-2.5	8.8	....	....	....	....	....	....	....
InvesNAT Balanced Fund	10.1	-0.8	....	....	....	....	....	....	....	....
InvesNAT Equity Fund	3.4	1.4	....	....	....	....	....	....	....	....
Investors Cdn Equity Fund	6.6	2.1	9.1	-6.9	10.1	27.9	25.5	....	....	....
Investors Income Plus Port	10.9	3.5	....	....	....	....	....	....	....	....
Investors Income Portfolio	14.2	4.5	....	....	....	....	....	....	....	....
Investors Pooled Equity	4.3	-1.1	12.2	-3.0	15.7	15.4	27.0	-4.8	64.9	-27.0
Investors Real Property Fund	5.3	7.3	11.7	9.4	10.0	10.0	9.8	....	....	....
Investors Retire Plus Port	6.7	3.4	....	....	....	....	....	....	....	....
Investors Retirement Mutual	1.9	-2.7	12.7	4.6	20.4	13.6	26.7	-3.9	58.3	-27.0
Investors Summa Fund	1.9	-3.3	12.5	-3.1	....	....	....	....	....	....
Jarislowsky Finsco Balanced	6.5	....	....	....	....	....	....	....	....	....
Jarislowsky Finsco Cdn Eqt	3.6	-0.8	13.5	-9.2	13.3	....	....	....	....	....
Jones Heward Cdn Balanced	7.8	0.2	8.1	-2.3	6.4	22.0	18.4	....	....	....
Jones Heward Fund	4.5	-9.7	10.7	-3.9	11.8	29.4	31.6	-5.7	73.8	-34.7
Landmark Canadian	7.5	-0.1	....	....	....	....	....	....	....	....
London Life Diversified Fund	5.7	1.0	12.4	....	....	....	....	....	....	....
London Life Equity Fund	1.1	-8.1	15.0	-0.3	21.0	19.0	28.7	-3.8	65.3	-21.3
Lotus Fund	7.6	0.4	9.0	-6.1	10.4	19.6	25.7	....	....	....
MD Equity Fund	0.9	0.1	10.6	6.1	20.5	20.5	33.9	2.3	62.0	-12.1
MD Realty Fund A	-0.1	14.4	14.8	7.7	19.9	5.4	10.1	8.3	....	....
Mackenzie Equity Fund	-8.6	-7.1	6.5	4.8	20.8	23.1	29.6	3.0	67.9	-26.8
Mackenzie Sentinel Cda Eqt	-6.1	-4.4	6.1	-13.0	22.4	....	....	....	....	....
Manulife 1 Capital Gains	2.3	0.3	11.8	-8.0	24.3	14.4	28.6	....	....	....
Manulife 1 Diversified	6.4	0.5	10.7	-1.2	18.3	13.1	21.6	-2.9	46.5	-3.2
Manulife 1 Equity	3.7	-1.9	10.5	-6.1	20.3	9.8	22.5	-7.3	63.4	-19.1
Manulife 2 Capital Gains	1.5	-0.4	11.0	-8.7	23.4	13.6	27.7	....	....	....
Manulife 2 Diversified	5.6	-0.3	9.9	-2.0	17.5	12.3	20.7	-3.6	45.5	-3.9
Manulife 2 Equity	2.9	-2.7	9.7	-6.8	19.4	9.0	21.6	-8.0	62.3	-19.7
Margin of Safety Canadian	3.7	....	....	....	....	....	....	....	....	....
Maritime Life Balanced Fund	8.7	0.7	11.2	1.9	....	....	....	....	....	....
Maritime Life Growth Fund	-1.0	-4.0	13.5	-11.1	15.2	24.7	34.8	-2.8	73.2	-30.9
Marlborough Fund	-6.5	-6.9	11.6	-16.0	13.7	23.0	25.5	-10.4	74.0	-32.3
McLean Budden Balanced Fund	5.9	1.6	13.4	-5.3	10.8	23.1	27.3	-0.7	45.7	-4.9
McLean Budden Balanced Growth	9.3	2.8	....	....	....	....	....	....	....	....
McLean Budden Equity Growth	1.1	-2.7	....	....	....	....	....	....	....	....
MetLife MVP Balanced	5.5	2.2	11.0	-4.1	....	....	....	....	....	....
MetLife MVP Equity	-1.5	-0.5	12.9	-11.8	....	....	....	....	....	....
Metfin Real Estate Growth Fd	10.3	-6.1	9.0	10.3	24.9	11.5	7.0	....	....	....
Metropolitan Balanced Growth	6.4	0.1	9.1	-17.1	7.0	24.7	18.9	-4.1	54.7	-31.6
Metropolitan Cdn Mutual Fund	-0.8	-3.2	10.4	-13.6	10.5	26.4	....	....	....	....
Montreal Trust Balanced	9.0	8.4	....	....	....	....	....	....	....	....
Montreal Trust Equity Fund	5.8	-2.0	10.1	-3.9	22.3	14.6	24.5	-9.6	66.1	-30.2
Montreal Trust RRSP-Balanced	8.6	6.7	....	....	....	....	....	....	....	....
Montreal Trust RRSP-Equity	4.4	-2.0	11.7	-6.1	20.9	17.7	25.0	-9.7	69.3	-29.5
Montreal Trust RRSP-Tot Ret	10.4	1.0	....	....	....	....	....	....	....	....
Montreal Trust Total Return	11.4	1.7	....	....	....	....	....	....	....	....
Multiple Opportunities Fund	-3.9	27.3	-35.9	-27.2	93.5	....	....	....	....	....
Mutual Canadian Index Fund	1.0	-0.4	10.4	....	....	....	....	....	....	....
Mutual Diversifund 25	9.0	1.5	11.1	3.0	7.0	15.9	....	....	....	....
Mutual Diversifund 40	6.3	-2.9	14.1	0.6	6.9	19.7	....	....	....	....

Fund	1991	1990	1989	1988	1987	1986	1985	1984	1983	1982
Mutual Diversifund 55	3.9	-4.2	16.0	-1.0	7.8	20.9	....	....	....	....
Mutual Equifund	-1.9	-8.3	20.4	-6.2	7.9	26.7	....	....	....	....
NN Balanced Fund	5.8	0.3	8.1	-0.9	....	....	....	....	....	....
NN Canadian 35 Index Fund	1.2	-2.3	....	....	....	....	....	....	....	....
NN Canadian Growth Fund	4.7	-6.5	9.9	-16.6	20.3	14.6	34.9	-5.6	85.3	-17.3
NN Gold Bullion Fund	2.5	-10.6	-17.7	....	....	....	....	....	....	....
NW Canadian Fund	7.2	3.3	12.1	-8.0	18.4	35.0	32.0	-7.4	83.8	-29.4
National Trust Equity Fund	6.7	0.8	10.9	-9.7	14.6	24.9	31.0	-5.9	50.9	-20.5
Natural Resources Growth Fund	-8.9	-15.4	-2.7	-12.4	50.3	-8.1	0.1	-11.1	41.6	-10.1
O.I.Q. Fonds d'Actions	6.5	-0.3	13.1	-2.8	23.7	17.0	30.8	-7.6	85.3	-37.6
O.I.Q. Fonds d'Equilibre	12.3	3.6	10.2	2.8	17.2	16.1	25.8	-0.5	51.6	-14.9
Ont Teachers Grp Balanced	7.5	3.5	12.1	1.8	13.3	....	....	....	....	....
Ont Teachers Grp Diversified	-1.4	-0.4	16.9	-4.7	17.3	21.3	34.7	-4.8	68.2	-26.6
Ont Teachers Grp Growth	-0.6	1.2	18.9	-4.5	18.4	24.8	38.4	-5.4	75.3	-28.9
PH&N Balanced Fund	9.5	5.7	....	....	....	....	....	....	....	....
PH&N Canadian Fund	1.3	4.1	18.2	-2.9	16.1	29.7	28.1	-5.5	88.7	-40.9
PH&N Pooled Pension Trust	1.9	3.6	14.9	-4.7	18.7	23.8	28.6	-3.5	85.8	-34.6
PH&N RRSP Fund	1.1	5.2	17.9	-6.3	16.5	29.0	29.3	-7.2	95.3	-38.9
Protected American Fd	9.1	6.3	5.4	7.2	3.1	....	....	....	....	....
Prudential Diversified Inv	9.6	-2.3	13.7	....	....	....	....	....	....	....
Prudential Growth Fund	-1.0	-4.0	12.1	-15.6	27.9	23.7	27.9	-5.8	74.7	-35.5
Prudential Natural Resource	-6.5	14.4	18.7	....	....	....	....	....	....	....
Prudential Precious Metals	-15.8	12.2	2.1	....	....	....	....	....	....	....
Pursuit Cdn Equity Fund	11.1	-9.6	-2.2	-13.9	5.9	66.4	22.8	-4.7	....	....
RoyFund Balanced Fund	4.3	3.8	9.8	....	....	....	....	....	....	....
RoyFund Equity Ltd	-6.3	0.1	10.2	-8.3	12.1	34.9	35.2	-0.9	82.1	-40.7
Royal Life Balanced Fund	11.8	....	....	....	....	....	....	....	....	....
Royal Life Equity Fund	11.6	....	....	....	....	....	....	....	....	....
Royal Trust Adv Balanced Fd	8.4	3.3	17.1	0.2	....	....	....	....	....	....
Royal Trust Cdn Stock Fund	2.6	-4.3	15.1	-5.7	17.8	11.3	24.6	-8.6	79.0	-34.1
Royal Trust Energy Fund	-7.4	9.4	5.3	-11.4	66.6	-23.7	0.1	-10.3	39.2	-41.8
Royal Trust Precious Metals	-3.1	-7.7	....	....	....	....	....	....	....	....
Roycom-Summit Realty Fund	7.7	12.1	10.7	....	....	....	....	....	....	....
Roycom-Summit TDF Fund	7.2	9.9	12.5	14.6	....	....	....	....	....	....
Saxon Balanced Fund	3.9	-8.0	3.9	-13.1	4.5	....	....	....	....	....
Saxon Small Cap	-2.0	-13.4	9.0	-9.1	11.8	....	....	....	....	....
Saxon Stock Fund	1.5	-5.4	2.0	-12.9	5.5	....	....	....	....	....
Sceptre Balanced Fund	8.7	0.9	11.7	3.4	13.4	....	....	....	....	....
Sceptre Equity Fund	3.2	-0.1	13.4	4.4	....	....	....	....	....	....
Scotia Canadian Balance Fd	3.6	1.3	9.2	-5.0	....	....	....	....	....	....
Scotia Canadian Eqt Growth Fd	7.6	-2.4	9.9	-10.9	....	....	....	....	....	....
Scotia Stock & Bond Fund	4.3	0.6	12.5	-0.9	....	....	....	....	....	....
Sovereign Growth Equity Fund	-0.5	1.6	9.3	-7.9	....	....	....	....	....	....
Sovereign Revenue Growth Fund	7.3	-0.1	11.3	4.4	....	....	....	....	....	....
Sovereign Save & Prosper	8.3	3.7	5.6	8.9	8.2	-5.8	4.7	5.2	9.1	....
Special Opportunities Fund	5.9	-15.6	3.5	....	....	....	....	....	....	....
Spectrum Canadian Equity Fd	2.6	-4.3	10.1	-3.3	....	....	....	....	....	....
Spectrum Diversified Fund	7.2	-0.1	10.2	1.6	....	....	....	....	....	....
St-Laurent Fonds d'Actions	0.4	-4.0	12.2	-13.6	16.4	....	....	....	....	....
St-Laurent Fonds de Retraite	8.5	0.0	12.3	5.0	8.1	....	....	....	....	....
Standard Life Bal 2000	11.7	3.1	10.2	1.0	....	....	....	....	....	....
Standard Life Equity 2000	6.7	2.5	9.4	-7.5	....	....	....	....	....	....
Strata Fund 60	7.4	-1.9	....	....	....	....	....	....	....	....
Strata Growth Fund	2.8	-5.1	....	....	....	....	....	....	....	....
StrataFund 40	10.2	-0.6	....	....	....	....	....	....	....	....
Talvest Diversified Fund	8.4	3.2	9.1	6.3	13.9	....	....	....	....	....
Talvest Growth Fund	10.6	-1.3	8.8	-0.6	25.7	15.4	27.5	-2.8	52.8	-29.8
Templeton Heritage Retirement	-3.4	-1.0	....	....	....	....	....	....	....	....
Top Fifty Equity Fund	2.2	-5.3	....	....	....	....	....	....	....	....
Tradex Investment Fund Ltd	1.1	0.4	12.1	-3.2	20.4	20.8	26.1	-2.4	67.1	-26.2
Trans-Canada Equity Fund	1.4	-1.0	10.9	-1.0	26.1	47.0	34.2	-0.3	54.0	-25.5
Trans-Canada Income	5.0	-1.9	10.8	3.5	16.9	30.3	32.4	2.7	27.7	-3.8
Trans-Canada Pension Fund	6.4	1.4	10.2	-6.0	15.4	23.2	25.6	7.7	....	....
Trimark Canadian Fund	5.1	3.1	16.9	1.6	19.6	18.1	31.5	-0.9	85.1	....
Trimark Income Growth Fund	7.2	2.7	13.2	....	....	....	....	....	....	....
Trimark Select Balanced	10.2	....	....	....	....	....	....	....	....	....
Trimark Select Canada Fund	7.9	2.4	....	....	....	....	....	....	....	....
Trust General Balanced Fund	7.6	-1.3	12.0	-0.2	....	....	....	....	....	....

APPENDIX FOUR 159

Fund	1991	1990	1989	1988	1987	1986	1985	1984	1983	1982
Trust General Canadian Equity	2.3	-5.8	10.9	-8.2	14.8	19.7	26.1	-4.9	63.5	-36.2
Trust General Growth Fund	2.7	-10.5	25.2	....	....	....	....	....	....	....
Trust La Laurentienne Action	3.0	-5.8	17.0	-6.0	13.4	....	....	....	....	....
Trust La Laurentienne Equilibr	9.8	....	....	....	....	....	....	....	....	....
Trust Pret Revenu Canadien	3.0	-3.2	12.5	-14.8	17.8	11.1	12.2	-3.8	78.4	-35.6
Trust Pret Revenu Retraite	8.9	3.7	10.0	-1.4	11.1	16.0	17.2	3.6	44.5	-7.9
United Accumulative Retirement	9.5	-4.3	16.0	-2.2	4.8	22.3	42.9	2.4	54.4	-29.0
United Portfolio of RSP Fds	12.4	-0.1	....	....	....	....	....	....	....	....
United Venture Retirement Fund	3.3	-11.9	13.1	-9.8	13.7	28.9	31.9	-4.5	66.9	-40.5
Universal Canadian Equity	-6.5	-7.0	7.6	11.0	17.1	24.3	31.1	1.3	54.4	-13.4
Universal Canadian Resource	-14.0	-3.6	-8.8	-4.1	51.2	-11.7	4.3	-3.6	81.6	-39.2
Viking Canadian Fund Ltd	1.6	-11.2	16.9	-2.6	11.1	20.6	25.9	-2.4	66.8	-29.8
Vintage Fund	10.5	12.9	17.7	-10.2	25.1	....	....	....	....	....
Waltaine Balanced Fund	9.8	1.5	12.0	1.0	13.3	16.0	21.9	1.5	37.1	1.6
Waltaine Dividend Growth Fd	5.7	-0.2	13.2	-2.6	....	....	....	....	....	....
Working Ventures Cdn Fund	8.5	....	....	....	....	....	....	....	....	....
HIGHEST IN GROUP	27.1	27.3	32.7	17.3	93.5	66.4	43.9	40.5	95.3	13.0
LOWEST IN GROUP	-19.3	-39.4	-50.3	-31.4	1.9	-23.7	-18.4	-14.2	5.0	-52.4
AVERAGE IN GROUP	4.3	-0.2	10.3	-4.2	18.0	19.6	23.8	-2.1	63.2	-23.2

Equity Funds Not RRSP-Eligible

Fund	1991	1990	1989	1988	1987	1986	1985	1984	1983	1982
20/20 Amer Tact Asset Allocati	4.7	4.2	....	....	....	....	....	....	....	....
20/20 US Growth Fund	5.1	10.8	....	....	....	....	....	....	....	....
20/20 World Fund	-11.6	10.5	4.3	....	....	....	....	....	....	....
AGF American Growth Fund	-2.6	5.0	21.2	-15.0	8.4	27.0	33.3	-6.0	62.9	-5.3
AGF Japan Fund	-16.3	16.1	-6.8	4.6	31.8	92.9	15.9	22.6	32.4	-21.0
AGF Special Fund	4.7	8.2	15.3	-8.2	10.5	31.2	23.4	-10.3	96.1	-12.6
AIC Value Fund	3.7	....	....	....	....	....	....	....	....	....
Admax American Performance	-2.5	....	....	....	....	....	....	....	....	....
Allied International Fund	10.9	-9.6	-2.6	-27.7	47.0	....	....	....	....	....
Altamira Diversified Fund	-10.2	-9.3	5.7	-23.0	3.2	42.5	....	....	....	....
BPI American Equity Growth	6.6	13.1	-17.9	....	....	....	....	....	....	....
BPI Europe & Far East Fund	-25.3	4.0	-9.6	....	....	....	....	....	....	....
BPI Global Equity Fund	-2.5	17.8	11.8	....	....	....	....	....	....	....
BPI Option Equity Fund	-7.4	-6.0	10.2	....	....	....	....	....	....	....
Barrtor American Fund	2.5	28.0	24.9	-14.8	11.9	51.2	36.4	-28.9	96.8	....
Barrtor Intl Fund	-19.5	16.9	-2.5	-24.5	15.6	....	....	....	....	....
Bissett Special Fund	6.8	4.0	....	....	....	....	....	....	....	....
Bolton Tremblay International	-5.5	13.0	11.2	-15.2	19.5	41.1	25.4	1.1	67.6	-9.2
Bolton Tremblay Taurus Fund	2.1	5.3	14.0	-22.7	1.1	23.8	11.9	-4.3	58.2	-9.9
Bullock American Fund	22.4	32.1	15.8	-20.7	21.2	56.0	16.8	-16.2	62.6	-16.0
CB Global Fund	-6.8	....	....	....	....	....	....	....	....	....
CIBC Global Equity Fund	-10.7	13.4	5.4	....	....	....	....	....	....	....
Cambridge American Fund	-0.2	10.0	2.9	-14.7	....	....	....	....	....	....
Cambridge Diversified Fd	-6.9	-2.7	6.4	8.9	19.8	30.9	28.1	3.6	36.2	-12.0
Capstone International	4.4	14.5	10.4	-6.2	....	....	....	....	....	....
Cda Life U.S. & Intl Eqty S-34	3.0	13.3	17.1	-7.4	13.3	31.7	27.8	....	....	....
Century DJ Mutual Fund	3.3	17.7	5.1	-25.6	14.3	....	....	....	....	....
Cundill Value Fund	-5.8	1.7	10.4	10.4	16.5	22.4	13.5	5.5	67.2	-0.3
Developing Growth Stock Fd	-0.9	8.1	....	....	....	....	....	....	....	....
Dynamic American Fund	-4.0	7.5	16.4	-8.1	22.7	22.3	31.1	2.9	58.5	-11.1
Dynamic Europe 1992 Fund	-17.4	....	....	....	....	....	....	....	....	....
EIF International Fund	9.6	-21.3	8.9	....	....	....	....	....	....	....
Empire Group Equity Growth #6	9.8	-2.8	13.0	-3.2	12.1	....	....	....	....	....
Empire International Fund #9	3.2	13.2	....	....	....	....	....	....	....	....
Endurance Global Equity	-2.6	....	....	....	....	....	....	....	....	....
Everest International Fund	-8.1	26.0	30.0	....	....	....	....	....	....	....
Extro International	-13.2	17.4	-1.6	....	....	....	....	....	....	....
Extro Tiger Fund	-8.9	....	....	....	....	....	....	....	....	....
F.M.O.Q. Fonds de Placement	13.3	7.7	7.8	-0.8	23.3	12.7	21.4	....	....	....
Fidelity Intl Portfolio Fund	-7.4	22.8	11.6	....	....	....	....	....	....	....
Fonds Desjardins International	-2.1	15.8	17.1	-17.0	9.5	43.4	19.9	-7.4	37.4	-4.4
GBC International Growth	-12.5	....	....	....	....	....	....	....	....	....
GBC North American Growth	-5.5	-1.8	14.2	-7.2	11.2	29.0	23.6	-14.1	88.5	-28.7
Global Strategy Europe	-13.0	14.4	11.5	-25.7	....	....	....	....	....	....
Global Strategy Far East	-10.0	19.7	12.1	-8.8	....	....	....	....	....	....
Global Strategy Fund	-7.3	12.1	11.3	-17.3	24.7	....	....	....	....	....

Fund	1991	1990	1989	1988	1987	1986	1985	1984	1983	1982
Global Strategy Intl Real Est	-14.3	....	....	....	....	....	....	....	....	....
GoldFund	-1.1	3.4	-20.4	-20.0	63.8	7.8	-10.6	-3.4	96.2	-28.1
Green Line U.S. Index	5.4	14.0	17.8	-7.8	....	....	....	....	....	....
Guardian American Equity	4.2	11.3	12.3	-13.1	12.8	22.1	10.5	-12.7	41.1	-7.4
Guardian Global Equity Fd	-12.1	10.0	8.8	-13.9	13.3	51.3	20.2	-7.6	39.1	-20.0
Guardian North American Fund	0.3	5.7	14.5	-24.0	3.1	24.7	13.1	-12.3	45.1	-1.6
Guardian Pacific Rim Corp	-6.2	1.9	-2.1	....	....	....	....	....	....	....
Guardian Vantage International	-9.6	-5.0	....	....	....	....	....	....	....	....
Guardian Vantage U.S. Equity	6.7	12.1	....	....	....	....	....	....	....	....
Hyperion Asian Trust	-11.7	....	....	....	....	....	....	....	....	....
Imperial Growth N.A. Equity	-12.1	-5.7	12.1	-6.8	24.2	24.3	28.0	-8.9	75.8	-28.9
Industrial American Fund	-1.1	7.7	8.3	-6.3	18.4	26.3	29.9	-1.3	55.9	-5.1
Industrial Global Fund	-14.1	8.6	2.8	-1.4	32.1	....	....	....	....	....
Investors Global Fund Ltd	-6.4	20.5	3.2	-14.9	....	....	....	....	....	....
Investors Growth Plus Port	5.2	4.9	....	....	....	....	....	....	....	....
Investors Growth Portfolio	-1.2	7.1	....	....	....	....	....	....	....	....
Investors Japanese Growth	-9.5	-1.7	-2.6	4.5	31.8	87.9	7.2	14.4	34.3	-15.7
Investors Mutual of Canada	8.1	-0.7	11.6	-1.9	18.4	12.7	21.6	-5.9	68.6	-19.7
Investors N.A. Growth Fund	7.3	7.9	21.8	-9.8	18.8	25.5	28.5	-7.4	69.2	-23.7
Investors Retire Growth Port	2.7	0.9	....	....	....	....	....	....	....	....
Investors Special Fund	9.4	11.9	18.3	-10.0	16.6	21.3	17.7	-17.9	89.6	-30.2
Investors U.S. Growth Fund	8.0	7.7	15.8	-14.4	18.5	25.3	27.2	-12.2	66.5	-14.8
Jarislowsky Finsco Amer Eqt	6.0	9.1	5.6	-14.8	11.9	....	....	....	....	....
Jones Heward American Fund	3.6	5.1	20.9	-17.5	14.6	39.0	20.2	2.2	....	....
Landmark American	7.4	7.0	....	....	....	....	....	....	....	....
Landmark International	0.1	16.7	....	....	....	....	....	....	....	....
London Life U.S. Equity Fund	-2.9	-7.4	18.6	....	....	....	....	....	....	....
MD Growth Investment	-9.5	10.1	8.7	-5.2	25.8	36.9	37.2	0.7	74.3	-16.9
MD Realty Fund B	-0.7	14.4	14.8	7.5	19.1	4.1	8.7	7.9	....	....
Mackenzie Sentinel Amer Eqt	-3.7	10.2	19.7	....	....	....	....	....	....	....
Mackenzie Sentinel Global	-15.3	10.0	4.7	-21.3	....	....	....	....	....	....
Margin of Safety Fund	16.3	5.2	....	....	....	....	....	....	....	....
McLean Budden Amer Growth	15.2	18.0	....	....	....	....	....	....	....	....
Metropolitan Collective Mutual	0.5	15.1	11.3	-27.7	6.1	28.9	14.9	-1.0	60.0	-5.4
Metropolitan Speculators	1.4	16.0	7.8	-20.6	29.1	....	....	....	....	....
Metropolitan Venture Fund	-0.9	14.8	8.8	-21.6	17.8	35.1	11.9	-12.0	45.7	-5.7
Montreal Trust Intl Fund	-1.3	12.9	7.1	-15.7	18.7	37.8	36.1	-4.1	42.6	-1.7
Mutual Amerifund	-2.6	3.4	10.4	-3.6	9.3	....	....	....	....	....
NN Global Fund	-16.8	9.9	6.1	-18.5	....	....	....	....	....	....
NW Equity Fund Ltd	8.7	20.4	14.6	-15.1	6.3	26.1	26.6	-7.4	55.0	-5.5
PH&N U.S. Fund	9.7	17.6	13.1	-10.6	8.1	28.8	32.4	-15.8	86.2	-4.2
PH&N U.S. Pooled Pension Fund	10.5	19.4	13.8	-8.8	8.7	28.7	33.4	-8.4	82.0	-3.6
Pursuit American Fund	21.9	12.1	6.9	-18.1	....	....	....	....	....	....
Royal Trust Adv Growth Fund	5.8	2.9	10.7	-4.4	....	....	....	....	....	....
Royal Trust American Stock	1.8	18.2	16.1	-15.6	16.8	31.8	21.9	-11.9	45.4	-5.6
Royal Trust European Growth	-11.8	0.3	3.4	....	....	....	....	....	....	....
Royal Trust Japanese Stock	-8.5	-4.7	-6.9	-4.7	42.4	87.7	....	....	....	....
Saxon World Growth	-5.3	-5.1	29.0	-10.8	31.6	....	....	....	....	....
Sceptre International Fund	-4.7	19.1	19.5	-4.6	....	....	....	....	....	....
Scotia Amer Eqt Growth Fd	6.8	11.4	-5.9	-22.8	....	....	....	....	....	....
Spectrum Intl Equity Fund	-5.1	11.2	6.9	-17.7	....	....	....	....	....	....
Talvest American Fund	-8.8	9.5	7.8	-14.3	15.9	....	....	....	....	....
Talvest Global Diversified	-8.0	14.9	6.1	....	....	....	....	....	....	....
Templeton Growth Fund	-4.0	11.0	15.4	-10.4	19.3	31.8	28.1	6.7	56.2	-14.1
Templeton Heritage Fd	-5.7	7.9	....	....	....	....	....	....	....	....
Trimark Fund	0.7	8.6	14.9	-0.5	17.5	31.2	26.5	-1.6	82.8	....
Trimark Select Growth Fd	0.0	11.4	....	....	....	....	....	....	....	....
Trust General International	-10.2	21.5	....	....	....	....	....	....	....	....
Trust General U.S. Equity	-0.3	10.5	19.2	-20.9	18.3	39.9	29.6	-14.1	....	....
Trust Pret Revenu American	3.1	13.6	11.2	-22.3	15.0	35.4	24.3	-3.5	37.0	-7.5
United Accumulative Fund	8.4	3.4	25.7	-14.9	11.7	34.3	32.7	10.6	39.8	-17.9
United American Fund Ltd	12.6	2.2	19.9	-17.3	6.3	32.3	29.2	9.3	38.7	-10.0
United Portfolio of Funds	9.8	2.2	....	....	....	....	....	....	....	....
United Venture Fund Ltd	-2.5	-14.5	11.2	-18.5	4.3	27.4	30.3	-3.1	55.5	-31.5
Universal American	0.0	9.4	8.8	-5.8	18.9	26.8	27.6	2.5	37.4	4.2
Universal Global	2.2	10.8	2.9	-11.4	19.0	....	....	....	....	....
Universal Pacific	-7.0	21.4	2.0	-8.0	34.8	110.0	12.0	10.1	23.4	....
Universal Sector American	-1.3	8.5	8.1	....	....	....	....	....	....	....

APPENDIX FOUR 161

Fund	1991	1990	1989	1988	1987	1986	1985	1984	1983	1982
Universal Sector Canadian	-6.5	-7.4	7.4	....	....	....	....	....	....	....
Universal Sector Global	2.3	10.4	2.2	....	....	....	....	....	....	....
Universal Sector Pacific	-7.0	20.6	1.8	....	....	....	....	....	....	....
Universal Sector Resource	-12.7	-4.3	-9.0	....	....	....	....	....	....	....
Viking Commonwealth Fund	-1.7	6.5	14.4	-3.4	21.2	30.4	24.3	0.7	55.0	-7.7
Viking Growth Fund	-4.3	1.4	15.6	-8.5	15.2	42.3	27.6	-2.6	50.7	-17.3
Viking International Fund	-4.8	9.3	9.9	-5.2	10.4	32.4	21.1	6.0	54.2	-14.5
HIGHEST IN GROUP	22.4	32.1	30.0	10.4	63.8	110.0	37.2	22.6	96.8	4.2
LOWEST IN GROUP	-25.3	-21.3	-20.4	-27.7	1.1	4.1	-10.6	-28.9	23.4	-31.5
AVERAGE IN GROUP	-1.6	8.7	9.5	-11.9	18.1	35.6	22.9	-3.5	58.8	-12.6

Bond and Mortgage Funds

Fund	1991	1990	1989	1988	1987	1986	1985	1984	1983	1982
20/20 Income Fund	10.3	1.7	8.9	1.3	12.0	....	....	....	....	....
AGF Canadian Bond Fund	10.0	1.4	12.2	7.5	5.8	20.4	31.6	3.5	31.2	18.4
AGF Global Govt Bond*	4.4	11.2	2.6	1.6	....	....	....	....	....	....
Admax Canadian Income	10.3	3.1	....	....	....	....	....	....	....	....
All-Canadian Revenue Growth	9.6	9.3	8.9	6.6	9.0	6.1	20.0	5.5	22.5	11.3
Allied Income Fund	11.4	5.9	10.2	5.9	16.2	....	....	....	....	....
Altamira Bond Fund	11.7	3.6	11.9	....	....	....	....	....	....	....
Altamira Income Fund	14.9	5.8	13.6	10.4	7.5	11.8	21.8	3.2	26.8	13.8
BPI Canadian Bond Fund	9.4	3.8	8.2	....	....	....	....	....	....	....
BPI Global Income Fund*	1.0	-0.2	0.7	....	....	....	....	....	....	....
Batirente-Section Obligations	12.8	-0.1	13.7	....	....	....	....	....	....	....
Bissett Fiduciary Fund	14.4	2.6	11.8	8.1	....	....	....	....	....	....
Bolton Tremblay Bond	14.6	2.5	12.0	....	....	....	....	....	....	....
Bullock Bond Fund	12.7	1.4	8.0	6.1	4.0	9.2	11.0	9.3	10.7	6.8
CDA RSP Bond & Mortgage	14.1	6.2	10.6	8.2	8.1	14.0	21.2	4.8	32.2	15.3
CIBC Fixed Income Fund	12.8	2.6	11.3	....	....	....	....	....	....	....
CIBC Mortgage Income	17.1	7.2	9.4	7.5	8.8	10.3	15.3	8.6	21.6	15.4
Cda Life Fixed Income S-19	12.3	3.4	9.4	6.9	6.4	14.8	24.7	2.5	37.0	12.8
Cda Trust Income Investments	13.8	2.1	10.4	7.5	6.0	13.4	22.9	4.9	25.1	16.1
Cda Trust Inv Fund Income	8.2	4.4	9.5	6.6	6.8	17.1	26.7	4.6	27.6	14.3
Cda Trust RRSP Income	12.4	2.0	9.9	6.9	6.8	16.8	25.8	7.3	26.7	14.2
Cda Trust RRSP Mortgage	15.4	8.4	9.2	9.1	8.4	11.0	17.0	7.9	20.4	17.7
Central Guaranty Income	12.5	0.1	12.9	1.8	4.9	16.9	23.0	2.8	35.1	12.9
Central Guaranty Mortgage	14.2	6.7	7.9	8.8	7.3	9.2	15.1	6.8	19.5	18.5
Church Street Income	13.6	2.5	10.3	....	....	....	....	....	....	....
Confed Mortgage Fund	14.5	9.5	9.1	8.8	8.4	10.4	17.1	8.8	25.4	15.4
Crown Life Pensions Bond Fund	13.0	4.1	10.7	7.7	3.9	15.7	20.1	-6.0	33.6	7.5
Crown Life Pensions Mortgage	16.5	6.2	10.4	8.6	8.6	13.2	21.7	7.8	38.4	15.8
Dynamic Global Bond Fund	-0.7	5.4	2.3	....	....	....	....	....	....	....
Dynamic Income Fund	11.6	4.8	13.9	6.6	8.2	14.1	30.3	1.5	36.3	6.4
Elliot & Page Bond Fund	11.7	6.1	11.8	....	....	....	....	....	....	....
Empire Bond Fund #2	14.0	2.6	11.4	3.0	6.5	....	....	....	....	....
Empire Fixed Income Fund #4	15.6	2.5	12.9	9.1	6.1	....	....	....	....	....
Endurance Government Bond	13.8	4.6	....	....	....	....	....	....	....	....
Everest Bond Fund	12.0	2.9	13.3	10.8	....	....	....	....	....	....
Everest US Bond Fund*	-1.5	....	....	....	....	....	....	....	....	....
Fd Des Prof Du Que-Bonds	15.5	3.7	10.3	....	....	....	....	....	....	....
Fidelity Cap Conservation Fd	6.5	4.6	7.0	....	....	....	....	....	....	....
Finsco Bond Fund	11.4	1.6	9.5	7.8	5.0	14.9	....	....	....	....
First Canadian Bond Fund	13.6	0.9	10.1	....	....	....	....	....	....	....
First Canadian Mortgage Fund	19.2	7.8	9.0	9.2	9.2	11.5	18.4	8.5	21.4	18.4
First City Income Fund	13.1	7.9	10.3	6.5	....	....	....	....	....	....
Fonds Desjardins Hypotheques	14.8	8.6	9.1	9.5	8.8	11.2	18.9	5.8	25.1	17.3
Fonds Desjardins Obligations	13.9	1.1	10.8	7.1	5.4	15.9	29.8	-3.2	37.6	13.7
Fonds Ficadre Obligations	12.3	....	....	....	....	....	....	....	....	....
Fonds SNF obligations	14.1	2.3	10.4	....	....	....	....	....	....	....
FuturLink Government Bond	11.4	-0.8	12.8	....	....	....	....	....	....	....
FuturLink Mortgage Fund	15.0	11.8	....	....	....	....	....	....	....	....
GBC Canadian Bond	14.0	1.4	13.1	8.9	7.0	16.1	....	....	....	....
Global Strategy World Bond*	7.0	1.4	6.3	....	....	....	....	....	....	....
Great-West Life Bond Invest	13.3	0.0	10.6	7.4	5.9	14.7	26.0	1.9	29.0	10.1
Great-West Life Mortgage	13.3	3.5	10.8	7.8	6.7	12.5	18.8	5.3	24.9	15.7
Green Line Canadian Bond	12.2	2.5	7.4	....	....	....	....	....	....	....
Green Line Mortgage	16.2	7.0	11.6	9.7	8.5	10.5	13.7	8.7	22.1	18.3
Guardian Canada Bond Fund	11.4	10.8	10.3	7.0	....	....	....	....	....	....

Fund	1991	1990	1989	1988	1987	1986	1985	1984	1983	1982
Guardian Intl Income Fund	3.9	3.4	2.1	-1.4	....	....	....	....	....	....
Guardian Vantage Bond	10.9	10.8	....	....	....	....	....	....	....	....
Gyro Bond	12.5	....	....	....	....	....	....	....	....	....
Hyperion Fixed Income	12.3	....	....	....	....	....	....	....	....	....
Industrial Bond Fund	12.6	1.2	....	....	....	....	....	....	....	....
Industrial Income Fund	8.8	-1.4	12.6	13.2	12.3	18.6	38.0	-0.5	39.0	5.9
InvesNAT Income Fund	14.1	2.6	....	....	....	....	....	....	....	....
Investors Bond Fund	13.3	3.3	11.5	7.4	6.4	16.3	28.5	0.0	28.3	13.7
Investors Mortgage Fund	15.7	7.1	9.0	8.8	8.4	11.4	18.5	7.0	23.8	16.7
Investors Pooled Bond	15.3	3.8	12.7	9.4	8.3	17.4	29.5	0.6	30.8	14.4
Investors Pooled Mortgage	16.8	8.7	9.9	9.5	9.3	12.4	20.4	7.1	27.4	15.1
Jones Heward Bond	12.4	2.4	11.5	7.7	....	....	....	....	....	....
Landmark Bond	12.9	2.3	....	....	....	....	....	....	....	....
London Life Bond Fund	5.2	3.2	13.2	5.3	4.2	21.2	41.3	2.0	31.6	13.5
London Life Mortgage Fund	16.4	7.5	8.9	8.7	9.3	13.7	22.9	5.3	41.9	15.5
Mackenzie Income Fund	9.6	-0.9	12.9	13.0	12.5	17.6	30.3	4.3	27.6	14.2
Mackenzie Sentinel Cda Bond	12.3	0.6	10.8	6.5	8.0	....	....	....	....	....
Manulife 1 Bond	14.2	3.0	11.8	8.5	7.3	14.8	22.9	2.7	35.5	13.3
Manulife 2 Bond	13.4	2.2	11.0	7.7	6.6	14.0	22.0	1.9	34.5	12.5
Maritime Life Bond	13.4	....	....	....	....	....	....	....	....	....
McLean Budden Fixed Income	14.4	5.2	....	....	....	....	....	....	....	....
MetLife MVP Bond	12.3	3.8	11.2	2.1	....	....	....	....	....	....
Metropolitan Bond Fund	13.3	2.8	9.6	-3.2	7.9	13.3	27.1	-4.8	31.4	2.3
Montreal Trust Income Fund	13.2	0.9	11.8	6.6	7.7	19.5	25.1	-0.8	35.0	11.4
Montreal Trust Mortgage Fund	14.5	8.9	8.9	8.9	8.2	10.7	16.6	7.7	20.2	17.5
Montreal Trust RRSP-Income	12.6	0.2	11.2	6.7	8.2	17.9	23.1	2.8	43.6	9.5
Montreal Trust RRSP-Mortgage	14.6	7.9	8.7	8.5	8.2	10.5	16.4	7.6	19.9	17.0
NN Bond Fund	12.5	3.5	9.6	4.9	....	....	....	....	....	....
National Trust Income Fund	13.0	0.7	10.7	7.8	7.3	16.3	30.0	-2.3	43.0	9.6
O.I.Q. Fonds d'Obligations	11.1	4.7	11.2	6.3	8.4	15.3	26.2	1.8	45.7	13.9
PH&N Bond Fund	14.2	3.2	13.2	9.5	9.4	18.6	34.0	-3.2	44.8	9.0
Prudential Income Fund	12.5	1.7	13.2	9.3	7.3	13.3	22.6	4.9	32.1	11.7
Pursuit Income Fund	13.6	0.0	1.1	2.2	....	....	....	....	....	....
RoyFund Bond Fund	13.4	3.0	9.4	7.8	6.8	15.7	23.9	1.0	23.4	8.6
Royal Life Income Fund	10.0	....	....	....	....	....	....	....	....	....
Royal Trust Adv Income Fd	10.3	4.3	11.4	3.1	....	....	....	....	....	....
Royal Trust Bond Fund	13.6	1.9	11.0	7.3	6.2	16.5	30.0	1.3	35.5	11.7
Royal Trust Mortgage Fund	15.7	8.6	8.5	9.2	8.7	11.3	16.8	8.6	20.8	18.7
Sceptre Bond Fund	16.1	5.8	8.4	8.5	7.4	....	....	....	....	....
Scotia Defensive Income Fd	12.3	3.7	8.3	....	....	....	....	....	....	....
Scotia Income Fund	11.4	4.5	10.0	6.9	....	....	....	....	....	....
Sovereign Capital Sec Bond	11.9	4.3	9.8	7.1	....	....	....	....	....	....
Spectrum Government Bond	10.7	....	....	....	....	....	....	....	....	....
Spectrum Interest Fund	12.1	3.7	9.8	6.0	....	....	....	....	....	....
St-Laurent Fonds d'Obligation	12.1	0.4	12.8	7.9	7.4	....	....	....	....	....
Standard Life Bond 2000	15.1	3.4	10.7	10.3	....	....	....	....	....	....
Strata Income Fund	14.0	2.4	....	....	....	....	....	....	....	....
Talvest Bond Fund	12.9	2.3	11.6	8.0	9.3	15.9	30.2	2.5	40.7	12.3
Talvest Income Fund	13.5	5.6	9.1	8.3	8.6	10.3	19.1	5.8	22.3	16.6
Templeton Global Income*	10.0	9.7	....	....	....	....	....	....	....	....
Templeton Heritage Bond	8.6	....	....	....	....	....	....	....	....	....
Top 50 T-Bill/Bond Fund	11.7	10.4	....	....	....	....	....	....	....	....
Tradex Security Fund	11.3	....	....	....	....	....	....	....	....	....
Trans-Canada Bond Fund	11.8	3.9	6.2	9.0	....	....	....	....	....	....
Trust General Bond Fund	13.6	0.6	11.6	7.3	5.4	17.8	32.9	1.6	31.9	14.3
Trust General Mortgage Fund	15.2	8.0	8.0	7.9	9.1	12.7	21.7	7.7	23.9	17.1
Trust La Laurentienne Obligati	10.6	7.6	6.8	6.4	9.5	....	....	....	....	....
Trust Pret Revenu Fonds H	15.9	7.7	9.3	8.6	9.6	10.9	17.6	7.6	24.2	16.2
Trust Pret Revenu Obligat	12.6	4.4	8.6	....	....	....	....	....	....	....
United Mortgage	14.7	6.5	6.2	7.9	7.6	8.9	15.0	9.2	14.8	17.6
United Security Fund	16.3	8.4	2.5	5.2	8.1	15.0	27.0	-0.1	21.9	11.4
Universal Canadian Bond	12.0	0.9	13.6	12.1	7.0	15.7	36.4	-3.7	50.8	7.9
Viking Income Fund	13.0	2.5	10.4	7.7	7.3	16.5	30.9	0.5	37.9	10.9
Waltaine Income Fund	9.7	2.9	11.1	2.8	....	....	....	....	....	....
HIGHEST IN GROUP	19.2	11.8	13.9	13.2	16.2	21.2	41.3	9.3	50.8	18.7
LOWEST IN GROUP	-1.5	-1.4	0.7	-3.2	3.9	6.1	11.0	-6.0	10.7	2.3
AVERAGE IN GROUP	12.4	4.1	9.9	7.2	7.8	14.1	23.8	3.6	29.9	13.4

APPENDIX FOUR 163

Fund	1991	1990	1989	1988	1987	1986	1985	1984	1983	1982
Preferred Dividend Funds										
20/20 Dividend Fund	6.4	2.9	13.9	1.2	14.3	....	....	....	....	....
AGF High Income Fund	7.9	....	....	....	....	....	....	....	....	....
Allied Dividend Fund	-2.7	0.8	9.1	0.5	5.5	....	....	....	....	....
BPI High Yield Fund	2.6	2.1	6.3	....	....	....	....	....	....	....
Bolton Tremblay Income Fund	9.8	0.1	9.3	3.1	9.7	7.7	13.4	4.4	30.2	14.3
Bullock Dividend Fund	6.8	2.2	12.9	0.0	6.2	10.7	....	....	....	....
Dynamic Dividend Fund	7.2	2.0	10.1	5.9	11.1	....	....	....	....	....
FuturLink Income Fund	13.4	-0.1	13.3	....	....	....	....	....	....	....
Guardian Pref Dividend Fund	5.7	1.6	8.4	3.9	8.7	....	....	....	....	....
Investors Dividend Fund	10.6	1.5	12.9	3.6	9.9	9.8	24.2	2.5	55.3	-14.9
Montreal Trust Dividend Fund	9.3	0.4	10.1	-4.7	....	....	....	....	....	....
PH&N Dividend Income Fund	5.3	3.5	14.6	2.0	18.8	10.2	20.3	0.8	56.7	-11.1
Prudential Dividend Fund	5.5	-11.8	8.0	6.4	....	....	....	....	....	....
Royal Trust Pref Blue Chip	5.5	-0.6	11.0	0.7	7.2	....	....	....	....	....
Spectrum Dividend Fund	8.9	1.9	12.7	3.4	....	....	....	....	....	....
Viking Dividend Fund Ltd	6.2	2.2	13.5	3.5	11.5	15.3	23.5	6.2	55.4	-14.3
HIGHEST IN GROUP	13.4	3.5	14.6	6.4	18.8	15.3	24.2	6.2	56.7	14.3
LOWEST IN GROUP	-2.7	-11.8	6.3	-4.7	5.5	7.7	13.4	0.8	30.2	-14.9
AVERAGE IN GROUP	6.8	0.6	11.1	2.3	10.3	10.7	20.4	3.5	49.4	-6.5
Money Market Funds										
20/20 Money Market	10.9	....	....	....	....	....	....	....	....	....
AGF Money Market Account	11.3	12.1	10.4	8.4	7.8	9.3	10.8	9.4	12.0	18.2
Allied Money Fund	10.3	11.4	9.2	8.1	7.9	....	....	....	....	....
BPI Money Market Fund	10.9	12.1	8.8	....	....	....	....	....	....	....
Batirente-Section MMK	12.8	9.7	9.7	....	....	....	....	....	....	....
Bolton Tremblay Money Fund	11.5	12.3	10.5	8.7	8.2	9.4	11.0	9.1	11.7	....
Bullock Money Market Fund	10.2	11.3	9.9	....	....	....	....	....	....	....
CDA Money Market Fund	11.8	12.2	10.5	8.2	7.5	9.6	11.0	9.5	11.5	16.1
CIBC Money Market Fund	11.2	12.4	....	....	....	....	....	....	....	....
Capstone Cash Management	11.9	12.3	10.0	....	....	....	....	....	....	....
Cda Life Money Market S-29	11.7	11.1	9.7	7.3	6.0	7.7	10.0	9.3	12.4	17.2
Church Street Money Market	11.4	11.4	9.6	....	....	....	....	....	....	....
Crown Life Pen Short Term	11.8	12.6	9.3	9.3	7.4	10.0	10.8	9.0	11.3	17.1
Dynamic Money Market Fund	12.2	11.8	8.9	8.1	7.2	8.9	10.3	....	....	....
Elliott & Page Money Fund	12.4	12.6	10.8	8.6	8.5	10.1	....	....	....	....
Empire Money Market Fund #7	11.6	10.0	....	....	....	....	....	....	....	....
Everest Money Market Fund	11.8	12.6	11.5	8.1	....	....	....	....	....	....
F.M.O.Q. Monetaire	11.3	11.8	....	....	....	....	....	....	....	....
Fd Des Prof Du Que-Money Mkt	12.8	9.6	9.9	....	....	....	....	....	....	....
Finsco Cdn Money Mkt	11.3	12.2	9.8	8.4	7.9	9.5	....	....	....	....
Finsco Cdn T-Bill Fund	10.8	11.9	9.9	....	....	....	....	....	....	....
Finsco U.S. Dollar MMK*	6.5	7.9	7.2	6.3	....	....	....	....	....	....
First Canadian Money Market	11.0	11.1	9.2	....	....	....	....	....	....	....
First City Govt Money	11.5	....	....	....	....	....	....	....	....	....
Fonds Desjardins Marche Moneta	10.9	11.6	....	....	....	....	....	....	....	....
Fonds Ficadre Monetaire	9.6	11.7	9.6	7.0	7.5	9.0	....	....	....	....
FuturLink Money Market	11.3	12.2	....	....	....	....	....	....	....	....
GBC Money Market Fund	11.6	12.4	....	....	....	....	....	....	....	....
Global Strategy T-Bill Savings	9.6	11.4	9.7	....	....	....	....	....	....	....
Global Strategy US Money*	5.7	7.3	7.2	....	....	....	....	....	....	....
Global Strategy World Money	5.9	9.3	5.8	....	....	....	....	....	....	....
Great-West Life Money Market	10.9	12.0	9.9	7.8	7.0	8.9	10.7	8.6	11.3	17.7
Green Line Cdn Money Mkt	11.9	12.7	10.4	....	....	....	....	....	....	....
Green Line U.S. Money Mkt	6.6	7.8	....	....	....	....	....	....	....	....
Guardian Short Term Money Fund	11.8	13.0	10.9	8.7	7.7	9.3	10.7	9.3	11.4	17.7
Guardian US Money Market*	6.7	8.4	8.6	....	....	....	....	....	....	....
Hongkong Bank Money Mkt	10.7	....	....	....	....	....	....	....	....	....
Imperial Growth MMK Fund	10.9	10.1	....	....	....	....	....	....	....	....
Industrial Cash Management Fd	11.5	12.5	10.7	8.1	7.8	9.4	....	....	....	....
Investors Money Market Fund	11.1	11.6	10.1	8.3	7.2	8.9	....	....	....	....
Landmark Short Term Interest	9.5	10.4	....	....	....	....	....	....	....	....
London Life Money Market	11.6	....	....	....	....	....	....	....	....	....

Fund	1991	1990	1989	1988	1987	1986	1985	1984	1983	1982
MD Money Fund	11.4	11.6	9.3	7.6	7.1	9.0	10.5	9.3	11.6	17.5
Mackenzie Sentinel Cda MMK	11.6	11.8	8.4	9.7	....	....	....	....	....	....
Manulife 1 Short Term	11.6	11.9	10.2	8.0	7.6	8.9	10.4	....	....	....
Manulife 2 Short Term	10.7	11.1	9.4	7.2	6.8	8.1	9.6	....	....	....
Maritime Life Money Market	10.6	11.0	9.5	7.3	7.3	9.2	9.7	8.4	11.4	....
McLean Budden MMK Fund	11.1	10.8	....	....	....	....	....	....	....	....
Metropolitan Protection	10.2	10.7	7.1	....	....	....	....	....	....	....
Montreal Trust Money Market	11.3	12.0	10.4	....	....	....	....	....	....	....
Montreal Trust RRSP-MMK	11.5	11.6	10.1	....	....	....	....	....	....	....
Mutual Money Market Fund	10.7	11.3	9.9	7.7	6.8	8.1	....	....	....	....
O.I.Q. Fonds Monetaire	11.9	11.8	9.8	8.1	8.4	9.3	11.6	9.3	14.3	17.0
PH&N Money Market Fund	11.7	12.7	10.4	8.3	....	....	....	....	....	....
Prudential Money Market Fund	11.9	12.2	10.0	8.8	....	....	....	....	....	....
Pursuit Money Market Fund	11.4	11.6	8.7	....	....	....	....	....	....	....
RoyFund Money Market Fd	11.4	12.2	10.0	7.8	....	....	....	....	....	....
Royal Trust Cdn Money Mkt	11.4	11.4	9.7	....	....	....	....	....	....	....
Sceptre Money Market Fund	11.5	12.1	10.1	....	....	....	....	....	....	....
Spectrum Cash Reserve Fund	11.4	12.1	10.5	7.9	....	....	....	....	....	....
Spectrum Savings Fund*	11.5	12.5	10.8	....	....	....	....	....	....	....
St-Laurent Fonds d'Epargne	13.2	9.6	10.0	8.3	9.0	....	....	....	....	....
Strata Money Market Fd	10.7	11.1	....	....	....	....	....	....	....	....
Talvest Money Fund	12.0	12.2	10.8	7.9	4.6	....	....	....	....	....
Templeton Treasury Bill	11.6	12.3	10.3	....	....	....	....	....	....	....
Trans-Cda Money Market Fd	11.2	9.1	3.7	4.0	6.7	9.0	10.6	7.8	....	....
Trimark Interest Fund	11.5	12.7	9.6	8.6	....	....	....	....	....	....
Trust General Money Market	12.1	10.7	8.2	11.2	....	....	....	....	....	....
Trust Pret Revenu Money Mkt	11.4	11.1	....	....	....	....	....	....	....	....
United Cdn Money Market Fund	11.5	12.9	11.6	....	....	....	....	....	....	....
United US$ Money Market*	4.6	7.2	8.7	....	....	....	....	....	....	....
Universal Sector Currency*	6.8	7.1	5.1	....	....	....	....	....	....	....
Viking Money Market Fund	11.1	11.9	10.7	8.4	8.3	10.1	....	....	....	....
Waltaine Instant MMF	11.6	12.1	10.5	....	....	....	....	....	....	....
HIGHEST IN GROUP	13.2	13.0	11.6	11.2	9.0	10.1	11.6	9.5	14.3	18.2
LOWEST IN GROUP	4.6	7.1	3.7	4.0	4.6	7.7	9.6	7.8	11.3	16.1
AVERAGE IN GROUP	10.8	11.3	9.5	8.1	7.4	9.1	10.6	9.0	11.9	17.3

Market Indexes

91 Day Canada T Bill	10.9	12.8	11.1	8.7	8.0	9.3	10.7	10.0	10.7	16.5
Consumer Price Index	6.1	4.5	4.9	4.1	4.6	4.1	4.0	4.8	5.4	11.8
ScotiaMcLeod Universe Bond Ind	15.3	2.8	12.3	8.7	8.4	18.2	31.9	1.1	40.8	11.3
Standard & Poor's 500 Index	3.7	11.9	18.9	-15.2	20.6	38.2	34.9	2.2	53.3	-5.0
TSE Total Return Index	1.9	-2.4	13.5	-5.2	24.6	17.4	26.7	-5.7	86.9	-39.2

APPENDIX FIVE

Survey of Fund Volatility and Compound Performance*

(for periods ending June 30, 1991)

Fund	1yr	3yr	5yr	10yr	Assets	%	St.D.
Equity Funds – RRSP-eligible							
20/20 Cdn Asset Allocation	8.9	....	....	....	132	N/A	....
20/20 Cdn Growth Fund	7.7	....	....	....	20	N/A	....
20/20 RSP Growth Fund	7.2	....	....	....	15	N/A	....
20/20 Sunset Fund	9.0	8.3	7.4	....	94	16	2.06
ABC Fully Managed Fund	17.7	14.9	....	....	7	13	2.01
ABC Fundamental Value Fund	27.1	....	....	....	2	N/A	....
AGF Canadian Equity Fund	-1.2	-0.6	0.4	8.4	293	57	4.17
AGF Cdn Resources Fund	-11.8	-1.4	6.6	-2.1	35	98	5.85
AGF Convertible Income Fund	3.4	....	....	....	17	N/A	....
AGF Growth Equity Fund	2.4	0.8	0.5	3.9	89	92	5.20
AIC Advantage Fund	14.5	5.5	4.5	....	10	97	5.57
Admax Canadian Performance	-1.4	....	....	....	6	N/A	....
All-Canadian Compound Fund	3.3	4.3	3.5	8.5	12	33	2.83
All-Canadian Dividend Fund	3.2	4.3	3.5	8.2	14	33	2.84
Allied Canadian Fund	16.3	4.9	0.4	....	!	86	5.04
AltaFund	....	....	....	....	87	N/A	....
Altamira Balanced Fund	-0.9	0.7	-0.3	....	33	48	3.82
Altamira Capital Growth Fund	3.2	7.1	4.4	8.4	7	53	4.04
Altamira Equity Fund	13.7	21.2	....	....	65	44	3.47
Altamira Growth & Income Fund	10.8	8.8	10.2	....	22	11	1.96
Altamira Resource	8.7	....	....	....	4	N/A	....
Altamira Special Growth Fund	14.3	8.9	4.3	....	9	69	4.48
Associate Investors	6.0	5.5	6.1	10.1	8	41	3.26
BPI Cdn Equity Fund	-4.5	-0.2	....	....	3	54	4.05
BPI One Decision Fund	4.4	4.8	3.9	....	17	34	2.96
Barrtor Canadian Fund	10.8	8.4	7.0	....	4	15	2.03
Batirente-Section Action	-1.4	2.2	....	....	5	33	2.89
Batirente-Section Diversifiee	8.7	7.3	....	....	13	6	1.72
Bissett Canadian Fund	8.7	6.4	4.9	....	2	77	4.72
Bolton Tremblay Cda Cum Fund	-0.9	3.1	2.3	5.9	66	61	4.24
Bolton Tremblay Cdn Balanced	6.1	5.4	....	....	4	20	2.23
Bolton Tremblay Discovery	10.7	1.1	....	....	4	43	3.45
Bolton Tremblay Optimal Cdn	5.0	4.8	3.7	....	5	54	4.05
Bolton Tremblay Planned Res	7.3	3.5	3.6	3.8	18	99	5.99
Bullock Balanced Fund	5.6	5.2	....	....	1	6	1.68
Bullock Growth Fund	5.4	1.2	0.3	1.5	5	82	4.90
CDA RSP Balanced Fund	8.5	8.3	7.6	9.6	10	19	2.19
CDA RSP Common Stock Fund	5.1	6.3	6.9	11.7	34	59	4.19
CIBC Bal Income & Growth Fund	6.8	7.9	....	....	67	11	1.94
CIBC Canadian Equity Fund	1.4	....	....	....	36	N/A	....
Caisse de Sec du Spectacle	10.5	7.3	5.8	10.8	19	22	2.27
Caldwell Securities Associate	....	....	....	....	5	N/A	....
Cambridge Balanced Fund	12.7	7.7	8.1	12.7	6	4	1.45
Cambridge Growth Fund	6.3	7.6	9.4	13.5	27	43	3.43
Cambridge Pacific Fund	1.4	-17.3	-13.5	....	5	99	7.29
Cambridge Resource Fund	-8.4	-6.2	-0.6	5.0	2	89	5.12
Cambridge Special Equity	-19.3	-2.3	....	....	3	96	5.55

Fund	1yr	3yr	5yr	10yr	Assets	%	St.D.
Canadian Investment Fund	-1.4	4.5	3.2	7.7	66	69	4.48
Canadian Protected Fund	7.0	6.4	6.7	....	2	2	0.96
Capstone Investment Trust	10.3	8.5	4.7	10.2	7	39	3.14
Cda Life Bal Eqty Income E-2	2.4	4.0	5.2	10.4	28	75	4.70
Cda Life Cdn & Intl Equity S-9	0.7	3.6	5.2	9.5	194	67	4.41
Cda Life Managed Fund S-35	6.1	6.0	6.5	....	311	28	2.54
Cda Trust Inv Fund Equity	1.5	4.5	4.3	7.4	28	84	4.97
Cda Trust RRSP Equity	3.4	4.7	3.9	6.9	289	86	5.04
Cdn Anaesthetists Mutual Accum	1.7	4.6	5.8	9.1	57	56	4.11
Central Guaranty Equity	1.4	4.7	3.4	9.5	15	66	4.39
Central Guaranty Property Fd	2.3	8.6	8.8	....	20	2	1.02
Citadel Premier Fund	4.8	5.6	6.6	9.2	6	81	4.85
Colonia Growth Fund	2.6	0.6	....	....	21	30	2.72
Confed Growth Fund	-0.4	2.0	3.6	8.8	7	53	4.05
Corporate Investors Fund	1.7	3.0	5.6	8.5	9	42	3.38
Corporate Investors Stock Fund	5.1	-4.5	-7.4	1.8	10	83	4.93
Counsel Real Estate Fund	8.4	11.7	12.7	....	73	3	1.07
Crown Life Commitment Fund	2.6	3.5	....	....	6	59	4.19
Crown Life Pen Foreign Equity	0.7	6.5	6.2	11.2	26	65	4.36
Crown Life Pensions Balanced	8.0	7.6	7.2	....	53	10	1.91
Crown Life Pensions Equity	3.8	6.8	6.8	8.8	84	56	4.12
Cundill Security Fund	-1.8	1.0	5.2	8.0	16	41	3.30
Dynamic Fund of Canada	2.4	5.2	7.5	8.0	158	45	3.66
Dynamic Managed Portfolio	1.9	4.1	7.5	....	87	29	2.63
Dynamic Partners Fund	5.9	....	....	....	43	N/A	
Dynamic Precious Metals Fund	-3.6	-4.7	6.9	....	25	96	5.56
EIF Canadian Fund	12.9	-6.8	....	....	1	100	7.45
Elliott & Page Balanced Fund	9.0	6.7	....	....	3	17	2.17
Elliott & Page Equity Fund	8.6	7.0	....	....	6	49	3.95
Empire Balanced Fund #8	8.1	....	....	....	2	N/A	
Empire Equity Growth Fund #1	3.0	5.0	7.0	11.0	185	64	4.34
Empire Equity Growth Fund #3	6.1	6.4	5.4	12.1	23	60	4.20
Empire Equity Growth Fund #5	1.2	3.0	2.0	9.1	20	79	4.79
Endurance Cdn Balanced Fund	7.7	....	....	....	43	N/A	
Endurance Cdn Equity	3.4	....	....	....	11	N/A	
Ethical Growth Fund	7.3	9.0	10.0	....	60	31	2.72
Everest Balanced Fund	7.8	9.2	....	....	6	21	2.25
Everest North American	1.2	3.5	1.2	7.8	13	73	4.64
Everest Special Equity Fund	5.4	6.0	....	....	2	88	5.06
Everest Stock Fund	2.7	....	....	....	9	N/A	
F.M.O.Q. Omnibus	12.0	8.7	9.2	12.9	49	19	2.21
Fd Des Prof Du Que-Balanced	14.0	9.4	....	....	131	3	1.12
Fd Des Prof Du Que-Equity	4.7	4.9	....	....	18	30	2.66
Fidelity Cap Balanced Fund	6.7	5.9	....	....	18	28	2.55
Fidelity Capital Builder Fund	13.9	9.7	....	....	99	40	3.24
First Canadian Balanced Fund	8.4	5.9	....	....	23	16	2.05
First Canadian Equity Index	-0.5	2.1	....	....	36	44	3.54
First City Growth Fund	3.3	2.3	....	....	10	85	5.00
First City Realfund	3.7	7.7	10.1	....	211	4	1.15
Fonds Desjardins Actions	3.2	4.3	1.9	6.0	27	61	4.25
Fonds Desjardins Environ	....	....	....	....	5	N/A	
Fonds Desjardins Equilibre	8.6	7.1	....	....	24	12	1.98
Fonds Ficadre Actions	0.6	4.0	-0.6	....	3	62	4.26
Fonds Ficadre Equilibree	4.8	6.5	3.9	....	4	32	2.75
Fonds SNF actions	-2.9	-7.3	....	....	!	83	4.91
Fonds SNF equilibree	5.4	5.1	3.8	10.1	9	35	3.01
FuturLink Cdn Growth	1.8	5.1	....	....	125	39	3.13
FuturLink Select Fund	5.2	5.7	....	....	12	21	2.24
GBC Canadian Growth	15.2	....	....	....	9	N/A	
Global Strategy Americas	1.0	5.9	....	....	7	85	5.00
Global Strategy Canadian	4.2	5.5	....	....	93	18	2.18
Global Strategy Corp	13.5	8.3	5.6	....	1	58	4.18
Goldtrust	-3.2	-6.6	0.2	3.1	20	94	5.37
Great-West Life Diversified RS	6.0	6.4	6.2	....	50	14	2.02
Great-West Life Eqt/Bond	8.8	7.1	....	....	3	8	1.78
Great-West Life Equity	3.7	5.1	....	....	127	63	4.33
Great-West Life Equity Index	0.0	2.3	4.1	....	200	76	4.72
Great-West Life Real Estate	-4.3	5.4	6.8	8.2	323	1	0.81

APPENDIX FIVE 167

Fund	1yr	3yr	5yr	10yr	Assets	%	St.D.
Green Line Cdn Balanced	6.6	6.2	....	....	15	24	2.33
Green Line Cdn Equity	1.3	4.4	....	....	27	42	3.40
Green Line Cdn Index	0.5	2.7	4.6	....	34	76	4.72
Guardian Balanced Fund	12.2	9.2	9.6	11.7	18	7	1.77
Guardian Cdn Equity Fund	-2.4	0.0	1.1	7.0	25	75	4.70
Guardian Diversified Fund	6.9	....	....	....	4	N/A	....
Guardian Enterprise Fund	1.5	3.2	3.3	9.9	14	80	4.79
Guardian Growth Equity	4.2	....	....	....	2	N/A	....
Gyro Equity	-3.4	1.5	5.8	....	45	93	5.22
Hongkong Bank Balanced	5.0	....	....	....	2	N/A	....
Hongkong Bank Eqt Index	2.7	....	....	....	6	N/A	....
Hyperion Managed Trust	8.5	....	....	....	63	N/A	....
Imperial Growth Cdn Equity	3.0	7.3	13.7	13.5	81	94	5.28
Imperial Growth Diversified	7.4	....	....	....	8	N/A	....
Industrial Balanced	....	....	....	....	47	N/A	....
Industrial Dividend Fund	-8.7	-4.1	3.6	10.2	177	92	5.18
Industrial Equity Fund	-12.5	-9.6	-0.7	6.5	64	72	4.59
Industrial Future Fund	-0.9	2.3	....	....	113	37	3.10
Industrial Growth Fund	-1.5	1.3	6.8	12.0	1339	65	4.37
Industrial Horizon Fund	0.4	2.8	....	1511	36	3.06	....
Industrial Pension Fund	-9.8	-4.9	2.0	9.8	73	90	5.13
Integra Balanced Fund	8.6	4.9	....	....	13	11	1.97
InvesNAT Balanced Fund	10.1	....	....	....	4	N/A	....
InvesNAT Equity Fund	3.4	....	....	....	10	N/A	....
Investors Cdn Equity Fund	6.6	5.9	4.0	....	326	61	4.24
Investors Income Plus Port	10.9	....	....	....	433	N/A	....
Investors Income Portfolio	14.2	....	....	....	315	N/A	....
Investors Pooled Equity	4.3	5.0	5.4	8.1	69	55	4.10
Investors Real Property Fund	5.3	8.1	8.7	....	282	1	0.54
Investors Retire Plus Port	6.7	....	....	....	263	N/A	....
Investors Retirement Mutual	1.9	3.8	7.1	8.5	971	57	4.14
Investors Summa Fund	1.9	3.5	....	....	60	51	3.98
Jarislowsky Finsco Balanced	6.5	....	....	....	7	N/A	....
Jarislowsky Finsco Cdn Eqt	3.6	5.2	3.7	....	6	67	4.43
Jones Heward Cdn Balanced	7.8	5.3	4.0	....	5	25	2.37
Jones Heward Fund	4.5	1.5	2.3	7.4	42	89	5.07
Landmark Canadian	7.5	....	....	....	37	N/A	....
London Life Diversified Fund	5.7	6.3	....	....	133	17	2.06
London Life Equity Fund	1.1	2.2	5.2	9.5	170	71	4.56
Lotus Fund	7.6	5.6	4.1	....	38	37	3.09
MD Equity Fund	0.9	3.8	7.4	12.9	1071	45	3.66
MD Realty Fund A	-0.1	9.5	11.1	....	251	9	1.84
Mackenzie Equity Fund	-8.6	-3.3	2.7	8.7	57	80	4.82
Mackenzie Sentinel Cda Eqt	-6.1	-1.6	0.3	....	29	87	5.04
Manulife 1 Capital Gains	2.3	4.7	5.6	....	40	88	5.06
Manulife 1 Diversified	6.4	5.8	6.7	10.1	379	31	2.72
Manulife 1 Equity	3.7	4.0	4.9	7.7	228	94	5.31
Manulife 2 Capital Gains	1.5	3.9	4.8	....	40	90	5.12
Manulife 2 Diversified	5.6	5.0	5.9	9.3	379	40	3.22
Manulife 2 Equity	2.9	3.2	4.1	6.8	228	81	4.84
Marathon Equity Fund	....	....	....	....	!	N/A	....
Margin of Safety Canadian	3.7	....	....	....	!	N/A	....
Maritime Life Balanced Fund	8.7	6.8	....	....	70	27	2.47
Maritime Life Growth Fund	-1.0	2.6	2.0	8.0	166	72	4.62
Marlborough Fund	-6.5	-0.9	-1.5	4.2	2	97	5.75
McLean Budden Balanced Fund	5.9	6.9	5.1	10.7	8	35	3.03
McLean Budden Balanced Growth	9.3	....	....	....	!	N/A	....
McLean Budden Equity Growth	1.1	....	....	....	1	N/A	....
MetLife MVP Balanced	5.5	6.2	....	....	4	27	2.51
MetLife MVP Equity	-1.5	3.4	....	....	12	83	4.97
Metfin Real Estate Growth Fd	10.3	4.2	9.3	....	9	12	2.00
Metropolitan Balanced Growth	6.4	5.1	0.6	4.5	33	50	3.95
Metropolitan Cdn Mutual Fund	-0.8	2.0	0.2	....	26	70	4.52
Montreal Trust Balanced	9.0	....	....	....	1	N/A	....
Montreal Trust Equity Fund	5.8	4.5	6.0	7.2	17	56	4.11
Montreal Trust RRSP-Balanced	8.6	....	....	....	4	N/A	....
Montreal Trust RRSP-Equity	4.4	4.6	5.3	7.5	63	72	4.62
Montreal Trust RRSP-Tot Ret	10.4	....	....	....	3	N/A	....

Fund	1yr	3yr	5yr	10yr	Assets	%	St.D.
Montreal Trust Total Return	11.4	....	....	....	1	N/A	....
Multiple Opportunities Fund	-3.9	-7.7	2.0	....	5	100	8.48
Mutual Canadian Index Fund	1.0	3.6	....	....	5	44	3.50
Mutual Diversifund 25	9.0	7.1	6.3	....	14	6	1.71
Mutual Diversifund 40	6.3	5.6	4.8	....	121	28	2.53
Mutual Diversifund 55	3.9	4.9	4.3	....	67	36	3.06
Mutual Equifund	-1.9	2.7	1.9	....	68	79	4.79
NN Balanced Fund	5.8	4.7	....	....	8	25	2.39
NN Canadian 35 Index Fund	1.2	....	....	....	2	N/A	....
NN Canadian Growth Fund	4.7	2.5	1.5	9.2	46	62	4.27
NN Gold Bullion Fund	2.5	-9.0	....	....	!	49	3.92
NW Canadian Fund	7.2	7.5	6.2	11.2	5	82	4.86
National Trust Balanced	....	....	....	....	8	N/A	....
National Trust Equity Fund	6.7	6.0	4.3	8.6	106	87	5.04
Natural Resources Growth Fund	-8.9	-9.1	-0.2	0.3	5	93	5.26
O.I.Q. Fonds d'Actions	6.5	6.3	7.6	9.0	45	70	4.54
O.I.Q. Fonds d'Equilibre	12.3	8.6	9.1	11.2	48	17	2.16
Ont Teachers Grp Balanced	7.5	7.6	7.5	....	13	23	2.30
Ont Teachers Grp Diversified	-1.4	4.7	5.1	9.5	27	60	4.21
Ont Teachers Grp Growth	-0.6	6.1	6.2	10.7	15	63	4.33
PH&N Balanced Fund	9.5	....	....	....	74	N/A	....
PH&N Canadian Fund	1.3	7.6	7.0	9.4	56	74	4.67
PH&N Pooled Pension Trust	1.9	6.7	6.5	9.9	69	78	4.74
PH&N RRSP Fund	1.1	7.8	6.5	9.7	29	84	4.97
Polymetric Performance	....	....	....	....	51	N/A	....
Protected American Fd	9.1	6.9	6.2	....	5	5	1.59
Prudential Diversified Inv	9.6	6.8	....	....	6	8	1.84
Prudential Growth Fund	-1.0	2.1	2.8	6.8	61	91	5.15
Prudential Natural Resource	-6.5	8.3	....	....	6	52	4.02
Prudential Precious Metals	-15.8	-1.2	....	....	3	78	4.74
Pursuit Cdn Equity Fund	11.1	-0.6	-2.2	....	3	91	5.17
RoyFund Balanced Fund	4.3	6.0	....	....	67	5	1.61
RoyFund Equity Ltd	-6.3	1.1	1.2	7.6	679	52	4.01
Royal Life Balanced Fund	11.8	....	....	....	3	N/A	....
Royal Life Equity Fund	11.6	....	....	....	5	N/A	....
Royal Trust Adv Balanced Fd	8.4	9.4	....	....	133	24	2.31
Royal Trust Cdn Stock Fund	2.6	4.2	4.7	6.5	251	77	4.72
Royal Trust Energy Fund	-7.4	2.2	9.5	-1.3	24	98	5.88
Royal Trust Precious Metals	-3.1	....	....	....	5	N/A	....
Roycom-Summit Realty Fund	7.7	10.1	....	....	12	9	1.84
Roycom-Summit TDF Fund	7.2	9.8	....	....	10	22	2.28
Saxon Balanced Fund	3.9	-0.3	-2.1	....	1	34	2.98
Saxon Small Cap	-2.0	-2.5	-1.2	....	2	48	3.87
Saxon Stock Fund	1.5	-0.7	-2.1	....	!	39	3.15
Sceptre Balanced Fund	8.7	7.0	7.5	....	32	22	2.29
Sceptre Equity Fund	3.2	5.3	....	....	3	66	4.40
Scotia Canadian Balance Fd	3.6	4.7	....	....	9	38	3.11
Scotia Canadian Eqt Growth Fd	7.6	4.9	....	....	34	73	4.64
Scotia Stock & Bond Fund	4.3	5.7	....	....	32	14	2.01
Sovereign Growth Equity Fund	-0.5	3.4	....	....	2	71	4.56
Sovereign Revenue Growth Fund	7.3	6.1	....	....	!	10	1.90
Sovereign Save & Prosper	8.3	5.8	6.9	....	19	0	0.47
Special Opportunities Fund	5.9	-2.6	....	....	5	95	5.47
Spectrum Canadian Equity Fd	2.6	2.6	....	....	36	47	3.76
Spectrum Diversified Fund	7.2	5.7	....	....	55	15	2.03
St-Laurent Fonds d'Actions	0.4	2.6	1.7	....	!	46	3.71
St-Laurent Fonds de Retraite	8.5	6.8	6.7	....	6	7	1.73
Standard Life Bal 2000	11.7	8.3	....	....	8	26	2.40
Standard Life Equity 2000	6.7	6.2	....	....	7	68	4.46
Strata Fund 60	7.4	....	....	....	8	N/A	....
Strata Growth Fund	2.8	....	....	....	9	N/A	....
StrataFund 40	10.2	....	....	....	8	N/A	....
Talvest Diversified Fund	8.4	6.9	8.1	....	66	23	2.30
Talvest Growth Fund	10.6	5.9	8.2	8.6	64	55	4.08
Templeton Balanced Fund	....	....	....	....	36	N/A	....
Templeton Heritage Retirement	-3.4	....	....	....	5	N/A	....
Top Fifty Equity Fund	2.2	....	....	....	18	N/A	....
Tradex Investment Fund Ltd	1.1	4.4	5.8	9.3	45	50	3.96

APPENDIX FIVE

Fund	1yr	3yr	5yr	10yr	Assets	%	St.D.
Trans-Canada Equity Fund	1.4	3.6	6.8	12.1	16	45	3.59
Trans-Canada Income	5.0	4.5	6.7	11.6	6	29	2.59
Trans-Canada Pension Fund	6.4	5.9	5.2	....	!	67	4.41
Trimark Canadian Fund	5.1	8.2	9.0	....	489	68	4.48
Trimark Income Growth Fund	7.2	7.6	....	....	79	32	2.78
Trimark Select Balanced	10.2	....	....	....	113	N/A	....
Trimark Select Canada Fund	7.9	....	....	....	403	N/A	....
Trust General Balanced Fund	7.6	5.9	....	....	5	20	2.22
Trust General Canadian Equity	2.3	2.2	2.4	5.4	27	74	4.67
Trust General Growth Fund	2.7	4.8	....	....	!	47	3.80
Trust La Laurentienne Action	3.0	4.3	3.9	....	3	51	4.00
Trust La Laurentienne Equilibr	9.8	....	....	....	2	N/A	....
Trust Pret Revenu Canadien	3.0	3.9	2.4	4.5	13	78	4.72
Trust Pret Revenu Retraite	8.9	7.5	6.4	9.8	22	13	2.00
United Accumulative Retirement	9.5	6.7	4.5	9.3	146	38	3.11
United Portfolio of RSP Fds	12.4	....	....	....	24	N/A	....
United Venture Retirement Fund	3.3	1.0	1.1	5.4	41	58	4.18
Universal Canadian Equity	-6.5	-2.2	4.0	10.4	172	64	4.33
Universal Canadian Resource	-14.0	-8.9	1.9	0.7	18	95	5.55
Viking Canadian Fund Ltd	1.6	1.8	2.7	7.1	178	50	3.96
Vintage Fund	10.5	13.6	10.5	....	10	89	5.07
Waltaine Balanced Fund	9.8	7.7	7.4	11.1	46	18	2.18
Waltaine Dividend Growth Fd	5.7	6.1	....	....	5	26	2.43
Working Ventures Cdn Fund	8.5	....	....	....	5	N/A	....
HIGHEST IN GROUP	27.1	21.2	13.7	13.5			
LOWEST IN GROUP	-19.3	-17.3	-13.5	-2.1			
AVERAGE IN GROUP	4.3	4.2	4.6	8.3			

Equity Funds – Not RRSP-Eligible

Fund	1yr	3yr	5yr	10yr	Assets	%	St.D.
20/20 Amer Tact Asset Allocati	4.7	....	....	....	67	N/A	....
20/20 US Growth Fund	5.1	....	....	....	47	N/A	....
20/20 World Fund	-11.6	0.6	....	....	61	22	4.29
AGF American Growth Fund	-2.6	7.4	2.7	10.9	82	41	4.80
AGF Japan Fund	-16.3	-3.3	4.5	13.6	44	98	7.13
AGF Special Fund	4.7	9.3	5.8	12.7	134	62	5.18
AIC Value Fund	3.7	....	....	....	6	N/A	....
Admax American Performance	-2.5	....	....	....	19	N/A	....
Allied International Fund	10.9	-0.8	0.7	....	!	82	5.69
Altamira Diversified Fund	-10.2	-4.9	-7.3	....	15	28	4.41
BPI American Equity Growth	6.6	-0.3	....	....	2	49	5.02
BPI Europe & Far East Fund	-25.3	-11.1	....	....	!	74	5.51
BPI Global Equity Fund	-2.5	8.7	....	....	25	9	3.32
BPI Option Equity Fund	-7.4	-1.4	....	....	!	2	2.09
Barrtor American Fund	2.5	17.9	9.3	....	7	91	6.23
Barrtor Intl Fund	-19.5	-2.8	-4.4	....	5	56	5.08
Bissett Special Fund	6.8	....	....	....	1	N/A	....
Bolton Tremblay International	-5.5	5.9	3.8	12.6	177	30	4.49
Bolton Tremblay Taurus Fund	2.1	7.0	-0.9	6.1	20	51	5.03
Bullock American Fund	22.4	23.3	12.5	14.1	72	100	7.66
CB Global Fund	-6.8	....	....	....	6	N/A	....
CIBC Global Equity Fund	-10.7	2.2	....	....	15	14	3.61
Cambridge American Fund	-0.2	4.2	....	....	7	76	5.53
Cambridge Diversified Fd	-6.9	-1.2	4.7	10.1	8	6	3.21
Capstone International	4.4	9.7	....	....	!	13	3.52
Cda Life U.S. & Intl Eqty S-34	3.0	11.0	7.5	....	34	26	4.37
Century DJ Mutual Fund	3.3	8.5	1.7	....	!	73	5.51
Cundill Value Fund	-5.8	1.9	6.4	12.8	358	3	2.91
Developing Growth Stock Fd	-0.9	....	....	....	32	N/A	....
Dynamic American Fund	-4.0	6.3	6.2	12.2	48	23	4.29
Dynamic Europe 1992 Fund	-17.4	....	....	....	62	N/A	....
Dynamic Global Green Fd	....	....	....	....	7	N/A	....
EIF International Fund	9.6	-2.1	....	....	!	77	5.55
Empire Group Equity Growth #6	9.8	6.4	5.5	....	47	38	4.64
Empire International Fund #9	3.2	....	....	....	!	N/A	....
Endurance Global Equity	-2.6	....	....	....	12	N/A	....
Everest International Fund	-8.1	14.6	....	....	4	16	4.00
Everest U.S. Equity	....	....	....	....	10	N/A	....

Fund	1yr	3yr	5yr	10yr	Assets	%	St.D.
Extro International	-13.2	0.1	....	....	18	20	4.22
Extro Tiger Fund	-8.9	....	....	....	6	N/A	....
F.M.O.Q. Fonds de Placement	13.3	9.6	10.0	....	2	7	3.22
Fidelity Growth America	....	....	....	....	72	N/A	....
Fidelity Intl Portfolio Fund	-7.4	8.2	....	....	88	21	4.26
Fonds Desjardins International	-2.1	9.9	3.8	9.7	5	37	4.63
GBC International Growth	-12.5	....	....	....	5	N/A	....
GBC North American Growth	-5.5	1.9	1.8	7.2	123	80	5.68
Global Strategy Europe	-13.0	3.5	....	....	26	40	4.76
Global Strategy Far East	-10.0	6.5	....	....	20	89	6.02
Global Strategy Fund	-7.3	5.0	3.6	....	134	31	4.54
Global Strategy Intl Real Est	-14.3	....	....	....	7	N/A	....
GoldFund	-1.1	-6.6	1.3	3.4	7	95	6.35
Green Line U.S. Index	5.4	12.3	....	....	37	55	5.08
Guardian American Equity	4.2	9.2	5.0	7.0	18	69	5.30
Guardian Global Equity Fd	-12.1	1.7	0.5	6.7	4	71	5.36
Guardian North American Fund	0.3	6.7	-1.0	5.3	2	87	5.90
Guardian Pacific Rim Corp	-6.2	-2.2	....	....	3	90	6.19
Guardian Vantage International	-9.6	....	....	....	!	N/A	....
Guardian Vantage U.S. Equity	6.7	....	....	....	!	N/A	....
Hyperion Asian Trust	-11.7	....	....	....	32	N/A	....
Hyperion European Trust	....	....	....	....	11	N/A	....
Imperial Growth N.A. Equity	-12.1	-2.4	1.4	6.9	3	53	5.07
Industrial American Fund	-1.1	4.9	5.1	11.9	273	72	5.49
Industrial Global Fund	-14.1	-1.4	4.5	....	154	29	4.42
Investors European Growth	....	....	....	....	28	N/A	....
Investors Global Fund Ltd	-6.4	5.2	....	....	280	34	4.58
Investors Growth Plus Port	5.2	....	....	....	114	N/A	....
Investors Growth Portfolio	-1.2	....	....	....	142	N/A	....
Investors Japanese Growth	-9.5	-4.7	3.6	12.0	227	96	6.70
Investors Mutual of Canada	8.1	6.2	6.8	9.3	321	11	3.44
Investors N.A. Growth Fund	7.3	12.1	8.6	11.3	524	43	4.82
Investors Pacific Intl	....	....	....	....	48	N/A	....
Investors Retire Growth Port	2.7	....	....	....	110	N/A	....
Investors Special Fund	9.4	13.1	8.7	9.0	84	70	5.31
Investors U.S. Growth Fund	8.0	10.4	6.4	10.5	255	60	5.13
Jarislowsky Finsco Amer Eqt	6.0	6.9	3.1	....	7	24	4.32
Jones Heward American Fund	3.6	9.6	4.5	....	7	81	5.68
Landmark American	7.4	....	....	....	31	N/A	....
Landmark International	0.1	....	....	....	26	N/A	....
London Life U.S. Equity Fund	-2.9	2.2	....	....	27	19	4.19
MD Growth Investment	-9.5	2.7	5.3	13.5	786	65	5.22
MD Realty Fund B	-0.7	9.3	10.8	....	160	1	1.85
Mackenzie Sentinel Amer Eqt	-3.7	8.3	....	....	14	64	5.22
Mackenzie Sentinel Global	-15.3	-0.8	....	....	20	63	5.21
Margin of Safety Fund	16.3	....	....	....	4	N/A	....
McLean Budden Amer Growth	15.2	....	....	....	6	N/A	....
Metropolitan Collective Mutual	0.5	8.8	-0.2	8.2	26	46	4.92
Metropolitan Speculators	1.4	8.2	5.4	....	2	67	5.23
Metropolitan Venture Fund	-0.9	7.3	2.7	7.6	20	48	5.02
Montreal Trust Intl Fund	-1.3	6.1	3.6	11.6	18	50	5.03
Mutual Amerifund	-2.6	3.6	3.2	....	7	82	5.69
NN Global Fund	-16.8	-1.0	....	....	5	68	5.27
NW Equity Fund Ltd	8.7	14.5	6.2	11.4	2	97	6.70
PH&N U.S. Fund	9.7	13.5	7.1	13.7	88	93	6.28
PH&N U.S. Pooled Pension Fund	10.5	14.5	8.3	15.2	237	94	6.30
Pursuit American Fund	21.9	13.4	....	....	!	78	5.61
Royal Trust Adv Growth Fund	5.8	6.4	....	....	11	4	2.95
Royal Trust American Stock	1.8	11.8	6.6	10.3	59	59	5.13
Royal Trust European Growth	-11.8	-2.9	....	....	13	66	5.22
Royal Trust Japanese Stock	-8.5	-6.7	2.0	....	11	99	7.48
Saxon World Growth	-5.3	5.0	6.3	....	4	86	5.78
Sceptre International Fund	-4.7	10.7	....	....	7	79	5.64
Scotia Amer Eqt Growth Fd	6.8	3.9	....	....	20	52	5.05
Spectrum Intl Equity Fund	-5.1	4.1	....	....	7	32	4.56
Talvest American Fund	-8.8	2.5	1.3	....	3	45	4.85
Talvest Global Diversified	-8.0	3.9	....	....	28	5	3.08
Templeton Growth Fund	-4.0	7.1	5.6	12.3	1006	44	4.83

APPENDIX FIVE 171

Fund	1yr	3yr	5yr	10yr	Assets	%	St.D.
Templeton Heritage Fd	-5.7	....	....	....	36	N/A	....
Trimark Fund	0.7	7.9	8.0	....	606	84	5.69
Trimark Select Growth Fd	0.0	....	....	....	203	N/A	....
Trust General International	-10.2	....	....	....	2	N/A	....
Trust General U.S. Equity	-0.3	9.5	4.2	....	10	85	5.71
Trust Pret Revenu American	3.1	9.2	3.1	9.1	3	57	5.12
United Accumulative Fund	8.4	12.1	6.0	11.7	244	36	4.62
United American Fund Ltd	12.6	11.3	3.9	11.0	14	47	4.97
United Global Fund	....	....	....	....	4	N/A	....
United Portfolio of Funds	9.8	....	....	....	12	N/A	....
United Venture Fund Ltd	-2.5	-2.5	-4.7	3.0	14	54	5.07
Universal American	0.0	6.0	5.9	12.2	47	61	5.16
Universal Global	2.2	5.2	4.2	....	54	35	4.59
Universal Pacific	-7.0	4.8	7.4	....	84	88	6.01
Universal Sector American	-1.3	5.0	....	....	13	18	4.04
Universal Sector Canadian	-6.5	-2.4	....	....	7	10	3.39
Universal Sector Global	2.3	4.9	....	....	13	15	3.84
Universal Sector Pacific	-7.0	4.6	....	....	18	39	4.73
Universal Sector Resource	-12.7	-8.7	....	....	1	17	4.03
Viking Commonwealth Fund	-1.7	6.2	7.0	12.6	176	12	3.45
Viking Growth Fund	-4.3	3.9	3.4	10.0	96	27	4.39
Viking International Fund	-4.8	4.6	3.7	10.4	110	33	4.57
HIGHEST IN GROUP	22.4	23.3	12.5	15.2			
LOWEST IN GROUP	-25.3	-11.1	-7.3	3.0			
AVERAGE IN GROUP	-1.6	5.1	4.3	10.2			

Bond And Mortgage Funds

Fund	1yr	3yr	5yr	10yr	Assets	%	St.D.
20/20 Income Fund	10.3	6.9	6.8	....	67	65	1.72
AGF Canadian Bond Fund	10.0	7.8	7.3	13.7	476	91	2.27
AGF Global Govt Bond*	4.4	6.0	....	....	38	100	3.13
Admax Canadian Income	10.3	....	....	....	2	N/A	....
All-Canadian Revenue Growth	9.6	9.3	8.7	10.8	1	1	0.36
Allied Income Fund	11.4	9.1	9.8	....	!	98	2.72
Altamira Bond Fund	11.7	9.0	....	....	5	39	1.41
Altamira Income Fund	14.9	11.3	10.4	12.8	33	47	1.50
BPI Canadian Bond Fund	9.4	7.1	....	....	9	52	1.60
BPI Global Income Fund*	1.0	0.5	....	....	!	28	1.25
Batirente-Section Obligations	12.8	8.6	....	....	9	81	1.91
Bissett Fiduciary Fund	14.4	9.5	....	....	2	72	1.83
Bolton Tremblay Bond	14.6	9.6	....	....	20	44	1.45
Bullock Bond Fund	12.7	7.3	6.4	7.9	!	69	1.79
CDA RSP Bond & Mortgage	14.1	10.3	9.4	13.2	28	56	1.63
CIBC Fixed Income Fund	12.8	8.8	....	....	38	53	1.60
CIBC Mortgage Income	17.1	11.1	9.9	12.0	213	19	1.01
Cda Life Fixed Income S-19	12.3	8.3	7.6	12.6	81	54	1.61
Cda Trust Income Investments	13.8	8.7	7.9	12.0	38	59	1.65
Cda Trust Inv Fund Income	8.2	7.3	7.1	12.3	7	90	2.15
Cda Trust RRSP Income	12.4	8.0	7.6	12.6	125	62	1.70
Cda Trust RRSP Mortgage	15.4	11.0	10.1	12.4	132	14	0.73
Central Guaranty Income	12.5	8.3	6.3	11.8	3	99	2.79
Central Guaranty Mortgage	14.2	9.6	9.0	11.3	5	22	1.09
Church Street Income	13.6	8.7	....	....	2	38	1.41
Concorde Hypotheques	....	....	....	....	!	N/A	....
Confed Mortgage Fund	14.5	11.0	10.0	12.6	4	5	0.48
Crown Life Pensions Bond Fund	13.0	9.2	7.8	10.6	75	57	1.63
Crown Life Pensions Mortgage	16.5	10.9	10.0	14.4	83	20	1.06
Dynamic Global Bond Fund	-0.7	2.3	....	....	9	96	2.55
Dynamic Income Fund	11.6	10.0	9.0	12.9	110	31	1.30
Dynamic Strip Bond Fund	....	....	....	....	6	N/A	....
Elliot & Page Bond Fund	11.7	9.9	....	....	58	16	0.82
Empire Bond Fund #2	14.0	9.2	7.4	....	4	58	1.64
Empire Fixed Income Fund #4	15.6	10.2	9.1	....	25	33	1.33
Endurance Government Bond	13.8	....	....	....	31	N/A	....
Everest Bond Fund	12.0	9.3	....	....	42	60	1.69
Everest US Bond Fund*	-1.5	....	....	....	!	N/A	....
Fd Des Prof Du Que-Bonds	15.5	9.7	....	....	136	23	1.10
Fidelity Cap Conservation Fd	6.5	6.0	....	....	17	64	1.72

172 RRSPs 1992

Fund	1yr	3yr	5yr	10yr	Assets	%	St.D.
Finsco Bond Fund	11.4	7.4	7.0	....	10	46	1.50
First Canadian Bond Fund	13.6	8.1	....	....	24	55	1.61
First Canadian Mortgage Fund	19.2	11.9	10.8	13.1	659	11	0.67
First City Income Fund	13.1	10.4	....	....	16	93	2.42
Fonds Desjardins Hypotheques	14.8	10.8	10.1	12.8	107	4	0.46
Fonds Desjardins Obligations	13.9	8.5	7.6	12.6	31	86	2.02
Fonds Ficadre Obligations	12.3	....	....	....	1	N/A	....
Fonds SNF obligations	14.1	8.8	....	....	2	35	1.34
FuturLink Government Bond	11.4	7.6	....	....	39	88	2.07
FuturLink Mortgage Fund	15.0	....	....	....	31	N/A	....
GBC Canadian Bond	14.0	9.3	8.8	....	21	84	1.97
Global Strategy Income Fund	....	....	....	....	8	N/A	....
Global Strategy World Bond*	7.0	4.9	....	....	32	63	1.71
Great-West Life Bond Invest	13.3	7.8	7.3	11.5	293	74	1.83
Great-West Life Mortgage	13.3	9.1	8.4	11.8	311	24	1.14
Green Line Canadian Bond	12.2	7.3	....	....	24	78	1.87
Green Line Mortgage	16.2	11.5	10.5	12.5	105	27	1.24
Guardian Canada Bond Fund	11.4	10.8	....	....	24	2	0.40
Guardian Intl Income Fund	3.9	3.1	....	....	8	51	1.57
Guardian Vantage Bond	10.9	....	....	....	2	N/A	....
Gyro Bond	12.5	....	....	....	6	N/A	....
Hyperion Fixed Income	12.3	....	....	....	31	N/A	....
Industrial Bond Fund	12.6	....	....	....	946	N/A	....
Industrial Income Fund	8.8	6.5	8.9	13.9	234	89	2.07
InvesNAT Income Fund	14.1	....	....	....	6	N/A	....
Investors Bond Fund	13.3	9.3	8.3	12.5	1104	76	1.86
Investors Mortgage Fund	15.7	10.5	9.8	12.5	1613	10	0.64
Investors Pooled Bond	15.3	10.5	9.8	13.8	75	79	1.89
Investors Pooled Mortgage	16.8	11.8	10.8	13.5	170	8	0.60
Jones Heward Bond	12.4	8.7	....	....	4	30	1.27
Landmark Bond	12.9	....	....	....	71	N/A	....
London Life Bond Fund	5.2	7.1	6.2	13.4	196	97	2.66
London Life Mortgage Fund	16.4	10.8	10.1	14.6	115	7	0.60
Mackenzie Income Fund	9.6	7.0	9.3	13.7	324	87	2.05
Mackenzie Sentinel Cda Bond	12.3	7.8	7.5	....	23	92	2.34
Manulife 1 Bond	14.2	9.5	8.9	13.0	32	73	1.83
Manulife 2 Bond	13.4	8.7	8.1	12.2	32	75	1.84
Maritime Life Bond	13.4	....	....	....	28	N/A	....
McLean Budden Fixed Income	14.4	....	....	....	!	N/A	....
MetLife MVP Bond	12.3	9.0	....	....	3	26	1.21
Metropolitan Bond Fund	13.3	8.5	5.9	9.4	8	83	1.97
Montreal Trust Income Fund	13.2	8.5	8.0	12.6	15	67	1.73
Montreal Trust Mortgage Fund	14.5	10.7	9.8	12.1	11	15	0.79
Montreal Trust RRSP-Income	12.6	7.9	7.7	13.0	58	66	1.72
Montreal Trust RRSP-Mortgage	14.6	10.4	9.5	11.8	49	3	0.42
Mutual Bond Fund	....	....	....	....	4	N/A	....
NN Bond Fund	12.5	8.5	....	....	9	94	2.47
National Trust Income Fund	13.0	8.0	7.8	12.9	14	48	1.52
O.I.Q. Fonds d'Obligations	11.1	9.0	8.3	13.9	23	43	1.44
PH&N Bond Fund	14.2	10.1	9.9	14.5	177	60	1.69
Prudential Income Fund	12.5	9.0	8.7	12.6	45	42	1.44
Pursuit Income Fund	13.6	4.7	....	....	!	70	1.79
RoyFund Bond Fund	13.4	8.5	8.0	11.1	223	40	1.41
Royal Life Income Fund	10.0	....	....	....	7	N/A	....
Royal Trust Adv Income Fd	10.3	8.6	....	....	74	49	1.56
Royal Trust Bond Fund	13.6	8.7	7.9	13.0	409	80	1.89
Royal Trust Mortgage Fund	15.7	10.9	10.1	12.6	949	9	0.61
Sceptre Bond Fund	16.1	10.0	9.2	....	7	29	1.26
Scotia Defensive Income Fd	12.3	8.0	....	....	17	18	0.91
Scotia Income Fund	11.4	8.6	....	....	23	45	1.49
Sovereign Capital Sec Bond	11.9	8.6	....	....	!	36	1.36
Spectrum Government Bond	10.7	....	....	....	21	N/A	....
Spectrum Interest Fund	12.1	8.5	....	....	159	41	1.44
St-Laurent Fonds d'Obligation	12.1	8.3	8.0	....	1	77	1.87
Standard Life Bond 2000	15.1	9.6	....	....	4	95	2.50
Strata Income Fund	14.0	....	....	....	4	N/A	....
Talvest Bond Fund	12.9	8.9	8.8	14.1	89	68	1.78
Talvest Income Fund	13.5	9.3	9.0	11.8	12	17	0.85

APPENDIX FIVE   173

Fund	1yr	3yr	5yr	10yr	Assets	%	St.D.
Templeton Global Income*	10.0	....	....	....	22	N/A	....
Templeton Heritage Bond	8.6	....	....	....	20	N/A	....
Top 50 T-Bill/Bond Fund	11.7	....	....	....	9	N/A	....
Tradex Security Fund	11.3	....	....	....	10	N/A	....
Trans-Canada Bond Fund	11.8	7.3	....	....	10	34	1.33
Trust General Bond Fund	13.6	8.5	7.6	13.2	59	85	2.00
Trust General Mortgage Fund	15.2	10.4	9.6	13.0	32	12	0.70
Trust La Laurentienne Obligati	10.6	8.3	8.2	....	1	37	1.39
Trust Pret Revenu Fonds H	15.9	10.9	10.2	12.6	68	6	0.51
Trust Pret Revenu Obligat	12.6	8.5	....	....	4	25	1.17
United Mortgage	14.7	9.1	8.5	10.8	3	13	0.72
United Security Fund	16.3	9.0	8.0	11.3	23	21	1.09
Universal Canadian Bond	12.0	8.7	9.0	14.3	85	82	1.96
Viking Income Fund	13.0	8.5	8.1	13.2	98	71	1.80
Waltaine Income Fund	9.7	7.8	....	....	9	32	1.31
HIGHEST IN GROUP	19.2	11.9	10.8	14.6			
LOWEST IN GROUP	-1.5	0.5	5.9	7.0			
AVERAGE IN GROUP	12.4	8.7	8.6	12.5			

Preferred Dividend Funds

Fund	1yr	3yr	5yr	10yr	Assets	%	St.D.
20/20 Dividend Fund	6.4	7.6	7.6	....	18	N/A	2.61
AGF High Income Fund	7.9	....	....	....	121	N/A	....
Allied Dividend Fund	-2.7	2.3	2.6	....	1	N/A	1.45
BPI High Yield Fund	2.6	3.6	....	....	2	N/A	2.72
Bolton Tremblay Income Fund	9.8	6.3	6.3	9.9	32	N/A	1.41
Bullock Dividend Fund	6.8	7.2	5.5	....	!	N/A	1.95
Dynamic Dividend Fund	7.2	6.4	7.2	....	9	N/A	1.23
FuturLink Income Fund	13.4	8.7	....	....	4	N/A	2.58
Guardian Pref Dividend Fund	5.7	5.2	5.6	....	7	N/A	1.17
Investors Dividend Fund	10.6	8.2	7.6	10.3	1210	N/A	1.85
Montreal Trust Dividend Fund	9.3	6.5	....	....	6	N/A	2.06
PH&N Dividend Income Fund	5.3	7.7	8.6	10.9	17	N/A	3.23
Prudential Dividend Fund	5.5	0.2	....	....	3	N/A	2.46
Royal Trust Pref Blue Chip	5.5	5.2	4.7	....	12	N/A	1.74
Spectrum Dividend Fund	8.9	7.8	....	....	29	N/A	1.70
Viking Dividend Fund Ltd	6.2	7.2	7.3	11.1	146	N/A	2.32
HIGHEST IN GROUP	13.4	8.7	8.6	11.1			
LOWEST IN GROUP	-2.7	0.2	2.6	9.9			
AVERAGE IN GROUP	6.8	6.0	6.3	10.6			

Money Market Funds

Fund	1yr	3yr	5yr	10yr	Assets	%	St.D.
20/20 Money Market	10.9	....	....	....	52	N/A	....
AGF Money Market Account	11.3	11.3	10.0	10.9	212	N/A	0.15
AGF U.S. Money Market*	....	....	....	....	4	N/A	....
Allied Money Fund	10.3	10.3	9.4	....	1	N/A	0.13
BPI Money Market Fund	10.9	10.6	....	....	7	N/A	0.15
Batirente-Section MMK	12.8	10.7	....	....	1	N/A	0.33
Bolton Tremblay Money Fund	11.5	11.4	10.2	....	134	N/A	0.14
Bullock Money Market Fund	10.2	10.5	....	....	!	N/A	0.09
CDA Money Market Fund	11.8	11.5	10.0	10.8	24	N/A	0.22
CIBC Canadian T-Bill	....	....	....	....	208	N/A	....
CIBC Money Market Fund	11.2	....	....	....	1215	N/A	....
CIBC Premium T-Bill	....	....	....	....	380	N/A	....
Capstone Cash Management	11.9	11.4	....	....	5	N/A	0.23
Cda Life Money Market S-29	11.7	10.8	9.1	10.2	130	N/A	0.22
Church Street Money Market	11.4	10.8	....	....	2	N/A	0.12
Crown Life Pen Short Term	11.8	11.2	10.1	10.8	16	N/A	0.22
Dynamic Money Market Fund	12.2	10.9	9.6	....	107	N/A	0.17
Elliott & Page Money Fund	12.4	11.9	10.6	....	181	N/A	0.20
Empire Money Market Fund #7	11.6	....	....	....	5	N/A	....
Everest Money Market Fund	11.8	12.0	....	....	89	N/A	0.21
F.M.O.Q. Monetaire	11.3	....	....	....	3	N/A	....
Fd Des Prof Du Que-Money Mkt	12.8	10.8	....	....	11	N/A	0.23
Fidelity Short-Term Asset	....	....	....	....	11	N/A	....
Finsco Cdn Money Mkt	11.3	11.1	9.9	....	52	N/A	0.15
Finsco Cdn T-Bill Fund	10.8	10.9	....	....	259	N/A	0.12

174 RRSPs 1992

Fund	1yr	3yr	5yr	10yr	Assets	%	St.D.
Finsco U.S. Dollar MMK*	6.5	7.2	....	....	30	N/A	0.07
First Canadian Money Market	11.0	10.4	....	....	411	N/A	0.11
First City Govt Money	11.5	....	....	....	164	N/A	....
Fonds Desjardins Marche Moneta	10.9	....	....	....	9	N/A	....
Fonds Ficadre Monetaire	9.6	10.3	9.1	....	!	N/A	1.01
Fonds SNF Monetaire	....	....	....	....	3	N/A	....
FuturLink Money Market	11.3	....	....	....	325	N/A	....
GBC Money Market Fund	11.6	....	....	....	4	N/A	....
Global Strategy T-Bill Savings	9.6	10.2	....	....	2	N/A	0.20
Global Strategy US Money*	5.7	6.7	....	....	3	N/A	0.14
Global Strategy World Money	5.9	7.0	....	....	13	N/A	1.37
Great-West Life Money Market	10.9	10.9	9.5	10.4	175	N/A	0.19
Green Line Cdn Money Mkt	11.9	11.7	....	....	219	N/A	0.12
Green Line U.S. Money Mkt	6.6	....	....	....	23	N/A	....
Guardian Short Term Money Fund	11.8	11.9	10.4	11.0	26	N/A	0.21
Guardian US Money Market*	6.7	7.9	....	....	9	N/A	0.11
Hongkong Bank Money Mkt	10.7	....	....	....	4	N/A	....
Imperial Growth MMK Fund	10.9	....	....	....	7	N/A	....
Industrial Cash Management Fd	11.5	11.6	10.1	....	213	N/A	0.17
Industrial Short-Term	....	....	....	....	34	N/A	....
InvesNAT Money Market	....	....	....	....	105	N/A	....
InvesNAT T-Bill	....	....	....	....	131	N/A	....
Investors Money Market Fund	11.1	10.9	9.7	....	383	N/A	0.15
Landmark Short Term Interest	9.5	....	....	....	11	N/A	....
London Life Money Market	11.6	....	....	....	6	N/A	....
MD Money Fund	11.4	10.7	9.4	10.4	245	N/A	0.20
Mackenzie Sentinel Cda MMK	11.6	10.6	....	....	7	N/A	0.17
Manulife 1 Short Term	11.6	11.2	9.8	....	45	N/A	0.23
Manulife 2 Short Term	10.7	10.4	9.0	....	45	N/A	0.23
Maritime Life Money Market	10.6	10.4	9.1	....	49	N/A	1.01
McLean Budden MMK Fund	11.1	....	....	....	!	N/A	....
Metropolitan Protection	10.2	9.3	....	....	5	N/A	0.78
Montreal Trust Money Market	11.3	11.2	....	....	44	N/A	0.86
Montreal Trust RRSP-MMK	11.5	11.1	....	....	44	N/A	0.14
Mutual Money Market Fund	10.7	10.6	9.3	....	99	N/A	0.16
National Trust Money Mkt	....	....	....	....	22	N/A	....
O.I.Q. Fonds Monetaire	11.9	11.2	10.0	11.1	19	N/A	0.19
PH&N Money Market Fund	11.7	11.6	....	....	184	N/A	0.17
Prudential Money Market Fund	11.9	11.3	....	....	52	N/A	0.14
Pursuit Money Market Fund	11.4	10.5	....	....	!	N/A	0.51
RoyFund Cdn T-Bill	....	....	....	....	200	N/A	....
RoyFund Money Market Fd	11.4	11.2	....	....	516	N/A	0.17
RoyFund U.S. Money Market	....	....	....	....	39	N/A	....
Royal Trust Cdn Money Mkt	11.4	10.8	....	....	1287	N/A	0.12
Royal Trust US Money Mkt*	....	....	....	....	114	N/A	....
Sceptre Money Market Fund	11.5	11.2	....	....	7	N/A	0.14
Scotia Money Market	....	....	....	....	180	N/A	....
Spectrum Cash Reserve Fund	11.4	11.3	....	....	252	N/A	0.15
Spectrum Savings Fund*	11.5	11.6	....	....	52	N/A	0.15
St-Laurent Fonds d'Epargne	13.2	10.9	10.0	....	!	N/A	0.45
Strata Money Market Fd	10.7	....	....	....	23	N/A	....
Talvest Money Fund	12.0	11.7	9.5	....	15	N/A	0.38
Templeton Treasury Bill	11.6	11.4	....	....	16	N/A	0.13
Trans-Cda Money Market Fd	11.2	7.9	6.9	....	1	N/A	0.34
Trimark Interest Fund	11.5	11.3	....	....	68	N/A	0.16
Trust General Money Market	12.1	10.3	....	....	12	N/A	0.42
Trust Pret Revenu Money Mkt	11.4	....	....	....	12	N/A	....
United Cdn Money Market Fund	11.5	12.0	....	....	44	N/A	0.12
United US$ Money Market*	4.6	6.8	....	....	1	N/A	0.19
Universal Money Market	....	....	....	....	15	N/A	....
Universal Sector Currency*	6.8	6.3	....	....	3	N/A	0.28
Viking Money Market Fund	11.1	11.2	10.1	....	55	N/A	0.14
Waltaine Instant MMF	11.6	11.4	....	....	100	N/A	0.13
HIGHEST IN GROUP	13.2	12.0	10.6	11.1			
LOWEST IN GROUP	4.6	6.3	6.9	10.2			
AVERAGE IN GROUP	10.8	10.6	9.6	10.7			

APPENDIX FIVE 175

Fund	1yr	3yr	5yr	10yr	Assets	%	St.D.
Market Indexes							
91-Day Canada T-Bill	10.9	11.6	10.3	10.8			
Consumer Price Index	6.1	5.2	4.8	5.4			
ScotiaMcLeod Universe Bond Ind	15.3	10.0	9.4	14.5			
Standard & Poor's 500 Index	3.7	11.3	7.1	14.6			
TSE Total Return Index	1.9	4.1	5.9	7.8			

*This survey shows the average compound rate of return over three years, five years and ten years. The column labelled "Assets" is the net assets of the fund in millions of dollars. The column labelled "%" shows the percentile ranking by volatility within the grouping. For example, a percentile ranking of 5 for the fund means that 95% of the funds in the group are more volatile while 4% are less volatile. The column labelled "St. D" shows the standard deviation. This measure indicates the amount by which a fund's rate of return is likely to diverge from its average monthly rate of return. A fund with a standard deviation of 6 is twice as volatile as a fund with the same rate of return with a standard deviation of 3.

APPENDIX SIX

The Future Value of a Single Deposit of $1,000 Using Different Rates of Return

YEARS	1%	2%	3%	4%	5%	6%	7%	8%	9%	10%
1	1,010	1,020	1,030	1,040	1,050	1,060	1,070	1,080	1,090	1,100
2	1,020	1,040	1,061	1,082	1,103	1,124	1,145	1,166	1,188	1,210
3	1,030	1,061	1,093	1,125	1,158	1,191	1,225	1,260	1,295	1,331
4	1,041	1,082	1,126	1,170	1,216	1,262	1,311	1,360	1,412	1,464
5	1,051	1,104	1,159	1,217	1,276	1,338	1,403	1,469	1,539	1,611
6	1,062	1,126	1,194	1,265	1,340	1,419	1,501	1,587	1,677	1,772
7	1,072	1,149	1,230	1,316	1,407	1,504	1,606	1,714	1,828	1,949
8	1,083	1,172	1,267	1,369	1,477	1,594	1,718	1,851	1,993	2,144
9	1,094	1,195	1,305	1,423	1,551	1,689	1,838	1,999	2,172	2,358
10	1,105	1,219	1,344	1,480	1,629	1,791	1,967	2,159	2,367	2,594
11	1,116	1,243	1,384	1,539	1,710	1,898	2,105	2,332	2,580	2,853
12	1,127	1,268	1,426	1,601	1,796	2,012	2,252	2,518	2,813	3,138
13	1,138	1,294	1,469	1,665	1,886	2,133	2,410	2,720	3,066	3,452
14	1,149	1,319	1,513	1,732	1,980	2,261	2,579	2,937	3,342	3,797
15	1,161	1,346	1,558	1,801	2,079	2,397	2,759	3,172	3,642	4,177
16	1,173	1,373	1,605	1,873	2,183	2,540	2,952	3,426	3,970	4,595
17	1,184	1,400	1,653	1,948	2,292	2,693	3,159	3,700	4,328	5,054
18	1,196	1,428	1,702	2,026	2,407	2,854	3,380	3,996	4,717	5,560
19	1,208	1,457	1,754	2,107	2,527	3,026	3,617	4,316	5,142	6,116
20	1,220	1,486	1,806	2,191	2,653	3,207	3,870	4,661	5,604	6,727
21	1,232	1,516	1,860	2,279	2,786	3,400	4,141	5,034	6,109	7,400
22	1,245	1,546	1,916	2,370	2,925	3,604	4,430	5,437	6,659	8,140
23	1,257	1,577	1,974	2,465	3,072	3,820	4,741	5,871	7,258	8,954
24	1,270	1,608	2,033	2,563	3,225	4,049	5,072	6,341	7,911	9,850
25	1,282	1,641	2,094	2,666	3,386	4,292	5,427	6,848	8,623	10,835
26	1,295	1,673	2,157	2,772	3,556	4,549	5,807	7,396	9,399	11,918
27	1,308	1,707	2,221	2,883	3,733	4,822	6,214	7,988	10,245	13,110
28	1,321	1,741	2,288	2,999	3,920	5,112	6,649	8,627	11,167	14,421
29	1,335	1,776	2,357	3,119	4,116	5,418	7,114	9,317	12,172	15,863
30	1,348	1,811	2,427	3,243	4,322	5,743	7,612	10,063	13,268	17,449
31	1,361	1,848	2,500	3,373	4,538	6,088	8,145	10,868	14,462	19,194
32	1,375	1,885	2,575	3,508	4,765	6,453	8,715	11,737	15,763	21,114
33	1,389	1,922	2,652	3,648	5,003	6,841	9,325	12,676	17,182	23,225
34	1,403	1,961	2,732	3,794	5,253	7,251	9,978	13,690	18,728	25,548
35	1,417	2,000	2,814	3,946	5,516	7,686	10,677	14,785	20,414	28,102
36	1,431	2,040	2,898	4,104	5,792	8,147	11,424	15,968	22,251	30,913
37	1,445	2,081	2,985	4,268	6,081	8,636	12,224	17,246	24,254	34,004
38	1,460	2,122	3,075	4,439	6,385	9,154	13,079	18,625	26,437	37,404
39	1,474	2,165	3,167	4,616	6,705	9,704	13,995	20,115	28,816	41,145
40	1,489	2,208	3,262	4,801	7,040	10,286	14,974	21,725	31,409	45,259

YEARS	11%	12%	13%	14%	15%	16%	17%	18%	19%	20%
1	1,110	1,120	1,130	1,140	1,150	1,160	1,170	1,180	1,190	1,200
2	1,232	1,254	1,277	1,300	1,323	1,346	1,369	1,392	1,416	1,440
3	1,368	1,405	1,443	1,482	1,521	1,561	1,602	1,643	1,685	1,728
4	1,518	1,574	1,630	1,689	1,749	1,811	1,874	1,939	2,005	2,074
5	1,685	1,762	1,842	1,925	2,011	2,100	2,192	2,288	2,386	2,488
6	1,870	1,974	2,082	2,195	2,313	2,436	2,565	2,700	2,840	2,986
7	2,076	2,211	2,353	2,502	2,660	2,826	3,001	3,185	3,379	3,583
8	2,305	2,476	2,658	2,853	3,059	3,278	3,511	3,759	4,021	4,300
9	2,558	2,773	3,004	3,252	3,518	3,803	4,108	4,435	4,785	5,160
10	2,839	3,106	3,395	3,707	4,046	4,411	4,807	5,234	5,695	6,192
11	3,152	3,479	3,836	4,226	4,652	5,117	5,624	6,176	6,777	7,430
12	3,498	3,896	4,335	4,818	5,350	5,936	6,580	7,288	8,064	8,916
13	3,883	4,363	4,898	5,492	6,153	6,886	7,699	8,599	9,596	10,699
14	4,310	4,887	5,535	6,261	7,076	7,988	9,007	10,147	11,420	12,839
15	4,785	5,474	6,254	7,138	8,137	9,266	10,539	11,974	13,590	15,407
16	5,311	6,130	7,067	8,137	9,358	10,748	12,330	14,129	16,172	18,488
17	5,895	6,866	7,986	9,276	10,761	12,468	14,426	16,672	19,244	22,186
18	6,544	7,690	9,024	10,575	12,375	14,463	16,879	19,673	22,901	26,623
19	7,263	8,613	10,197	12,056	14,232	16,777	19,748	23,214	27,252	31,948
20	8,062	9,646	11,523	13,743	16,367	19,461	23,106	27,393	32,429	38,338
21	8,949	10,804	13,021	15,668	18,822	22,574	27,034	32,324	38,591	46,005
22	9,934	12,100	14,714	17,861	21,645	26,186	31,629	38,142	45,923	55,206
23	11,026	13,552	16,627	20,362	24,891	30,376	37,006	45,008	54,649	66,247
24	12,239	15,179	18,788	23,212	28,625	35,236	43,297	53,109	65,032	79,497
25	13,585	17,000	21,231	26,462	32,919	40,874	50,658	62,669	77,388	95,396
26	15,080	19,040	23,991	30,167	37,857	47,414	59,270	73,949	92,092	114,475
27	16,739	21,325	27,109	34,390	43,535	55,000	69,345	87,260	109,589	137,371
28	18,580	23,884	30,633	39,204	50,066	63,800	81,134	102,967	130,411	164,845
29	20,624	26,750	34,616	44,693	57,575	74,009	94,927	121,501	155,189	197,814
30	22,892	29,960	39,116	50,950	66,212	85,850	111,065	143,371	184,675	237,376
31	25,410	33,555	44,201	58,083	76,144	99,586	129,946	169,177	219,764	284,852
32	28,206	37,582	49,947	66,215	87,565	115,520	152,036	199,629	261,519	341,822
33	31,308	42,092	56,440	75,485	100,700	134,003	177,883	235,563	311,207	410,186
34	34,752	47,143	63,777	86,053	115,805	155,443	208,123	277,964	370,337	492,224
35	38,575	52,800	72,069	98,100	133,176	180,314	243,503	327,997	440,701	590,668
36	42,818	59,136	81,437	111,834	153,152	209,164	284,899	387,037	524,434	708,802
37	47,528	66,232	92,024	127,491	176,125	242,631	333,332	456,703	624,076	850,562
38	52,756	74,180	103,987	145,340	202,543	281,452	389,998	538,910	742,651	1,020,675
39	58,559	83,081	117,506	165,687	232,925	326,484	456,298	635,914	883,754	1,224,810
40	65,001	93,051	132,782	188,884	267,864	378,721	533,869	750,378	1,051,668	1,469,772

APPENDIX SEVEN

The Future Value of an Annual Investment of $1,000 a Year

YEARS	1%	2%	3%	4%	5%	6%	7%	8%	9%	10%
1	1,010	1,020	1,030	1,040	1,050	1,060	1,070	1,080	1,090	1,100
2	2,030	2,060	2,091	2,122	2,153	2,184	2,215	2,246	2,278	2,310
3	3,060	3,122	3,184	3,246	3,310	3,375	3,440	3,506	3,573	3,641
4	4,101	4,204	4,309	4,416	4,526	4,637	4,751	4,867	4,985	5,105
5	5,152	5,308	5,468	5,633	5,802	5,975	6,153	6,336	6,523	6,716
6	6,214	6,434	6,662	6,898	7,142	7,394	7,654	7,923	8,200	8,487
7	7,286	7,583	7,892	8,214	8,549	8,897	9,260	9,637	10,028	10,436
8	8,369	8,755	9,159	9,583	10,027	10,491	10,978	11,488	12,021	12,579
9	9,462	9,950	10,464	11,006	11,578	12,181	12,816	13,487	14,193	14,937
10	10,567	11,169	11,808	12,486	13,207	13,972	14,784	15,645	16,560	17,531
11	11,683	12,412	13,192	14,026	14,917	15,870	16,888	17,977	19,141	20,384
12	12,809	13,680	14,618	15,627	16,713	17,882	19,141	20,495	21,953	23,523
13	13,947	14,974	16,086	17,292	18,599	20,015	21,550	23,215	25,019	26,975
14	15,097	16,293	17,599	19,024	20,579	22,276	24,129	26,152	28,361	30,772
15	16,258	17,639	19,157	20,825	22,657	24,673	26,888	29,324	32,003	34,950
16	17,430	19,012	20,762	22,698	24,840	27,213	29,840	32,750	35,974	39,545
17	18,615	20,412	22,414	24,645	27,132	29,906	32,999	36,450	40,301	44,599
18	19,811	21,841	24,117	26,671	29,539	32,760	36,379	40,446	45,018	50,159
19	21,019	23,297	25,870	28,778	32,066	35,786	39,995	44,762	50,160	56,275
20	22,239	24,783	27,676	30,969	34,719	38,993	43,865	49,423	55,765	63,002
21	23,472	26,299	29,537	33,248	37,505	42,392	48,006	54,457	61,873	70,403
22	24,716	27,845	31,453	35,618	40,430	45,996	52,436	59,893	68,532	78,543
23	25,973	29,422	33,426	38,083	43,502	49,816	57,177	65,765	75,790	87,497
24	27,243	31,030	35,459	40,646	46,727	53,865	62,249	72,106	83,701	97,347
25	28,526	32,671	37,553	43,312	50,113	58,156	67,676	78,954	92,324	108,182
26	29,821	34,344	39,710	46,084	53,669	62,706	73,484	86,351	101,723	120,100
27	31,129	36,051	41,931	48,968	57,403	67,528	79,698	94,339	111,968	133,210
28	32,450	37,792	44,219	51,966	61,323	72,640	86,347	102,966	123,135	147,631
29	33,785	39,568	46,575	55,085	65,439	78,058	93,461	112,283	135,308	163,494
30	35,133	41,379	49,003	58,328	69,761	83,802	101,073	122,346	148,575	180,943
31	36,494	43,227	51,503	61,701	74,299	89,890	109,218	133,214	163,037	200,138
32	37,869	45,112	54,078	65,210	79,064	96,343	117,933	144,951	178,800	221,252
33	39,258	47,034	56,730	68,858	84,067	103,184	127,259	157,627	195,982	244,477
34	40,660	48,994	59,462	72,652	89,320	110,435	137,237	171,317	214,711	270,024
35	42,077	50,994	62,276	76,598	94,836	118,121	147,913	186,102	235,125	298,127
36	43,508	53,034	65,174	80,702	100,628	126,268	159,337	202,070	257,376	329,039
37	44,953	55,115	68,159	84,970	106,710	134,904	171,561	219,316	281,630	363,043
38	46,412	57,237	71,234	89,409	113,095	144,058	184,640	237,941	308,066	400,448
39	47,886	59,402	74,401	94,026	119,800	153,762	198,635	258,057	336,882	441,593
40	49,375	61,610	77,663	98,827	126,840	164,048	213,610	279,781	368,292	486,852

YEARS	11%	12%	13%	14%	15%	16%	17%	18%	19%	20%
1	1,110	1,120	1,130	1,140	1,150	1,160	1,170	1,180	1,190	1,200
2	2,342	2,374	2,407	2,440	2,473	2,506	2,539	2,572	2,606	2,640
3	3,710	3,779	3,850	3,921	3,993	4,066	4,141	4,215	4,291	4,368
4	5,228	5,353	5,480	5,610	5,742	5,877	6,014	6,154	6,297	6,442
5	6,913	7,115	7,323	7,536	7,754	7,977	8,207	8,442	8,683	8,930
6	8,783	9,089	9,405	9,730	10,067	10,414	10,772	11,142	11,523	11,916
7	10,859	11,300	11,757	12,233	12,727	13,240	13,773	14,327	14,902	15,499
8	13,164	13,776	14,416	15,085	15,786	16,519	17,285	18,086	18,923	19,799
9	15,722	16,549	17,420	18,337	19,304	20,321	21,393	22,521	23,709	24,959
10	18,561	19,655	20,814	22,045	23,349	24,733	26,200	27,755	29,404	31,150
11	21,713	23,133	24,650	26,271	28,002	29,850	31,824	33,931	36,180	38,581
12	25,212	27,029	28,985	31,089	33,352	35,786	38,404	41,219	44,244	47,497
13	29,095	31,393	33,883	36,581	39,505	42,672	46,103	49,818	53,841	58,196
14	33,405	36,280	39,417	42,842	46,580	50,660	55,110	59,965	65,261	71,035
15	38,190	41,753	45,672	49,980	54,717	59,925	65,649	71,939	78,850	86,442
16	43,501	47,884	52,739	58,118	64,075	70,673	77,979	86,068	95,022	104,931
17	49,396	54,750	60,725	67,394	74,836	83,141	92,406	102,740	114,266	127,117
18	55,939	62,440	69,749	77,969	87,212	97,603	109,285	122,414	137,166	153,740
19	63,203	71,052	79,947	90,025	101,444	114,380	129,033	145,628	164,418	185,688
20	71,265	80,699	91,470	103,768	117,810	133,841	152,139	173,021	196,847	224,026
21	80,214	91,503	104,491	119,436	136,632	156,415	179,172	205,345	235,438	270,031
22	90,148	103,603	119,205	137,297	158,276	182,601	210,801	243,487	281,362	325,237
23	101,174	117,155	135,831	157,659	183,168	212,978	247,808	288,494	336,010	391,484
24	113,413	132,334	154,620	180,871	211,793	248,214	291,105	341,603	401,042	470,981
25	126,999	149,334	175,850	207,333	244,712	289,088	341,763	404,272	478,431	566,377
26	142,079	168,374	199,841	237,499	282,569	336,502	401,032	478,221	570,522	680,853
27	158,817	189,699	226,950	271,889	326,104	391,503	470,378	565,481	680,112	818,223
28	177,397	213,583	257,583	311,094	376,170	455,303	551,512	668,447	810,523	983,068
29	198,021	240,333	292,199	355,787	433,745	529,312	646,439	789,948	965,712	1,180,882
30	220,913	270,293	331,315	406,737	499,957	615,162	757,504	933,319	1,150,387	1,418,258
31	246,324	303,848	375,516	464,820	576,100	714,747	887,449	1,102,496	1,370,151	1,703,109
32	274,529	341,429	425,463	531,035	663,666	830,267	1,039,486	1,302,125	1,631,670	2,044,931
33	305,837	383,521	481,903	606,520	764,365	964,270	1,217,368	1,537,688	1,942,877	2,455,118
34	340,590	430,663	545,681	692,573	880,170	1,119,713	1,425,491	1,815,652	2,313,214	2,947,341
35	379,164	483,463	617,749	790,673	1,013,346	1,300,027	1,668,994	2,143,649	2,753,914	3,538,009
36	421,982	542,599	699,187	902,507	1,166,498	1,509,191	1,953,894	2,530,686	3,278,348	4,246,811
37	469,511	608,831	791,211	1,029,998	1,342,622	1,751,822	2,287,225	2,987,389	3,902,424	5,097,373
38	522,267	683,010	895,198	1,175,338	1,545,165	2,033,273	2,677,224	3,526,299	4,645,075	6,118,048
39	580,826	766,091	1,012,704	1,341,025	1,778,090	2,359,757	3,133,522	4,162,213	5,528,829	7,342,858
40	645,827	859,142	1,145,486	1,529,909	2,045,954	2,738,478	3,667,391	4,912,591	6,580,496	8,812,629

Index

A
Annuities, 103
    flexible-premium guaranteed-interest, 39
    life annuities, 29, 106
    and poor health, 109
    rates, 106, 108
    single-premium deferred, 39

B
Balanced funds, 63 - 64
    and stability, 28
    and volatility, 59
Bankruptcy, 18 - 19
Benefit accrual rate, 10
Benefit entitlement, 10
Bond funds, 45
    and deposit insurance, 46
    and interest rates, 47 - 48
    management fees, 51
    portfolio management, 50
    and risk, 47
Bonds
    term to maturity and volatility, 49
Borrowing against your plan, 73
Borrowing to contribute, 118
Borrowing to invest, 81
    and RRSP gimmicks, 111

C
Canada Deposit Insurance Corp., 25
    See also Deposit insurance
Canada Savings Bonds (CSBs), 67
Carry-forward, 10 - 11, 80 - 81, 113
Choosing RRSP investments
    See Investment strategies
Claw-back (OAS), 98
Closed-end funds, 70
Contribution deadline, 8
Contribution limits, 4, 9
    carry-forward provision, 6

D
Deadline
    See Contribution deadline
Deferred profit sharing plans (DPSPs), 9, 10, 87 - 91
    and compensation package, 87
    contribution limits, 87
    eligible investments, 88 - 90
    rules for employers, 89
    as a tax shelter, 87
    and vesting, 88
Deposit insurance
    and bond and mortgage funds, 46
    and equity funds, 57
    and foreign currency plans, 36
    and RRIFs, 104
    and self-directed plans, 78
Diversification
    and risk reduction, 31

E
Earned income, 7 - 8
Eligibility to contribute, 7
Eligible investments, 11 - 12
Equities and RRSPs, 23
Equity funds, 55 - 62

cash component and risk, 58
comparative volatility, 28
and deposit insurance, 57
foreign securities limit, 56
investment objectives, 60
management, 57
and performance variation, 57
performance of eligible funds, 57
specialty funds, 59
and stock market indexes, 58
and volatility, 59

F
Financial Times of Canada, 52, 57
Fixed-income funds
   See Income funds
Foreign currencies as hedge, 75
Foreign currency plans, 36
Foreign investment limit, 11
   in self-directed plans, 70

G
Gimmicks, 111 - 114
   deferring contributions, 113
   overcontributions, 112
   "tax-free" withdrawals, 111
Goods and services tax (GST), 19
Government of Canada bonds, 49, 67
   as component of bond funds, 51
Graham, Benjamin, 74
Group RRSPs, 83 - 85
   advantages to employees, 83
   association plans, 85
   costs, 84 - 85
   and your investment objectives, 84
   services offered, 85
Guaranteed plans, 33 - 39
   credit unions and insurance, 34
   and deposit insurance, 34 - 35
   fees, 37
   how they work, 33
   money market fund, 37
   as temporary havens, 33
   two basic types, 35

H
Hedging and foreign currencies, 75

I
Income funds, 45 - 54
   advantages, 46
   fees, 54
   fund size and performance, 52
   management and objectives, 53
   portfolio structure, 48 - 49
   RRSPs and diversification, 53
   valuation, 47
   See also Bond funds; Mortgage funds
Income Tax Act, 7
Individual pension plans (IPPs), 90 - 91
Inflation
   and your retirement needs, 98
Interest rates
   and compounding period, 38
   and income funds, 45
   and mortgage markets, 50
Investment corporations
   See Closed-end funds
Investment objective
   and mutual fund type, 41
Investment strategies
   age as a basis, 26 - 27
   bond and mortgage funds, 26
   GICs and term deposits, 25
   guaranteed investments, 25
   investing for growth, 26
   preservation of capital, 27 - 28

L
Liquidity of investments, 22
Locked-in RRSPs, 13

M
Managed asset-mix funds
   See Balanced funds
Market cycles
   causes, 56

INDEX 183

and self-directed plans, 74
Money market funds, 37
Mortgage funds, 45
   and deposit insurance, 46
   and interest rates, 51
   management fees, 51
   and rate of return, 47
Mortgages
   as RRSP investments, 77 - 78
   in self-directed plans, 70
Mutual fund corporations, 70
Mutual funds
   advantages, 22, 42
   declining redemption fees, 42
   definition, 41
   evaluating past performance, 60
   fees, 42, 51, 59, 61, 116
   how to purchase, 30
   investment objectives, 41, 60
   purchase plans, 61
   RRSP-eligible funds, 24, 31, 41
   RRSPs and fees, 42 - 43
   and self-directed plans, 77
   survey of performance, 157
   where to find information, 43, 52
   See also Equity funds; Income funds; No-load funds; Real estate funds; Specialty funds

N
No-load funds, 42, 62
   and short-term trading, 61

O
Over-contributions, 15-16

P
Past service pension adjustments (PSPAs), 9 - 10
Pension reform, 4
Pensions, maximum payments, 4

Q
Quebec Insurance Board, 34

R
Rates of return
   effect on a regular deposit, 179
   effect on a single deposit, 177
   high returns and risk, 31
   and investment risk, 24 - 25
   TSE total return index, 57
Real estate funds, 64 - 66
   regulatory requirements, 64
   valuations, 65
Retirement needs, 97 - 99
Risk, 22
Roll-overs
   See Transfers, of pension to RRSPs
RRIFs, 29, 102 - 103
   and deposit insurance, 104
   income stream from $50,000, 156
   and insurance, 114
   and investment income, 29
   minimum amounts, 29
   and mutual funds, 104
   and risk, 104
   strategies, 105 - 106
   where to purchase, 104
   withdrawal regulations, 102
   and the younger spouse, 103
RRSPs
   advantages, 1 - 5
   age limits, 118
   assets as collateral, 16 - 17
   and bankruptcy, 18 - 19
   carry-forward, 80 - 81
   contribution limits, 117
   and death, 17 - 18
   disadvantages, 5 - 6
   early contribution, 79
   foreign property limit, 69
   and foreign residency, 110
   gimmicks, 111 - 114
   and the GST, 19
   guarantees vs. growth, 30
   income requirements, 117
   and mortgages, 77
   number of plans, 117

and pay cheque deductions, 79 - 80
and pension plans, 118
questions about, 117 - 119
risk and choice of investment, 115
rules, 7 - 19
and short-term savings, 81 - 82, 114
starting early, 80, 97
and tax savings, 30
trustee fees and taxation, 82
by type and institution, 121
and U.S. citizens, 18
See also Group RRSPs; Self-directed plans; Spousal plans

S

Securities as contribution, 12
Self-directed plans, 30, 67 - 78, 116
    administration fees, 68
    and changes in investments, 67
    choosing a trustee, 77
    eligible investments, 68 - 71
    and foreign holdings, 56, 72 - 73
    and guaranteed investments, 36
    ineligible investments, 70-71, 76
    by institution, 137
    and market cycles, 74
    minimum amounts, 76
    and mortgages, 75
    and mutual funds, 77
    penalties for ineligible investments, 72
    RRIFs, 105
Specialty funds, 66
    energy funds, 66
    ethical funds, 66
    precious metals funds, 66
    small-cap funds, 66
Spousal plans, 13, 14 -15, 93 - 95
    and common-law spouses, 93
    contribution limits, 94, 118
    tax liabilities, 94 - 95
    transfer limits, 93
    transfers, 118
Strip bonds, 68

T

Tax credits
    pension income amount, 101
Tax deferral, 5
Tax savings using RRSPs, 30
Taxation
    and borrowing to invest, 81
    of dividends, capital gains and interest, 29 - 30
Transfers
    between RRSPs, 12
    to a common-law spouse, 14
    of pension to RRSPs, 12
    of pension income to spousal RRSPs, 13
    of retiring allowance, 13
    to a spouse, 13
Trustee fees, 82
TSE 300 composite index, 55

U

U.S. citizens, 18
Unit benefit, 10
Unwinding your plan, 16, 101 - 110
    before retirement, 118
    RRIF vs. annuity, 107

V

Variable-rate plans, 36
Volatility, 22
    of stocks, 55
    and term to maturity, 49

W

Withholding tax, 17
    rates for Quebec, 17